What people are say

Jesus: A Life in Cl

Two of our most capable Marxist biblical interpreters offer a historical materialist life of Jesus, grounded in the social and material forces of Jesus' age rather than on efforts to read Jesus' mind. Precise, clear, accessible, and important. I can think of no better introduction to the historical Jesus for the general reader, no clearer statement on the legacy of the Jesus movement in the sweep of subsequent history, or a more worthy challenge to contemporary scholarship on Jesus and the rise of Christianity. **Neil Elliott**, author of *Liberating Paul: The Justice of God and the Politics of the Apostle* and *The Arrogance of Nations: Reading Romans in the Shadow of Empire*

A work of exceptional scholarship, the greatest story ever told as told from below is more compelling than ever. I was utterly engrossed. What impresses the most, though, is in how by demystifying an epic class struggle of the past lessons of strategic relevance to struggles for liberation in the present can be drawn. Essential stuff. **Ciara Cremin**, author of *The Future is Feminine: Capitalism and the Masculine Disorder* and *Totalled: Salvaging the Future from the Wreckage of Capitalism*

This account of the life of Jesus is neither a historical novel nor a scholarly monograph. It represents an excellent fusion of these approaches: copious and informed material information by way of well-wrought and well-written biographical narrative. The book conveys a sharp sense of the times and places, the issues and discussions, the difficulties and possibilities. A marvelous idea on the part of Crossley and Myles—altogether well done! **Fernando F. Segovia**, Oberlin Graduate Professor of New

Testament and Early Christianity, Vanderbilt University

This book moves on from the Third Quest for the historical Jesus, so focused on seeing Jesus as a great innovator within a particular cultural, religious and societal context. Seeing such portraits as romanticized and overly idealized, the interest here is on the social and economic forces that produced the Jesus movement, so that Jesus and his associates are seen as responding to the material upheavals of the time. **Joan E. Taylor**, Professor of Christian Origins and Second Temple Judaism, Kings College London

Crossley and Myles have recaptured the mind-blowing excitement generated by the original quest to distinguish the Jesus of history behind the myth. Although Jesus scholarship has struggled to let go of the fantasy of a man who dropped from the sky, this book places Jesus firmly on his feet, a product of his agrarian class and imperial repression. Crossley and Myles have found Jesus: in the Galilean dirt under his fingernails. **Deane Galbraith**, Lecturer in Religion, University of Otago

Jesus: A Life in Class Conflict

Jesus: A Life in Class Conflict

James Crossley

Robert J. Myles

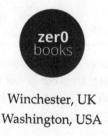

zer0
books

Winchester, UK
Washington, USA

JOHN HUNT PUBLISHING

First published by Zero Books, 2023
Zero Books is an imprint of John Hunt Publishing Ltd., No. 3 East St., Alresford,
Hampshire SO24 9EE, UK
office@jhpbooks.com
www.johnhuntpublishing.com
www.zero-books.net

For distributor details and how to order please visit the 'Ordering' section on our website.

Text copyright: James Crossley, Robert J. Myles 2022

ISBN: 978 1 80341 082 1
978 1 80341 083 8 (ebook)
Library of Congress Control Number: 2021947481

All rights reserved. Except for brief quotations in critical articles or reviews, no part of this
book may be reproduced in any manner without prior written permission from the publishers.

The rights of James Crossley, Robert J. Myles as author have been asserted in accordance with
the Copyright, Designs and Patents Act 1988.

A CIP catalogue record for this book is available from the British Library.

Design: Stuart Davies

UK: Printed and bound by CPI Group (UK) Ltd, Croydon, CR0 4YY
Printed in North America by CPI GPS partners

We operate a distinctive and ethical publishing philosophy in
all areas of our business, from our global network of authors to
production and worldwide distribution.

Contents

Preface

"What if the greatest event in human history was erased?" Such a question is posed by the promotional material for *Assassin 33 A.D.*, a 2020 "faith-based" thriller written and directed by Jim Carroll. The scintillating plot hinges on an Islamist terror conspiracy to go back in time to first-century Palestine and assassinate Jesus of Nazareth, and hence change the course of world history. "It's the ultimate jihad; eliminate Christianity by killing Jesus before the resurrection," says its title character, the inventor of the time machine, upon discovering the great conspiracy unfolding before his eyes.

Despite its one-dimensional and clichéd "war on terror" slant, not to mention the complicated paradoxes of time travel, and the obvious plot hole that Jesus was already put to death *before* reports of his resurrection, the film can be critiqued on another level: namely, its unquestioned premise that the course of world history pivots exclusively on the individual exploits of so-called Great Men. In direct opposition to this dominant ideology, we take the view that even if someone was able to successfully travel back in time and assassinate Jesus, they would not necessarily alter the course of human history. While details would obviously change, the same intersecting historical and material forces would still largely exist, and someone else would inevitably rise up to take his place.

The "Quest of the Historical Jesus" has an extensive intellectual history, beginning in the European Enlightenment and continuing into the twenty-first century. As with any number of scholarly enterprises, the Jesus quest overlaps with the rise of capitalism as a global force. The work you hold in your hands is the fruitful collaboration of two scholars of Jesus and early Christianity who have a shared interest in Marxist historiography and the ways in which struggles from the past may give us insight into the struggles we face today. We have written this book with the educated non-specialist in mind. We seek to unpack the life of Jesus and the early Jesus movement within its original historical context of first-century Palestine but in a way relevant for all interested in the history of class conflict, irrespective of individual religious sympathies or proclivities. An orienting assumption is: Jesus was not *just* a religious leader. And this prompts us to write not another dry biography of a "Great Man" from the past. Rather, there are important lessons about the broader unfolding of history when the study of Jesus is properly contextualized as a life in class conflict. We offer up this historical materialist life of Jesus as part of the "Next Quest" and as a deliberate point of contrast to the perpetual proliferation of the many "neoliberal lives" of Jesus produced, mass-marketed, and consumed over the past several decades.

The ideas presented in this book have benefited from the critical suggestions of several colleagues and friends. We forego the usual practice of naming a long list of specific individuals, but we have, as always, appreciated their help, and anticipate that, come the revolution, they will enjoy glorious reward.

We note here that when quoting the Bible, we follow the English text of the New Revised Standard Version. The various books that make up the New Testament were originally composed in Greek. Greek words have been transliterated into English for the aid of readers, but if readers want to consult the Greek text then we recommend the Nestle-Aland, *Novum Testamentum Graece*, 28th edition.

James Crossley
Barrow, England
Robert J. Myles
Perth, Western Australia

Select Abbreviations

For biblical books, we follow the John Hunt Publishing House Style (https://www.johnhuntpublishing.com/publishing-guide/appendices/house-style/). Other main abbreviations include:

1 Macc.	1 Maccabees
1QM	War Scroll (Dead Sea Scrolls)
1QpHab	Pesher Habakkuk (Dead Sea Scrolls)
1QS	Community Rule (Dead Sea Scrolls)
Bar.	Baruch
2 Macc.	2 Maccabees
3 Macc.	3 Maccabees
4 Macc.	4 Maccabees
4QpNah	Pesher Nahum (Dead Sea Scrolls)
11Q19	Temple Scroll (Dead Sea Scrolls)
Apion	Josephus, *Against Apion*
Antiquities	Josephus, *Antiquities of the Jews*
b.	Babylonian Talmud
CD	Damascus Document
OGIS	*Orientis Graeci Inscriptiones Selecta* (Greek inscriptions)
Life	Josephus, *The Life*
m.	Mishnah
NRSV	New Revised Standard Version (Bible)
Ps. Sol.	*Psalms of Solomon*
Pr. Man.	Prayer of Manasseh
Q	Quelle
Sir.	Sirach
Tob.	Tobit
t.	Tosefta
Thom.	Gospel of Thomas
War	Josephus, *Jewish War*

Wisd.	Wisdom of Solomon
y.	Palestinian (or: Jerusalem) Talmud

Chapter 1

Introduction: A Life in Class Conflict

The Quest of the Historical Materialist Jesus

This is not a religious book, but a historical materialist one. It is the purpose of this book to take up two related questions regarding the life of Jesus of Nazareth: First, what can we know about the historical Jesus and his movement? Second, how can we understand the emergence of the Jesus movement in terms of class conflict as a driver of historical change?

The "historical Jesus" refers to the Jesus modern historians can plausibly reconstruct from the earliest sources we have about him. In this book, we attempt a sober account of Jesus' life, sifting fact from fiction through the evidence left behind in our ancient sources, drawing on key archaeological findings from the time of Jesus, and highlighting the importance of class and material conditions for understanding why and how the Jesus movement emerged when and where it did.

Class conflict is much misunderstood in scholarly discussions of Christian origins generally and reconstructions of the life of Jesus specifically. Typically, class and class conflict are overlooked or dismissed as anachronistic. In one sense, there is good reason for this because when class and class conflict are acknowledged they are usually associated with, or in the service of, a romanticized reconstruction of Jesus as someone who had "woke" views on gender and even sexuality, was a Gandhi-like pacifist, a Che Guevara-style revolutionary, or established a system of village communes in the countryside. We would also add that the current penchant in scholarship for emphasizing "status" rather than "class," and the preference for looking at the performance of identities in different social settings, is likewise romanticized and more a reflection of current North

American-led interests in individualism and identity politics than a serious account of class as a structural factor that drives historical change.

This is not to say any of these positions are without merit. Clearly people do perform class-related identity differently in different social settings and clearly the early followers of Jesus did dream of a new and better world. However, to challenge the anachronisms of these readings, we employ Marxist notions of class as a way of understanding how people react (consciously or not) to the contradictions inherent within the mode of production of their day. This includes how Jesus and his contemporaries responded to, and emerged from within, the productive forces of the ancient world, as well as their entanglement within various social relations such as those governing property, power, and prosperity, as well as gender and ethnic associations, in the rapidly changing economic landscape of first-century Palestine. Theoretically, one could undertake a Marxist reading of any figure from history irrespective of their politics. Just as a Marxist reading of Hitler does not make Hitler a communist, a Marxist reading of Jesus does not necessarily make Jesus a socialist. Rather, such an approach is focused on understanding the chosen subject as a product of the social and material conditions of their time and place.

Of course, it is still common to read of, or hear about, claims that class and Marxism are a product of the Industrial Revolution, that they concern modern capitalist issues of the proletariat and bourgeoise, and thus have no application to the pre-capitalist world such as that of Jesus' time. But this is a reductive understanding of class and Marxism, and we stress the importance of historical materialism to counter this misreading. By historical materialism, we stand in the tradition of Marxist historians who explain long-term changes in human society without endless emphasizing of the epoch-changing actions of supposed Great Men. After all, Great Men are but the products of their society, and their individual ideas and genius would be impossible without the social conditions built before and during their lifetimes.

It is for this reason we seek to understand Jesus as part of a broader "Jesus movement." This refers to the nebulous collectivity gathered around Jesus during his adulthood and in the wake of his death, and through which individual members could share their dissatisfaction with the present state of affairs and their vision of a better order. Although Jesus emerged as a key organizer, and the movement later came to bear his name, Jesus himself did not invent the movement or mastermind its ideas. Rather what came to be known as the Jesus movement was one of many religious and social movements around first-century Palestine doing broadly similar things.

Typically, historical materialist approaches have determined how class antagonisms and technological developments drove the transformation from feudalism to capitalism, but they have also sought to understand the transformation from ancient societies to feudal ones. In other words, to explain the transition from one mode of production, and the distinct ways in which a particular socio-economic formation is structured or configured, to another. Obviously, this scope alone is too broad for understanding the historical figure of Jesus and the Jesus movement but what this approach does mean is we can situate Jesus in relation to the class antagonisms of his time and place and with an eye to social and cultural changes they generated. From this perspective, class antagonisms must be understood as occurring not under *capitalism* but configured to the social and economic relations in largely *agrarian* societies.

Accordingly, we use terms such as "peasantry" to denote a broad and internally diverse category of rural workers and non-elite actors closely associated with agricultural production of the land and water. This group made up the overwhelming majority of the total population in antiquity and can be positioned in dialectical opposition to a mostly urban-based minority of the "elite." The elite sustained their relatively lavish lifestyles in varying ways through the exploitation of the labor-power of the peasant masses and a system which included slave labor, land tenure, and tributary payment.[1] While we stress that "peasantry" is a useful category for cross-cultural comparison over time and place, it must be also understood in context-specific ways and related to the dominant mode of production; a medieval "serf" and a first-century field worker, for instance, both have shared things in common and significant differences. Within the first century too, a field worker, a day laborer, and a fisherman could be differentiated, but, as we will see, this did not undermine possibilities for class solidarity.

We will return to issues relating to economic production in Jesus' context in the following chapters. First, we want to establish ancient manifestations of class antagonism that were available to Jesus and establish how they do not always complement modern Leftist beliefs. Indeed, as will become clear elsewhere in this book, the category of "peasant" further helps us appreciate Jesus as more of a "traditionalist" than anything else. What mattered most was the preservation of traditional patterns of life, with all their accompanying agrarian hierarchies, in the face of a changing Galilee.

Millenarianism and Banditry

Palestine in the first century was under the direct or indirect rule of the Roman Empire, the most expansive and powerful political entity that had existed to date. Coming from an insignificant village in Galilee in northern Palestine on the margins of the Empire, it is perhaps no surprise Jesus was not remembered as having much to say about the high political, social, and economic questions of his day. Jesus did not hold considered opinions on factions seeking influence at royal court, establishing trade networks, levels of military presence needed to keep the populace calm, alliances with neighboring rulers, or more mundane topics of town planning and public building projects. However, he certainly was remembered as having much to say on issues we would recognize today as "political," such as social and economic inequalities and the promise of a dramatic reversal of the world order with the rich getting their comeuppance.

For a first-century CE non-elite Jew like Jesus, there were two obvious and related options available for framing or interpreting social, economic, and political discontent and antagonism in rural Galilee: Jewish millenarianism and banditry. Here we define "millenarianism" in the general sense of an expectation of impending destruction, radical or even revolutionary transformation of the social, economic, and political order, and the expectation of a Golden Age. This transition to a new age was thought to involve dramatic supernatural intervention and a divinely appointed human agent or agents, with prophetic figures claiming access to the truth of divine revelation.

Academics will always argue over definitions and the definition of millenarianism employed here can be qualified further, as will be done in Chapter 5 where we explain what we mean specifically by Jesus' curious brand of "revolutionary millennialism." This embodiment of millenarianism envisaged a radical overthrow of the existing world order but also tended to hit hard at class exploitation in the present. For now, Jewish millenarianism was a phenomenon common in the first century CE, at least as far as we can gather from Josephus, the Jewish historian writing toward the end of the century. Around the time of the initial organizing of the Jesus movement in the late 20s CE, John the Baptist was probably a more famous example of a millenarian figure, and we will discuss John in detail in Chapter 3. Others include the prophetic figure of Theudas who, in the 40s CE, led a popular movement to the River Jordan where he announced he would part the river thereby allowing people to pass over (Josephus, *Antiquities* 20.97-99). Why this story might be categorized as "millenarian" is because it envisaged radical transformation through a dramatic action by tapping into well-known themes from Jewish ancestral traditions about Moses (the most important and archetypal organizer of the Israelites) and his exodus from Egypt which involved guiding the enslaved Israelites across a divinely parted Red Sea to their freedom. These traditions were reapplied to the future of Jews living now under the shadow of Roman rule. Like John the Baptist, Theudas would eventually lose his head because he was a sufficient threat from the perspective of the elite in power. It is for this reason and others (see below) that we should link millenarianism with the related phenomenon of banditry.

Banditry could take on different forms. The classic definition of "social banditry" to describe those outlawed by the ruling classes, championed by the peasantry, upholders of traditional values and morality, and fighters against injustice reflects a phenomenon certainly attested in first-century Palestine.[2] Stories of social bandits, many of whom set themselves up as alternative kingly figures, are recounted by Josephus and may have come down to him (and us) as idealized stories. But whatever the lived realities behind the stories, they were live ideas present in the time of Jesus. Josephus has examples of the common cliché of social bandits as popular figures among the peasantry. Away from urban centers, villages could be a safe place to hide for bandits who robbed the representatives of Rome, with villagers loyal to the cause refusing to give them up (Josephus, *War* 2.228-231; *Antiquities* 20.113-117). A bandit called Eleazar ben Dinai was active in the mid-first century and managed to resist capture for 20 years before he, his followers, and numerous peasant supporters were crucified (*Antiquities* 20.121, 160-161; *War* 2.253).

Bandits were also arbiters of local justice. They were often tasked with settling localized disputes and vendettas, perhaps at times close to gangsterism (*War* 2.232-235; *Antiquities* 20.118-119, 232-235). As this might suggest, Jewish bandits were not always remembered in the romantic sense Robin Hood is thought of today. In plenty of instances they were regarded as self-serving thieves without any indication they were robbing the rich to give to the poor. A famous example is from the Parable of the Good Samaritan (see Chapter 7) where the victim was beaten, stripped and left for dead by bandits or robbers (Luke 10.30 uses the Greek word *lēstēs*, which is the same word used for "bandits") which reflects a sensible enough sentiment known from elsewhere: it was best to be armed when traveling (*War* 2.125).

Nevertheless, rural robbery can also tell us something about the socio-economic options open to the non-elite. We know, for instance, famine, unusually heavy taxation, and bad harvests could generate a rise in banditry (*Antiquities* 18.269-275; cf. *Antiquities* 16.271-272). In some cases there was simply no other option for survival. Those involved in banditry could be remembered as (former) slaves, shepherds, soldiers, sailors, as well as people more generally designated destitute and poor (*Antiquities* 17.270-284; *War* 2.60-65, 585-558; *Life* 66, 175, 372). Justice was out of the question for the poor, unless they could obtain the help of a powerful benefactor in exchange for a price, such as their freedom. Indeed, bandits were not always so loyal to their roots or support base, and Roman officials could sometimes recruit them as hired muscle or simply tolerate limited amounts of banditry in exchange for a cut from their spoils (*War* 2.272-276; *Antiquities* 20.255-257).

Jewish millenarians and prophets were not necessarily bandits in the sense of planning violence in the here and now; rather, if God was going to intervene then perhaps there was no need for physical violence by humans in the present. But some, such as the popular prophet called "the Egyptian," could combine the expectation of supernatural intervention with

7

violent subversion such as the overthrowing of Jerusalem (*War* 2.261-262; cf. Acts 21.38). Josephus gives us further indication such categories could be blurred in his presentation of the mid-first century. In an extended discussion of prophets, bandits, and assassins called the *sicarii*, he argued those with "divine inspiration" for "revolutionary changes" ushered crowds "out into the desert under the belief God would there give them tokens of deliverance." Such were their overlapping interests of prophets and bandits that Josephus further explained they made an alliance, incited revolution, promoted political independence, and threatened to murder those who submitted to Roman domination. Josephus adds that related groups looted the houses of the wealthy, killed the owners, and burned villages (*War* 2.254-265). Whatever the realities behind these recollections, Josephus viewed the categories of "prophet" (or, rather, false prophet, for Josephus) and "bandit" as representing similar and interrelated concerns.

Pre-Political Agitation

Why bring the world of bandits and millenarians to the fore in a book on the historical Jesus and class conflict? For a start, Jesus' death in the earliest narrative source we have, Mark's Gospel, is remembered as one reserved for militant bandits or insurrectionists. It is claimed the "whole cohort" (about 500 soldiers) were called in to deal with Jesus (Mark 15.16) and he was crucified between two "bandits" or "insurrectionists" (using the same Greek word in Luke 10.30, *lēstēs*) (Mark 15.27). Jesus the millenarian could be easily confused (deliberately or not) for a violent bandit or rebellious insurgent from the perspective of Roman power. And this provided the reason for his execution by means of violent crucifixion, a brutal form of capital punishment typically reserved for traitors to the Empire and those foreigners deemed insubordinate to the totalizing rule of Rome.

But we opened with this discussion of bandits and millenarians to make a more general point about social and economic agitation in Jesus' world because these sorts of tendencies have been described as "pre-political." We take (and develop) the phrase from the Marxist historian Eric Hobsbawm who, in his early work on southern Europe and Latin America, looked at how forms of social agitation adapted (or not) with the arrival of capitalism. For Hobsbawm, the phenomena of rural banditry (including the more benevolent Robin Hood-type) and peasant millenarianism were prime examples of pre-political resistance in the sense they were *pre-capitalist* forms of resistance.

This does not mean bandits and peasant millenarians showed no interest in politics. On the contrary, Hobsbawm argued these phenomena were pre-political in the sense they had to come to terms with a new world and be absorbed into more organized and bureaucratized resistance to capitalism, such as socialist or communist parties. Pre-political rebels could once provide defense against a world of unjust princes, tax collectors, and landlords. Similarly, millenarians could promise a dramatic new world free from perceived injustices of the current world order. It was this yearning for radical transformation that would feed into the revolutionary politics of the twentieth century, Hobsbawm argued.

Some of the specifics of Hobsbawm's argument have been strongly critiqued. For instance, some are not fond of his ideas about historical development and progression, though this criticism owes more to anti-Marxist backlash than understanding of Hobsbawm's argument. Certainly, his interest did not stretch further back than the influence of medieval forms of resistance on the modern world. We would add the cultural peculiarities of millenarianism from different times and places does not come through strongly in Hobsbawm's argument. But whatever the merits (or not) of such critiques, the general point about pre-political peasant rebellion in the form of banditry and millenarianism remains useful and relevant for understanding social movements in and around ancient Galilee (where they thrived), not least because it helps us guard against historical anachronism.

Concerns about anachronism should be obvious (and are common in historical Jesus studies) but the genre of the historical Jesus book will often provide, whether intentionally or not, arguments about Jesus' relevance for today. Readers may or may not find relevance for today from this book but that is not the point we wish to make. As critical historians, we want to retain Hobsbawm's stress on the material interests of millenarianism at the time of Jesus, but appreciate it manifested in an agrarian way of life and addressed injustices (perceived or otherwise) using expressions and concepts we might today find strange and unusual.

Furthermore, we understand the ongoing relevance of Jesus in a different way. The millenarianism associated with Jesus was connected to significant socio-economic changes in Galilee and Judea, provided a language or framework that functioned as a means of rallying socio-political discontents, and was influential in shaping dominant forms of millenarianism in the centuries that followed, including in the contexts Hobsbawm himself studied. In the shorter term, however, it was the Jewish millenarian themes associated with Jesus, quite alien to most (but not all) social movements today, that would lead to the mobilization of a movement in his name. These millenarian themes permeated the organizational apparatus that kept the movement going and would be eventually absorbed and transformed into the official ruling ideology of the Roman Empire itself.

What is the "Historical Jesus" and How Do We Know?

But we are now getting ahead of ourselves. Before proceeding any further, we need to address what is actually meant by the "historical Jesus." As noted above, the "historical Jesus" refers to the Jesus who historians reconstruct from the earliest accounts we have about him. The implication is the work we have to do as critical historians is to assess the extent to which our earliest presentations of Jesus tell us something about the individual figure who was alive in Galilee and Judea during the first 3 decades of the first century. To do this, we need to understand the usefulness as well as the limitations of our evidence.

The four canonical Gospels in the Christian New Testament are attributed to Matthew, Mark, Luke, and John, though it is not entirely clear whether these are later attributions, pseudonymous attributions, or whether there were even any names originally attributed to these texts. The author of Luke also wrote a second volume narrating the expansion of the early church, the Acts of the Apostles, to which the same uncertainties apply. Except for the letters attributed to Paul, which provide fleeting guidance into the life of the historical Jesus, the canonical Gospels are the earliest known sources we have. Most scholars date them to the second half of the first century, though some scholars date Luke and John into the early second. The earliest Gospel, Mark, is usually dated to around the year 70 CE, though a minority position puts it a few decades earlier. What this means is our earliest sources about Jesus' life were written some decades after his death in approximately 30 CE. As with the growth of any social or religious movement over time, the initial themes associated with the early movement had evolved to address new and distinct situations. But the complications do not stop there: while Matthew and Luke were likely composed in the last decades of the first century, they both copied Mark, often word-for-word. This means the Gospels themselves cannot be treated at face value as independent sources.

Both Matthew and Luke also share similar material that is not found in Mark, and this is usually thought to come from a hypothetical source which goes by the label "Q" from the

German word *Quelle*, which means "source." An alternative explanation to the Q hypothesis is that material common to Matthew and Luke but not Mark came about because Luke used Matthew as a source. It is also possible to combine these two views in the sense that Luke used Mark and Q and knew of Matthew (cf. Luke 1.1-4). Within the dominant theory, known as the "four-source hypothesis," Matthew and Luke also drew on independent traditions that are labeled "M" and "L" respectively (see figure 1).

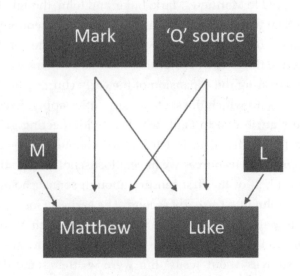

Figure 1.
The Four-Source Hypothesis is a scholarly construct that attempts to explain the literary relationship between the Gospels of Matthew, Mark, and Luke

Are the Gospels factual depictions of events, fanciful fables, or something in-between? The answer to this question is not straightforward. A "Gospel" is not a distinctive genre. It literally means "good news" and while it initially referred to the millenarian proclamation *of* Jesus and the Jesus movement, it later came to refer to a proclamation *about* Jesus by the Christian community. Later still, it became affixed to the texts we now call the Gospels as it can be found in the title of our earliest Gospel, Mark, which commences: "The beginning of the good news (i.e., gospel) of Jesus Christ, the Son of God" (Mark 1.1). So what kind of literature are the Gospels? Figuring out the answer to this question is crucial if we are to assess their usefulness in reconstructing the life of the historical Jesus.

Recent scholarship has sought to clarify the ways in which the Gospels are comparable to ancient biographies or lives (*bioi*) of other "great" figures of the Greco-Roman period.[3] There are numerous examples of such literature, including works by famous Roman authors like Plutarch, Suetonius, and Tacitus. Such literature was akin to ancient propaganda. At the most basic level, then, this means the Gospels cannot be taken naïvely as a straightforward transcription of historical events, but equally we should avoid the temptation to quickly dismiss them as the purely mythical inventions of their authors. Although the Gospels are concerned with presenting the "truth" of their contents, they do so according to specific and highly stylized literary conventions which tend to accentuate a focus on the individual agency of the protagonist as the main driver of historical events. For example, in ancient biography, protagonists are portrayed according to pre-existing stereotypes: powerful politicians who lived within and often controlled the structures of society; or conversely, philosophers who lived outside those structures and challenged them from without. Moreover, chronology functioned primarily to organize the external facts of a person's life, not as an explanation of individual behavior.

Accordingly, we need to look elsewhere (such as to the materialist categories discussed above) to best determine the historical explanations for Jesus and the broader movement's motivations and actions. The intersecting historical and economic forces in Jesus' day sparked a range of different beliefs and responses and, as we will see in the following chapters,

Jesus and the Jesus movement were very much a product of shifting material interests in Galilee. We regard Jesus not as the innovative founder of a new religious or social movement *per se*, but rather as someone who emerges as a religious organizer from within the amorphous collective of the peasantry responding to these upheavals.

Moreover, by approaching the study of the historical Jesus in this way, we also want to turn a related bourgeois emphasis in the history of modern Jesus research on its head. Ever since its origins during the European Enlightenment, the quest for the historical Jesus has stood firmly in the tradition of Great Men as pivotal figures of historical change. In his book *Jesus and the Rise of Nationalism*, Halvor Moxnes points out that Jesus books written in the nineteenth century were presented as biographies which appealed to "the emerging culture of a bourgeois elite" in the expression of their ideas.[4] In its effort to solidify its "universal" claims to private property, the aspiring bourgeoisie were historically necessitated to *invent* individual persons with rights and identities, that would legally, and indeed morally, bind them to their private property.[5] Jesus was a perfect subject for undertaking this broader discursive project, given the immense influence Christianity exerted over Western culture and, at that time, politics too. And this scholarly and popular tradition of Jesus the Great Man continues today. Indeed, we only need to observe the ways in which books on Jesus sell to scholarly *and* popular audiences in ways that, say, books on Obadiah do not.

These issues aside, only three of the four Gospels (Matthew, Mark, and Luke) are our main written sources for reconstructing the life of the historical Jesus. They are known as the Synoptics, because they can be "seen together" with their many striking similarities. Mark, as the earliest narrative, is to be privileged. The Gospel of John is probably later than the Synoptics and, as with Matthew and Luke, is dependent on earlier sources.

Whether John is directly dependent on the other New Testament Gospels or simply aware of their stories and general storyline,[6] it is of limited use for reconstructing the life of the historical Jesus (though as we will see, it is possible to reconstruct earlier history in light of changes or differences in John's Gospel).

Why is John's Gospel so problematic? Unlike Matthew, Mark or Luke, John presents Jesus as a figure so elevated in the divine hierarchy he is effectively equal to God. John's exalted view of Jesus as not merely a mortal but a divine man sent down from heaven was controversial and manifests as a conflict in John's story of Jesus with a generic character/group labeled "the Jews" (or a roughly equivalent translation, "the Judeans," according to some scholars). According to John 5.18, for instance, "the Jews were seeking all the more to kill him, because he was not only breaking the Sabbath, but was also calling God his own Father, thereby making himself equal to God." Similarly, according to John 10.33, "the Jews" are said to claim, "It is not for a good work that we are going to stone you, but for blasphemy, because you, though only a human being, are making yourself God." While many Christians today think of Jesus as equal or equivalent to God, and these ideas are implied through John (e.g., 1.1-18, 20.28), such sentiments are not palpable in Matthew, Mark, or Luke who would not have excluded such controversial material had it been available to them. The obvious conclusion is, on this major theme at least, John reflects a heightened level of theological speculation about Jesus somewhat removed from earlier reflections and is therefore less likely to tell us much about the *historical* Jesus.

Similar conclusions can be drawn from other differences between John and the Synoptics. For example, the phrase "kingdom of God" is common in the Synoptics (Matthew's Gospel tends to use the equivalent "kingdom of Heaven") but appears only twice in John's Gospel where it is no longer used with reference to end times but to being "born again" as a follower of Jesus (John 3.3,

5). But the contrast does not end there. The Gospels of Matthew and Mark in particular stress the coming of the divine kingdom to earth is imminent whereas the Gospel of John omits all such sayings and replaces them with the idea that Jesus' "kingdom is not from this world" (John 18.36). Furthermore, the Synoptic Gospels expect the Second Coming of Jesus (a belief that Jesus would return to judge the world after his ascension into heaven) within the lifetime of Jesus' original audience (see Mark 13; Matt. 24; Luke 21) whereas John 21 explains why this is no longer the case. The obvious explanation is the Gospel of John's presentation of "eschatology" (that is, the theology of the end-time) reflects a later moment in the development of the tradition where predictions relating to imminent end-time events were not being fulfilled as previously expected and so were being revised accordingly (see also 2 Peter 3).

Key differences in John's chronology of Jesus' life also point to its complicated use in historical reconstruction. The earliest known narrative account of the immediate cause of Jesus' death comes from Mark 11.15-18 (and is followed by Matthew and Luke), namely, the account of Jesus overturning the tables of the moneychangers and the seats of the dove-sellers in Jerusalem during the festival of Passover. The Gospel of John, on the other hand, places the Temple disturbance near the beginning of the narrative (John 2.13-16) and instead has as the immediate cause of Jesus' arrest and execution his miraculous resurrection of Lazarus (John 11). When any Gospel author has good theological reasons for including certain material, scholars will quickly raise questions about its historicity. Whatever we make of the reliability of the account of the Temple disturbance in Mark 11.15-18, it is not inherently implausible to the critical historian as an event that could have led to Jesus' arrest and death. A supernatural explanation like that found in John 11, however, appears more likely a fictional creation than the accounts attested in the Synoptics. Much more could be said about John but collectively these are the sorts of arguments that count strongly against relying on it extensively in the reconstruction of a life of Jesus.

It does not automatically follow, however, that we now have something like the words and actions of the historical Jesus in the Synoptic Gospels, even if they form our best collection for such reconstruction. Indeed, in the next chapter, we will see their severe limitations in the reconstruction of Jesus' birth and upbringing. Until recently, it was common to use a set of "criteria of authenticity" to establish whether words or actions were said or done by the historical Jesus.[7] For instance, a common argument was that if a similar theme or saying was found independently in two or more sources (e.g., Mark and Q), and perhaps in two or more different subgenres (e.g., parables, controversy stories) then we are likely in touch with the historical Jesus. As is increasingly recognized, this sort of reasoning only tells us if certain ideas *predated* the Gospels, not that they necessarily go back to the life of Jesus (though they may). We also know ancient writers could copy material without much elaboration and could also create fictional accounts without too much concern.

We prefer, then, to look at specific themes and issues on a case-by-case basis and work out from there whether a given theme or issue has proximity to the historical Jesus. We should state we are skeptical about what we can know *with confidence* and so we prefer to think in terms of whether ideas about Jesus were early or late and whether they were particular to his geographical location or beyond. In the absence of more sources from closer to the time of Jesus we have no grounds for certitude in the reconstruction of his life. We stress this because it will become cumbersome to repeat throughout the book and the reader should always remember we are providing what we think are the earliest narratives about Jesus or themes associated with the Jesus movement. Jesus, like certain bandits, soon came to be idealized.

There have been other suggestions of useful sources, such as the second-century collection of Jesus' sayings called the Gospel of Thomas. Although this text is likely dependent on earlier Gospels, it is also possible the author of Thomas had access to some independent sayings attributed to Jesus, though this does not typically add much to what we already know. Other non-canonical and/or so-called "Gnostic" Gospels are of no real use in reconstructing the life of the historical Jesus because they tell us more about theological concerns and interests from the second century onwards or fill in the narrative gaps in the life of Jesus with creative storytelling. Sources, of course, have other uses than potential mines of older biographical information but given our interests are in the historical Jesus we stress specific references to Jesus in non-Christian sources, such as the asides found in Josephus and Tacitus, are of no serious value for understanding the historical Jesus, not least because they are based on speculations and rumors about what Christians believed.

But, as we have seen already, the Jewish historian Josephus provides plenty of other useful details on the political and social history of the first century, though this too needs to be critically assessed. Josephus' extensive account of the Jewish War fought with Rome (66-73 CE), based on his own first-hand knowledge of the events, is particularly interesting for its coloring of the context more generally as a hotbed of social and ideological conflict. Such conflict boiled over into full-scale insurrectionary revolt in 66 CE when the Jewish leaders declared independence from Roman rule. A bitter and violent struggle between Jewish radicals and Roman legions was fought for several years and culminated in a Roman siege on Jerusalem in 70 CE, destroying the city and its Holy Temple. These events, as well as many less dramatic clashes between Rome and the Jewish population during the first century, would have been electrifying, and in many cases fueled millenarian hopes and dreams.

Josephus was himself a vivid storyteller with an apologetic

agenda (in the sense of providing a formal defense of one's conduct and views), and his historical work needs to be analyzed alongside archaeological evidence which likewise gives us material insight into the social world of Jesus. But like Josephus and the Gospels, archaeological evidence needs to be understood critically as it typically privileges the durable lives of the elite over the lives of itinerant figures like Jesus and the more precarious members of his movement. We will generally refer to the ancient literary sources we use, as well as archaeological remains coming from the elite such as coins and monumental structures, as forming part of the *ideological imperial apparatus*, that is, the "soft power" that generated and regulated the ideas and perspectives of the ruling elite. After all, as Marx put it, "the ideas of the ruling class are in every epoch the ruling ideas, i.e., the class which is the ruling material force of society, is at the same time its ruling intellectual force."[8]

Even so, elite sources should not be discarded simply because they typically favor different class interests. Such sources not only provide evidence for reconstructing history from below, but they can also tell us about elite perceptions of popular movements and thus how a figure like Jesus was understood by his class enemies. There are ancient sources which provide us with information about lives from below, though this is usually limited. Papyri, for instance, provide insights into lives spent in agricultural work, laboring, and fishing, though such material typically comes from Roman Egypt and there is disagreement over the extent to which it can be used to make generalizations about Galilee and Judea.

Among the most plentiful sources available to us are Jewish ones which deal with issues we would typically label "religious" or "theological," and so are directly relevant for contextualizing a Jewish millenarian figure like Jesus. Rabbinic literature was codified from around 200 CE onward but contains huge amounts of information relating to the interpretation of Jewish scriptures, including claims about rabbis and Pharisees from the first century. Because it is of a comparably late date, rabbinic literature needs to be used cautiously when reconstructing ideas from the first century. But it can be done.

Though often reflecting certain sectarian interests, the Dead Sea Scrolls from Qumran are among the best of Jewish sources because they were collected, written, and interpreted before and around the time of Jesus. This means they provide another window into the diverse world of first-century Judaism. They are particularly useful for determining how, for instance, apocalypticism and the interpretation of the Jewish Scriptures were being discussed at the time. No New Testament documents were among the scrolls, and conspiracy theories about them containing coded references to Jesus cannot be taken seriously, but it should be noted some scholars have speculated about possible connections between John the Baptist and Qumran given the mutual interests in water purification rituals and asceticism in the wilderness.

These Jewish texts from antiquity may appear to cover "religious" and "theological" issues but this does not mean they were removed from "class" or "political" concerns, whether or not authors, texts, and interpreters obfuscate such connections. The popular distinction between religion and politics is, of course, a modern one, and in antiquity people freely blended political and class concerns with theological ones. Religion was not a private matter of personal devotion or restricted to "spiritual" matters as opposed to "worldly" ones. Rather it concerned all of life. Accordingly, we will use a range of sources to provide not only the most plausible reconstruction of the historical Jesus and his world but, against the reductive trend in bourgeois scholarship, we will also provide an explanation about why class is central to understanding the life of a first-century millenarian prophet and the movement that was called by his name.

A Précis

It remains to offer a précis for our life of Jesus of Nazareth. Our historical reconstruction begins by looking at Jesus' upbringing against the backdrop of changing social and economic conditions in first-century Galilee. We introduce antagonistic influences on the ordinary Jewish population (e.g., urbanization projects in Galilee) as well as the influence of other popular movements from the time (e.g., John the Baptist), and we assess how these impacted the direction of Jesus' adult life.

As noted above, instead of romanticizing the enigmatic person of Jesus as a Great Man of history, we seek to reconstruct his lifework more plausibly as a socially credible religious organizer, emerging from the non-elite Jewish classes, and as a figure who was dependent on and a suitable conduit for the interests of the peasantry in Galilee and Judea. In doing so, we seek to uncover the social and economic origins behind the formation of the collective "Jesus movement" he was a part of and which, in turn, formed him as a leader.

The aims and objectives of the Jesus movement were clear, at least in the initial stages. Caught up in millenarian and messianic beliefs about God imminently and dramatically intervening in human history to transform the world for the better, the Jesus movement would act as a vanguard political party with its own politburo and would be installed through decisive divine judgment as the custodians of a new theocracy, a dictatorship serving the interests of the peasantry. Come the revolution, the fortunes of the agrarian world would be turned upside down: non-elite sectors of Jewish society were guaranteed a life of plenty; the rich, however, would have to relinquish their wealth or suffer ruinous consequences. As part of its work in Galilee, the Jesus movement organized a controversial "mission to the rich" to get some of the wealthy onboard, and it was moderately successful in these attempts.

The Jesus movement's credibility among the Galilean peasantry

21

was due to its emphasis on traditional peasant values, generous acts of healing, culturally serious interpretations of Jewish scriptures, and strict group discipline, all of which provided a dignified alternative in a changing Galilee. As households were broken up due to elite-sponsored building projects in nearby urban centers, the Jesus movement formed its own alternative household, respectfully mimicking traditional family roles. However, this also provoked reaction and ridicule and the movement was dismissed by outsiders as "effeminate" and "unmanly." These allegations were ironically embraced by the Jesus movement.

Alongside this, the movement looked for opportunities to self-present as tough, muscular, hard, and manly (mostly through a redefinition of terms) so as not to be out of step with the hegemonic masculinity of their wider world. As the Jesus movement gained renown, Jesus and others drew on Jewish traditions of "righteous martyrs" to develop ideas about dying a glorious death for the sake of God and country. Martyrdom, which involved "taking it like a man," would feature as a defining public presentation of their masculinity, but it also spurred them into further skirmishes with the elite.

With time being short, and passions high, the Jesus movement converged on Jerusalem, located to the south of Galilee in the Roman province of Judea. Their fateful trip to the holy city, where the Temple was located, took place during the festival of Passover when underlying social and political anxieties would regularly flare up. History from below continues as we contextualize Jesus and the movement's entanglements at Jerusalem with the volatile and unpredictable Passover crowds. As is well known, Jesus' participation in incendiary activities was used by the authorities as the reason to arrest and crucify him. His maimed body hung on a cross under a sign displaying his charge, "Jesus of Nazareth, the King of the Jews"; he was put to death as a deranged royal pretender.

But this was not the end of the story, or the movement for

that matter. Not long after Jesus' martyred corpse was laid in a tomb by Joseph of Arimathea (one of several success stories of the movement's "mission to the rich"), key figures in the vanguard sincerely believed God had resurrected him back to life. This was not a completely unexpected outcome of Jesus' gruesome but manly execution as a martyr. Quite the opposite: it confirmed the end times were truly at hand!

That Jesus' associates and sympathizers reported seeing him after his death is one important reason for the survival of the movement. Ultimately, however, the revolution envisaged by the movement failed. It became clear God would not intervene quite as imminently as they had predicted. We accordingly end our story by gesturing to Jesus' role in longer-term historical developments, not as a prime mover, but swept up in the historical materialist process itself. Radical and fanatical objectives of the initial movement transcended their original historical context of first century Galilee. We suggest the inherent tensions uncovered in earlier chapters between the Jesus movement's revolutionary and reactionary impulses would be raised back to life, in various guises and places, over the centuries to follow.

Chapter 2

Growing Up in a Gentrifying Galilee

It is difficult enough to reconstruct the adult life of Jesus. It is more difficult still to reconstruct details of his birth and childhood. This is because of a lack of consistent evidence. In the earliest material, Jesus' life as a child and young adult are effectively silent years to us, though it is possible to establish some general points about his birthplace, hometown, parentage, and basic chronology.

While there is a distinct lack of biographical detail, we can fill in gaps with historical evidence of what the small village of Nazareth and the expansive region of Galilee in northern Palestine were like as Jesus and his peers were growing up against the backdrop of direct and indirect Roman power. This should not be seen as trivial background which adds a little color to Jesus' upbringing. Rather, it enables us to return to the issues raised in the previous chapter by identifying important socio-economic changes taking place at the time, and the dislocations and disruptions to village life that were happening as a result. These changes also provided daily reminders of the inequalities of a world backed by Roman imperial power, and such reminders would occasionally clash with deep-seated memories or traditions of Jewish calls for national sovereignty and a renewed political order.

Accordingly, in this chapter, we examine how these material shifts in first-century Galilee were impacting the lives of peasants and artisans in the countryside. Class conflicts in Galilee would continue to shape the rest of Jesus' life (and death) and explain why the millenarian Jesus movement appeared in that time and place. Before we come to such issues, however, we should investigate what we can deduce about his earliest biographical

24

details. As we will see, although the evidence in our primary sources is inconsistent, we can make several relatively firm determinations about his birth and upbringing.

Jesus from Nazareth

In the Gospel of Mark, Jesus first appears as a fully-grown adult whose hometown is Nazareth in the Jewish region of Galilee (Mark 6.1-6). Mark, the earliest biography of Jesus, either ignores or is ignorant of the circumstances of Jesus' birth and childhood. In John's Gospel, after an abstract and philosophical prologue (John 1.1-18), the narrative proper likewise begins with Jesus as an adult from Nazareth, with no indication he was born anywhere else. This is one reason why it is commonly argued Jesus was born and raised in Nazareth.

The conclusion is supported by the insignificance of Nazareth, which was not the sort of place that would be invented as the origin of someone deemed special or important. Nazareth is not mentioned in the Old Testament/Hebrew Bible, Josephus, Dead Sea Scrolls, or later rabbinic writings. John's Gospel, although not particularly reliable on historical detail, provided one creative way of dealing with the problem of an insignificant Nazareth by claiming Jesus exceeded all expectations:

> Nathanael said to him, "Can anything good come out of Nazareth?" Philip said to him, "Come and see." When Jesus saw Nathanael coming towards him, he said of him, "Here is truly an Israelite in whom there is no deceit!" (John 1.46-47)

Alongside this, in the Gospels of Matthew and Luke we find the famous infancy stories that claim Jesus was born in Bethlehem and was miraculously conceived when his mother Mary was a virgin. These stories also include extended and idealized genealogies, various angelic appearances, wise men following stars to a precise location, an unborn child leaping in the womb at some good news, and a 12-year-old Jesus dazzling the experienced teachers in the Jerusalem Temple.

As critical scholarship has long recognized, these infancy narratives are of limited use for the historian reconstructing Jesus' first days, months, and years because they fit into a general tendency in the ancient world to provide dramatic origin stories of figures deemed Great Men (e.g., emperors, philosophers, patriarchs). For example, the details surrounding Jesus' birth look like later attempts to shift Jesus' birthplace to somewhere more fitting for a Jewish Messiah, as Bethlehem was the supposed hometown of David, the most famous king of ancient Israel (and whose exploits are chronicled in 1 Samuel 16.13-1 Kings 2.12). To help amplify their protagonist's own greatness, Matthew and Luke placed Jesus' birth in Bethlehem so he fulfilled a prophecy about a future ruler of Israel descended from the royal line of David (Matt. 1.1-18; 2.1-6; Luke 1.26-33; 2.4; 3.23-38). As the prophet Micah foretold:

But you, O Bethlehem of Ephrathah,
who are one of the little clans of Judah,
from you shall come forth for me
one who is to rule in Israel,
whose origin is from of old,
from ancient days. (Mic. 5.2).

But while Matthew and Luke both seek to explain how a known resident of Nazareth came to be born in Bethlehem, their explanations are also strikingly inconsistent, as we shall see.

On the one hand, Matthew depicts Jesus' family initially resident in Bethlehem and arriving in Nazareth only after fleeing to Egypt to avoid the upheaval of King Herod, the ruler of Palestine (see below), setting about killing boys aged 2 years and under in and around Bethlehem (Matt. 2.16-18). After an angel informed Joseph (Mary's betrothed) of Herod's death, the family was able to safely leave Egypt and return to Palestine. As Judea was still deemed too dangerous, however, they made their way north to Nazareth in Galilee (Matt. 2.19-23).

This is an exaggerated case of Matthean fiction. The narrative employs a typological reusing of the story of Moses' birth and exodus from Egypt to align Jesus with another Great Man (cf. Deut. 34.10) and a founding myth of the Israelite tradition (Ex. 1.22-2.10; 13-15.21). And while Matthew's tale is certainly useful for highlighting the political and social instability of Judea at the time, it lacks corroborating evidence. Archaeological discoveries suggest infanticide was routinely employed in other parts of the Roman Empire as a method of population control, yet there is no material evidence for such an episode occurring in Bethlehem. Nor is there any independent mention of Herod ordering the mass murder of children (or the backlash it would have likely provoked). Herod was certainly capable of acts of brutality, but he also tried to keep order and an unprovoked act like this would have led to serious unrest. It is the kind of scintillating story Josephus would not have left out of his history of the Jewish people had it happened.

On the other hand, and in direct contrast to Matthew, Luke has Jesus' immediate family in Nazareth to begin with and so must explain why they traveled to Bethlehem. Luke does this by claiming the displacement was due to a census under the Roman governor Quirinius and according to a decree of the Roman Emperor for "all the world" to be registered. This required Joseph to travel from his hometown of Nazareth to the town of Bethlehem where his remote ancestors had apparently lived (Luke 2.1-5; 3.31-32).

Many scholars think Luke's description of the census requirements is unfeasible, not least because no census took place around the time Jesus was supposed to be born. According to Josephus, a census was, in fact, conducted several years later as part of the reorganization of Judea after the fall of Herod's son and successor Archelaus in 6 CE. Quirinius was tasked with assessing Judea for the Roman tax take, triggering the revolt of Judas the Galilean (see below). Yet elsewhere, Luke 1.5 suggests the events surrounding Jesus' birth took place "in the days of King Herod" who had died in 4 CE. It appears Luke may have shifted the historical detail about the census from its original context to explain why Jesus was born in accordance with a prophecy about a great ruler from Bethlehem.

The most straightforward explanations are, in general, better. It is reasonable, therefore, to go with the assumption of our earliest Gospel of Mark that Jesus was, in fact, born in Nazareth. This makes better sense than Mark somehow being unaware or ignoring a dramatic and impressive origins story of the sort found in Matthew or Luke.

While there are historical problems with the birth and infancy stories, this does not mean they are completely without use. First, if the chronological information is roughly correct, then Jesus was born toward the end of the reign of Herod the Great (Matt. 2.1, 16, 19; cf. Luke 1.5) who died in 4 BCE. This means, ironically, Jesus was born earlier than the dating system which divided all of history based on his life into the years before Christ "BC" and *Anno Domini* "AD" (Latin for "in the year of the Lord"). The system originates from the sixth century CE and appears to have miscalculated the year Jesus was born.

Second, Luke claims John the Baptist began his public career in the "fifteenth year of the reign of Emperor Tiberius" (Luke 3.1), which would be around 29 CE, and that Jesus was about 30 when he began his own work (Luke 3.23). Luke places the beginning of the Jesus movement's organizing directly after John's. These dates do not match up with Matthew, but we are not dealing with the lives of kings or officials where we could expect more precise records. We can be content with the general point that Jesus was born toward the end of the first century BCE and his movement rose to public prominence toward the end of the 20s CE.

What's in a Name?

From the Gospels we can make further observations about Jesus' birth and upbringing. The name "Jesus" comes from the Greek *Iēsous*, which is a translation of the Hebrew name *Yēshua*ʾ, "Joshua." As Matthew 1.21 implies, the basic meaning of the name is "God (or Yahweh) saves" and it was the name of Moses' successor who led the Israelite conquest of Canaan according to the book of Joshua. Quite how much significance was given to Jesus' name by his family beyond a general identification with Jewish tradition is impossible to say. However, such names were part of the constant reminders of ideas that came to undergird the revolutionary millenarianism of the Jesus movement: specifically, that God had liberated Israel from slavery under Pharaoh once before and would do it again; this time by liberating the Jewish people from their Roman-backed overlords and installing a new political order in its place.

We can make an educated guess that Jesus' father, Joseph, was older than his mother. It was common for husbands to be older than their wives (note how often widows are mentioned in the New Testament). The fact that Joseph is conspicuously absent when Jesus was an adult suggests he was dead by this time. We know marginally more about Jesus' mother, Mary (or Miriam, named after the sister of Moses), who outlived Jesus and, according to Acts 1.5, was part of the ongoing movement after his death. If Mark's Gospel is to be believed, however, the familial relationship was not without its difficulties, an issue we return to in Chapter 6. One possible reason for this was that Jesus, as the eldest son, would have been expected to become head of the household after Joseph's death and provide for the family, rather than wandering through the countryside with his itinerant movement.

Mark 6.3 and the parallel text in Matthew 13.55-56 claim Jesus had sisters (whose names are not given) and brothers named James (or Jacob), Joses (or Joseph), Judas, and Simon.

The New Testament letter of Jude was attributed to Jesus' younger brother by that name, although scholars continue to debate whether this attribution is pseudonymous. Jesus' most famous brother, James, would become the leading Jerusalem-based figure in the Jesus movement after his death. We do not know how James reacted to the Jesus movement initially or whether he became involved after his brother's martyrdom. It is possible James was already in Jerusalem as a prominent figure in his own right. Given the interests in socio-economic issues in the letter attributed to him, he may have been part of another branch which organized its own millenarian response to the changes in Galilee and Judea.[1]

By far the simplest explanation of Jesus' parentage is that he was the eldest son of Joseph and Mary, who had other children. Speculations about alternative explanations of the parentage of Jesus and his brothers and sisters are later developments. One is worth noting, if only for its ongoing notoriety. It is sometimes argued one function of the birth and infancy stories in Matthew and Luke was to hide a problematic fact: Jesus was the product of a brutal rape and, moreover, his father was actually a Roman soldier called Panthera.[2]

The earliest overt version of the story of Panthera dates to the late second century and the critic of Christianity, Celsus (Origen, *Contra Celsus* 1.32). Related claims were later taken up by some Jewish opponents of Christianity, as John's Gospel perhaps already implies (John 8.39-47). Such claims should be understood as later polemics against Christianity rather than reflections of first-century realities. Of course, it is not impossible that Mary got pregnant by having sex (consensual or not) with someone other than her betrothed. The Romans did ransack nearby Sepphoris in 4 BCE (see below), where soldiers would have raped the defeated population, and if the birth and infancy narratives in the Gospels did want to hide the reality of Jesus' parentage and did a successful job of it, then we may never know. But these sorts of speculations are just that: speculations.

It remains there is no *early* evidence that Jesus' birth was deemed dishonorable, the infancy stories of Matthew and Luke coming later. Our earliest Gospel, Mark, saw no need to defend Jesus or Mary from such criticism. It is sometimes claimed that when Jesus was referred to as the "son of Mary" in his hometown of Nazareth (Mark 6.3), it was dishonorable because he should have been called the "son of Joseph," given the patriarchal expectations of the time (cf. John 6.42). However, the reason for this labeling was not due to his dubious parentage, but simply because Joseph was probably long dead, or perhaps also to insinuate Jesus was not living up to his obligations to provide for his mother in his role as the new head of the household. Besides, the notion that Jewish men could not be referred to with reference to their mothers generalizes too much about gendered expectations in early Judaism. Given Mary plays a prominent role in the Gospels, it is hardly surprising that this connection is highlighted. As it happens, references to mothers occur in other Jewish sources, particularly if they were deemed important, including the high priest of 17-18 CE, Simon son of Kamith (Josephus, *Antiquities* 18.34), and his parentage was not up for dispute.

Growing up in Nazareth

While the biographical evidence for Jesus' early years is basic, we can say much more about the political and social world he was born into. For much of the rest of this chapter, we discuss in detail the historical background of a gentrifying Galilee, as can be gathered from the writings of Josephus and with reference to the archaeological record. This also allows us to profile Jesus' own class background, and to think about how he and his peers responded to the changes and upheavals taking place around them.

Herod the Great ruled a client-kingdom by the grace of

Rome from 37 BCE until his death in 4 BCE. As governor of Galilee, before he was inaugurated "King of the Jews," Herod successfully campaigned against Galilean bandits, executing their leaders, and enhancing his status in the eyes of Rome. During his reign as monarch, Herod expressed unrelenting loyalty to Rome, and embarked on large-scale building projects such as the grandiose refurbishment of the Jerusalem Temple. Various inscriptions found on the Acropolis in Athens attest to Herod's reputation through the Empire as a "Friend of the Romans" and "Friend of the Emperor" (*OGIS* nos. 414; 427).

After Herod the Great's death, the kingdom was divided among his three sons: Antipas became tetrarch (governor of one of four divisions of a province) of Galilee and Perea and is the "Herod" mentioned in the Gospels when Jesus was an adult; Philip became tetrarch of the northeasterly parts of Herod's kingdom; and Archelaus became ethnarch (governor of an ethnic group) of Judea, Samaria, and Idumea. Archelaus was quickly judged incompetent by the Romans and in 6 CE was replaced by a series of Roman prefects (i.e., placed under direct Roman rule), the most famous of whom was the man ultimately responsible for Jesus' death, Pontius Pilate, who took power in 26 CE.

Pilate was based on the coast of Roman Judea at Caesarea Maritima but would come to Jerusalem with a military presence for major occasions such as Passover. Here the situation was particularly tense as Jews celebrated the founding myth of the escape from slavery under Pharaoh, and some expected history to repeat itself, and soon. As Josephus noted, it was during festivals that insurrections were most likely to happen (*War* 1.88).

The devastation left by Roman military power was a lingering memory for Galileans after the city of Sepphoris (6 kilometers or about an hour's walk from Nazareth) was sacked and razed and its inhabitants enslaved in 4 BCE by Varus, the Roman governor of Syria (*Antiquities* 17.271-87; *War* 2.56-69). This was to suppress an uprising led by Judas, son of the bandit Ezekias. The rebels had made an assault on the palace, seizing weapons and plundering spoils. If Jesus was born by this time, he would have been just a toddler, but we can imagine local stories about freedom fighters were being circulated in the years following, alongside traumatic accounts of the retaliatory threat of Roman suppression.

Nevertheless, there was not a *direct* Roman presence in Galilee for the rest of Jesus' life. Galilee was effectively left for Antipas, son of Herod the Great, to rule as a client-kingdom of Rome with relative independence until he was exiled in 39 CE, several years *after* Jesus had been crucified. Under Antipas, there is no evidence that taxation was problematic enough to provoke another full-scale uprising, though resentments and class interests manifested themselves in other ways, as we will see. In Galilee, as elsewhere, the small urban-based elite of the governing class and their retainers dominated the overwhelmingly rural population who lived in small villages. The elite were able to live in relative comfort off the exploitation of agrarian labor of the peasantry, and many farmers would have been just one crop failure away from famine or a life of banditry.

Nazareth itself was a small Galilean village located between the southern shores of the Sea of Galilee (actually a freshwater lake) to the east and the Mediterranean Sea to the west, with a population estimated at no more than 400, though some scholars suggest up to 2000. Nazareth was unremarkable in the sense it was in an area with irrigation and terracing, undertook agricultural produce (e.g., cereals, olives, figs, grapes), and grazed livestock (e.g., cattle, goats, sheep). From the surplus of resources created by the labor-power of the peasantry, tithes were relinquished to sustain the priesthood, rents went to absentee landowners, and taxes were paid to Antipas who in turn offered tribute to Rome.

From what we know of its archaeology, Nazareth was a conventional enough Jewish village of its time and place.

Houses were basic and consisted of a small group of rooms around a central courtyard. Although no layout of the village or its houses has been produced, and no remains with Greek symbolism have been unearthed, there is evidence that stone vessels were used for maintaining Jewish purity laws. There is thus no reason to think that Jesus had anything other than a conventional Jewish upbringing in that he would have been circumcised, eaten kosher, rested on the Sabbath, heard stories about the history of Israel from Jewish scriptures, and cited daily a reminder of who Jews believed was rightfully in charge of the world: "Hear, O Israel: The Lord is our God, the Lord alone. You shall love the Lord your God with all your heart, and with all your soul, and with all your might" (Deut. 6.4-5). Some of these beliefs and practices were learned at home and became everyday cultural assumptions. Some were acquired at the local synagogue. In a small village like Nazareth, we should probably visualize the synagogue as a gathering in a convenient space, rather than one of the more formally named buildings present elsewhere in Palestine.

Illiterate Peasant?

While Greek was the common language of the eastern Roman Empire, in Galilee the primary language was Aramaic with a Galilean dialect (Matt. 26.73). That Jesus spoke Aramaic was assumed by the Gospel writers who, although themselves writing in Greek, provided explanations for several Aramaic phrases. Whether Jesus spoke the words attributed to him or not, Mark 5.41 gives a clear example of this assumption when Mark accurately explains the Aramaic term, *talitha qum*: "He took her by the hand and said to her, 'Talitha cum,' which means, 'Little girl, get up!'" As we will see, understanding the Aramaic of Jesus can provide (admittedly modest) help in determining some of the nuances of the Jesus movement's ideas.

Jesus may have also known Hebrew to some degree as it was

the main language of the scriptural and related texts transmitted in Palestine, most famously the Dead Sea Scrolls. By the time of the first century, a Greek translation of the Hebrew scriptures, the Septuagint, was also in use. Work on this translation had begun in the third century BCE in Alexandria, Egypt. The name derives from the Greek word for "seventy" (hence, its abbreviation "LXX," the number 70 in Roman numerals), referring to a legend that the translation was undertaken by 72 Jewish interpreters bought to Egypt by the ruler Ptolemy.

It is thus possible Jesus knew at least some Greek. Despite a lack of specific evidence with regard to Jesus, Jews throughout the Roman Empire, and no doubt some in Galilee too, could happily use Greek and embrace Greek philosophy and culture without necessarily seeing any contradiction with their Jewish identity. But in Galilee, Aramaic and Hebrew may have also functioned as a linguistic and cultural identity marker against Greco-Roman culture. This may have been broadly assumed but there is a hint of this in the Gospels when Jesus used the phrase "hypocrite" to attack his opponents. *Hypocritēs* was not an Aramaic term but a Greek one meaning "actor" of the sort found in a Greco-Roman theater. It is possible Jesus polemically (and, arguably, unfairly) used this Greek term to attack scribes and Pharisees. The Pharisees, who we will encounter again in Chapter 7, were a group of particularly observant and influential Jews in the first century, popularly regarded as visible upholders of Jewish practices and identity in larger towns where what was understood to be Greco-Roman culture was more embedded (*Antiquities* 18.15).

Another reason behind the speculation that Jesus may have acquired some Greek was possible work opportunities in nearby Sepphoris or through the trade of goods produced by his household. Nazareth was itself not far from a major trade route to Egypt, the *Via Maris*. We should be cautious of such speculation, however, as modern "entrepreneurial" categories tend to obscure our comprehension of the regular and mostly inward-looking work-patterns of rural villagers, as we will see below. What mattered most was sustaining traditional ways of life, not making a quick denarius at their expense.

In any case, Jesus is famous for his occupation as a carpenter, and it is possible he did work with wood. The English word "carpenter" translates the Greek *tektōn* of Mark 6.3, which also described skills beyond carpentry, including stonemasonry, as well as the labor of a manual worker or an artisan. At least some people would have expected Jesus to remain a *tektōn* for the rest of his life. A telling example comes from a Jewish text from before Jesus' time which reveals class-based assumptions about the division of labor in the world:

> The wisdom of the scribe depends on the opportunity of leisure...How can one become wise who handles the plough, who glories in the shaft of a goad, who drives oxen and is occupied with their work, and whose talk is about bulls?...So too is every artisan (*tektōn*) and master artisan who labours by night as well as by day...So too is the smith sitting by his anvil, intent on his iron work...So too is the potter sitting at his work and turning the wheel with his feet...All these rely on their hands and all are skilful in their own work. Without them no city can be inhabited...Yet they are not sought out for their council of the people, nor do they attain eminence in the public assembly. They do not sit in the judge's seat, nor do they understand the decisions of the courts; they cannot expound discipline or judgement, and they are not found among the rulers. But they maintain the fabric of the world, and their concern is for the exercise of their trade. How different the one who devotes himself to the study of the law of the Most High! (Sirach 38.24-34)

In this romanticized, elite justification of the world, a basic reality is at play: someone like Jesus should not be involved with intellectual matters and should know his place as a rural manual worker.

But does it follow that Jesus was a peasant (or an artisan closely aligned with the peasantry) without sufficient literacy skills to read (for example) Jewish scriptures? This is a difficult problem to resolve, with arguments and counter arguments regularly put forward by scholars. Estimates that non-elite workers were overwhelmingly unlikely to be able to read or write are important, and texts like Matthew 23.1-3 imply ordinary people needed scribal assistance if they wanted to learn about the Jewish scriptures. But it does not automatically follow all people from such backgrounds were illiterate in the sense of being unable to read extended texts; Jesus could, theoretically, have been in the minority.

Phrases attributed to Jesus in the Gospels like "have you not read...?" (e.g., Mark 2.25), if taken literally, imply a shared assumption that both Jesus and his opponents could read. Alternatively, this could be understood as a sarcastic riposte by Jesus. Another option is these words reflect more the concerns of later scribes who penned the Gospels and who had an interest in portraying Jesus as literate (see below). Whatever the case, we should take seriously the point that Jesus and James, brought up in the same household, were later remembered as teachers and exegetes of Jewish scriptures, which at least suggests a background conducive to such developments.[3] But all this knowledge could have been acquired aurally, from family members or from the synagogue.

Much more could be said, and Chris Keith provides the most significant treatment of these issues.[4] Keith highlights a particularly important point: the development of Gospel themes concerning Jesus' trade and social standing shift from a lower-status manual worker in Mark through to a more elite scribal figure in Luke. The story in Mark 6.3 has Jesus return to Nazareth to teach in the synagogue to the amazement of the villagers. They wondered about his authority to teach and rejected him with explicit reference to his trade as a *tektōn*.

Matthew, working from Mark's text, transferred the occupation to Joseph: "Is this not the carpenters' son?" (Matt. 13.55). Though this was not exactly an inaccurate reading of Mark (who presumably would have agreed that Joseph was a *tektōn*), it does subtly distance Jesus from the trade. The reason for Matthew's change was possibly because a manual trade was not sufficiently elevated. Indeed, later opponents of Christianity sometimes thought fit to ridicule Christians on the basis of Jesus' occupation (e.g., Origen, *Contra Celsus* 6, 34). Luke went further still in his substantially rewritten version of the rejection at Nazareth (Luke 4.16-30). Not only did he drop reference to *tektōn* altogether (Jesus is now "Joseph's son"), but Jesus himself reads aloud from a scroll of Isaiah, a detail which is completely absent from the other Gospels.

None of this decisively disproves that the historical Jesus could have read extensively from Jewish scriptures. It is theoretically possible the author of Luke wanted to make clear what Mark (and Matthew) merely assumed. But, on balance, attempts to explain why Jesus was sufficiently educated, or at least downplay his role as a rural manual worker, suggest a more likely option is that he was not, by elite assumptions at least, the type of person who should expound Jewish scripture in public. This became an uncomfortable problem that had to be dealt with by the various Gospel writers after Mark.

There is, admittedly, no definitive answer to the question of the extent of Jesus' literacy. However, whether he was a literate peasant does not ultimately affect our historical reconstruction. If the general Gospel portrayal is right that Jesus knew the Jewish scriptures in detail, then this could have been through hearing them regularly expounded as he was growing up. And even if he could read at length, the point remains that among the earliest perceptions of him, he was remembered as a rural manual worker who did not fit into what was expected of the scribal elite. On the contrary: he was occasionally viewed as getting above his station.

Either way, we now have another important question to address: how did someone from Jesus' unremarkable background come to have a movement form around him? To understand this, we need to grasp the social and economic changes taking place in Galilee as he was growing up. Making sense of the class antagonisms in Galilee will in turn form a crucial basis for unpacking the rest of Jesus' life presented in this book.

A World Turning Upside Down

Despite it being widely known that wealth in the Roman world was concentrated among an aristocratic few, and that much of the peasantry lived on a knife's edge, class and class conflict is frequently distorted in bourgeois and liberal scholarship on Jesus. In some cases, class is brushed aside as a modern category that would have been unrecognizable to Galileans primarily interested in issues of family and kinship. Again, we stress that historians should not ignore differing claims to status in terms of kinship, nor indeed gender, prestige, and other markers of social status and identity in the ancient world (see Chapter 6). But we should not be afraid to be suspicious of, or to demystify, ancient constructions of social status and the order of things, just as critical historians have been suspicious of, and have demystified, Gospel claims about Jesus.

A persistent myth, for instance, that rural artisans like Jesus were "middle class" is not only anachronistic but has been mobilized in certain streams of scholarship to erode possibilities for class conflict in Galilee. While it is true manual workers were classed well below the small minority of the elite and in some cases were marginally better off than others in the peasantry, especially those with more chaotic work-patterns like a day laborer, it is misleading to speak of such folk as belonging to the middle class. In fact, there was nothing equivalent to a middle class in antiquity. Most workers were born, lived, and died in what would be today considered modest economic circumstances, circumstances geared toward subsistence living.

Moreover, we should avoid the credulous idea that because certain rulers were especially skilled at keeping the peace then everybody was more-or-less happy with the situation. Resentments could fester under the surface, especially during periods of effective suppression. It is worth remembering, too, that a reductive focus on supposedly isolated cases of violence or disorder can all-too-easily overlook the systemic violence that is inherent to the "normal" state of things. However people may have expressed their concerns, understood the world, and negotiated the complexities of social strata, we still have to explain why the rich stayed rich and the poor stayed poor, why palaces were built, why rents were charged, why taxes were collected, why there were occasional outbursts of discontent about taxes, why peasants were more likely to starve than aristocrats, and why some people looked forward to the rich suffering terribly in the afterlife.

But there is another reason why class as a motor for historical change is dismissed by historians of Jesus and Galilee: the apparent lack of *explicit* evidence of class conflict in Galilee as Jesus was growing up. There is a respectable and influential strand of scholarship which has argued the Galilean economy under Antipas was relatively prosperous, and his building projects would have, if anything, benefited the populace, assuming a kind of "trickle-down" logic to the ancient economy. One of the most influential historical Jesus scholars in the past 40 years, E. P. Sanders, argued:

the lack of uprisings also indicates that Antipas was not

excessively oppressive and did not levy exorbitant taxes... he undertook large building projects that helped reduce unemployment. Galileans in Jesus' lifetime did not feel that things most dear to them were seriously threatened: their religion, their national traditions and their livelihoods.[5]

More recently, scholars such as Morten Hørning Jensen and Helen K. Bond have developed this argument, likewise claiming archaeological evidence suggests Galilee under Antipas was relatively tranquil.[6]

Such scholarship is obviously an important corrective to popular perceptions that Galilee was especially oppressed under Herod Antipas. However, this does not mean we should reject understanding the emergence of the Jesus movement in terms of class conflict. As noted in the previous chapter, archaeology and literary texts tend to favor the lives and perspectives of the elite and so only tell us so much about conflict and class in Galilee. If there was extensive evidence of material damage, it would no doubt help the case, but the absence of such evidence does not mean an absence of discontents under Antipas. The disgruntled masses do not always destroy buildings!

The framing of the debate in terms of an unambiguous rise or fall in the standards of living among the peasantry is also misleading. Unrest, rebellions, critiques of authority, and so on, do not (though they may) have to be reactions to, or the result of, an unambiguous decline in the general standard of living, or a reaction to the overall population being even more exploited than usual. The situation could have been a more complex mix of reactions, from anger through opportunism to accepting change against personal economic interests. Indeed, we shall see there is good evidence for this sort of scenario in Galilee as Jesus was growing up.

The discussion of class, class conflict, and historical change in Galilee therefore needs to be nuanced. The older Marxist work of the ancient Roman historian G. E. M. de Ste. Croix in his monumental *The Class Struggle in the Ancient Greek World* has recently reemerged in scholarship of Christian origins. This includes debates over whether a slave economy, unfree labor, the tributary system, or some combination of these, constituted the dominant mode of production in the ancient world, including first-century Palestine.[7]

These issues are too vast and uncertain for proper engagement here. What we can say is in Galilee and Judea, as we might expect in more advanced agrarian societies, the town-countryside relationship formed one aspect of production which, as we will see, was particularly crucial for understanding local class conflict and disruptions. One point is especially worth repeating: elites in urban centers maintained the tributary system and their extravagant lifestyles by extracting surplus from the labor-power and agrarian produce of the villages in the surrounding countryside, as we saw implied in the passage from Sirach quoted above.

In some respects, Antipas faithfully carried on the legacy of his father before him in the form of large-scale building projects. Crucially, we know of two urbanization projects in Galilee as Jesus was growing up: the rebuilding of Sepphoris and the building of Tiberias. Tiberias was built near the Sea of Galilee and was completed around 19 CE. With a reminder of the power behind Antipas, it was named after the Roman emperor Tiberius. First-century material remains suggest Roman influence in Galilee more broadly included the introduction of certain "Roman" features in monumental public buildings, such as Roman-style frescoes in Sepphoris, as well as limited amounts of imported fine Italian wares.[8]

Sepphoris itself was especially significant given its proximity to Nazareth. After it was razed by the Romans, Antipas had it rebuilt and refortified to the extent Josephus could refer to it as "the ornament of all Galilee" and possibly its capital (*Antiquities*

18.27; *War* 2.511). Elsewhere Josephus noted it was "situated in the heart of Galilee, surrounded by many villages" (*Life* 346). Among these surrounding villages was Nazareth, which may have contributed labor and surplus for the ornamentation of Sepphoris and its elites. With the development of the water system, including from the time of Antipas, Sepphoris also dominated water resources in the area.[9]

The claim made by Sanders and others that these urbanization projects increased employment is unnuanced and needs to be tempered against what else we know of the dynamics of peasant life. While such projects obviously required skilled artisans, the assumption that villagers were unthreatened by the changes is unsubstantiated and sounds suspiciously like the wishful thinking of a disconnected elite. While it is certainly possible that Jesus as a *tektōn* worked on nearby building sites, it is equally possible he was content producing wares to sustain Nazareth. In addition to the already busy and village-centric lives of rural artisans, such speculation about the "feelings" of ordinary Galileans renders invisible other issues perhaps of more concern to the non-elite, such as the likely use of forced labor (i.e., slavery) and that these projects were usually paid for by the resident population through higher taxes and levies. While some of the peasantry would have certainly benefited materially from these changes, others would not have fared quite so well.

Indeed, alongside increased demands and competition on their time and labor, sat the possibility of land dislocation to make way for the changes. As labor and materials had to be produced, elite demand for luxury goods increased, and land was acquired or reallocated. In such settings, the creation or perpetuation of landless peasants, precarious day laborers, indebtedness to landlords, banditry, and flat-out destitution was very real. Indeed, Josephus' description of the building of Tiberias indicates a more complex situation than the scholarship on the apparent prosperity of Galilee implies. We learn that displacement benefited some with gifts of lands while removing others from theirs:

> The new settlers were a promiscuous rabble, no small contingent being Galilean, with such as were drafted from territory subject to him (Antipas) and brought forcibly to the new foundation. Some of these were magistrates. Herod (Antipas) accepted as participants even poor men who were brought in to join the others from any and all places of origin. It was in question whether some were even free beyond cavil. These latter he often and in large bodies liberated and benefited imposing the condition that they should not quit the city, by equipping houses at his own expense and adding new gifts of land. (*Antiquities* 18.36-38)

This passage would support a nuanced account of class and the material changes in Galilee, one inclusive of the perception that significant upheavals were happening to ordinary people's lives, and evidently in many cases against their wishes.

Of course, we should add to this the possibility that after the major construction works had been completed in Tiberias around 19 CE, there was a sudden change in labor requirements. The precise impact on the peasantry is hard to determine, but it is worth flagging up in any case. Josephus mentions that when the refurbishment of the Temple was completed in the early 60s CE, more than 18,000 workmen were suddenly unemployed, and "in want, because they had earned their labors about the temple." King Agrippa, who had the care of the Temple committed to him by Caesar, intentionally created more work by having them pave the Jerusalem streets with white stone (*Antiquities* 20.219-222). We do not know whether Antipas engaged in similar "work creation" initiatives after the bulk of his urbanization projects had been completed by the 20s. If not, sudden underemployment would have exacerbated the destabilizing economic effects. It would have been yet another contributing factor to a disaffected peasantry in the surrounding villages.

Regardless of how we nuance the situation for workers, we should also keep in mind the classic materialist point typically ignored in debates about Galilee, namely, that even cases of a material rise in living standards can involve antagonisms between classes. The situation of unequal distribution of resources remains; it will not satisfy all, and rises for some can lead to further demands. Potential reactions to changes in production, labor, household relocations, and land use because of urbanization could, then, take on many different, even contradictory, forms.

As some social historians have argued, social unrest or rebellion and accompanying millenarianism was more likely to erupt in agrarian societies when urbanization, modest commercial activity, and accompanying demands intensified, with calls for change ranging from the reactionary to the revolutionary. Eric Hobsbawm, the social historian introduced in the previous chapter who was especially influential for the framing of debates on peasant unrest in first-century Galilee, stressed peasant reactions were typically due to alienation (e.g., land occupations) which peasants did not perceive to be valid.[10]

This stress on *perception*, although frequently overlooked, is important because much of the debate on Galilee wrongly assumes a direct correlation between a rise or fall in the standard of living and the temperament of the general population. In the rebuilding of Sepphoris and the building of Tiberias, we can acknowledge the socio-economic world was significantly altered for Galileans like Jesus' family and not everyone would have *perceived* social and cultural changes in traditional lifestyles for the better.

In the longer run, it is of some gravity that there was a full-scale Jewish revolt against Rome in 66-73 CE, at the beginning of which debt records were burned which Josephus suggested was "to cause a rising of poor against the rich" (*War* 2.427-248). The tensions that exploded in the Jewish revolt had built up over decades and were exacerbated by Roman mishandling of the region in the period *after* Jesus' death. It is interesting, however, that Josephus himself traces the revolt's roots in 66 CE back 6 decades to the rebellion instigated by Judas the Galilean and Zadok the Pharisee in 6 CE (*Antiquities* 18.23), thereby situating events squarely within Antipas' reign and at the time Jesus was growing up. Judas the Galilean claimed taxation was no better than slavery and called for liberty from imperial rule. In his personal recollections of the revolt in Galilee, Josephus also reported great hatred leveled at Sepphoris and Tiberias (e.g., *Life* 30, 39, 66-68, 99, 374-84).

It is clear from other sources that such tensions were already rising in Galilee around the time of Jesus. The Gospel tradition itself suggests the world had not improved for the better and that a new order therefore had to be envisaged. Hence, the concern with the interrelated themes of an end-time reversal of rich and poor, debt, the opposition of God and Mammon, dubious property management, hostility toward "soft" clothing and eating well, and a concern for those without food, drink, clothing, and community. Such emphases were likely generated by perceptions of what was happening as a direct result of the changes in land use, dislocation, and labor in Galilee.

We will revisit these issues in the next chapters, but it is also worth observing two further details in the Gospels: the first is the curious absence of any references to Sepphoris and Tiberias, despite them being imposing centers within the vicinity of the Jesus movement's organizing. Perhaps the reason for this was a deliberate avoidance by Jesus of the centers associated with discontents, and this was certainly an argument put forward by de Ste. Croix, who located Jesus "outside the area of Graeco-Roman civilization proper" by observing that, apart from Jerusalem,

Jesus' mission took place exclusively in rural villages.[11]

Second, in the Gospel of Matthew, Jesus reproached the townships of Chorazin, Bethsaida, and Capernaum for failing to heed his teachings and thus threatened them with a terrible fate on the day of judgment (Matt. 11.20-24). Irrespective of whether Jesus actually said this, that Matthew refers to these marginal fishing villages in Galilee as "cities" (*poleis*) is suggestive given the term held political associations of the city-state. Was there a common perception Galilee had become overly gentrified and encroached by elite interests?

Whatever the reason for these details, we should not doubt that Antipas' urbanization projects in Galilee marked a change in the everyday life of rural Galilee, even if at the level of ideological construction of the world. Such changes unlocked inherited tensions and anxieties already present when Jesus was born and would later propel the Jesus movement and its revolutionary millenarianism into existence. As we shall see, millenarian thinking and language was a culturally fitting avenue for expressing discontent in the context of these changes taking place throughout the region.

Religious Organizers

In agrarian worlds, discontent did not always move beyond specific localized concerns. In many cases, the broader dissemination of ideas required assistance from the intelligentsia, and occasionally, agents from outside the peasantry. Indeed, the perpetuation of the Jesus movement in Galilee after Jesus' death owes much to scribal or administrative "middling" roles, as Sarah Rollens has argued.[12] But in the case of Jesus, given the likelihood he was a manual worker who was not trained as a scribe, we should look more to his role as a religious organizer.

By "religious organizer" we are developing a cross-cultural observation about figures who are assigned authority, whether through official channels or by popular support, to mediate between groups of people and the divine.[13] These might be priests who broadly support the status quo but it can also cover those who stand outside the official system and utilize traditions of wealth redistribution to address the material needs of the lower orders and critique those in power. Like prophets, who in ancient Israel were outspoken opponents of injustice and poured out bitter condemnation on the elite, the latter type of religious organizer can pose challenges to the status quo and its ideological apparatus through personal access to the divine.

By way of an illustrative comparison, we might think about the role of anticlericalism of the lower clergy in peasant unrest in Medieval Europe, including figures such as the dissident priest John Ball in the English uprising of 1381. Figures like Ball drew on biblical traditions of radical socio-economic and apocalyptic reversal (including supporting the decapitation of senior political and religious authorities). In doing so, they authorized and propagated ideas for a new world order far beyond localized peasant complaints. Come the transformation, rural workers would enjoy access to the land and political representation under a just king (see Chapter 5).[14]

Closer to the time and culture of Jesus, there were various options for channeling discontent, some violent, some not (at least until God, it was hoped, would dramatically intervene). We will continue to look at the overlapping concerns of bandits, insurrectionists, and millenarians in Galilee and Judea in the remaining chapters but for now we note the Jesus movement could similarly draw upon, and reapply to their specific situation, Jewish traditions of radical socio-economic reversal accompanied by popular expectations of an imminent divine intervention to right the world's wrongs. Of course, no two historical situations are the same and we should modify any comparisons accordingly, particularly cross-cultural ones. But thinking of Jesus' role as a religious organizer is useful not least because his popular authority was remembered as coming directly from God and deemed problematic enough for questions to be raised about it and answered (e.g., Mark 1.23-27; 2.6-10; 3.22-30; 6.1-6; Matt. 12.28//Luke 11.20).

Accordingly, Jesus as a religious organizer in the context of economic changes in Galilee will be important for understanding his adult life in the following chapters. It will help us to comprehend, among other things, how a person and his allegiant millenarians could channel the collective interests of the peasantry. Why the transfer of wealth into their hands could serve as a form of communal insurance against the "damned" rich. What they thought would happen at the end times when God would dramatically intervene in human history. And ultimately how Jesus himself could end up on a Roman cross as a willing martyr for the cause.

Before we get there, though, we need to turn to the inception of Jesus' public career. This started around the age of 30 if Luke 3.23 is to be believed. And before he joined with others to form a vanguard party, Jesus' ideological training as a religious organizer owed much to another organizer active around the same time. The movement was likewise concerned with a radical reordering of the world and an expectation of an imminent divine intervention. And the popular authority of its leader was arguably much greater than that of Jesus (cf. Mark 11.27-33): John the Baptist.

Chapter 3

Ideological Training with John the Baptist

Around the end of the 20s CE, John the Baptist emerged as a popular prophet. The prophets of ancient Israel were not simply "predictors" of future events, as sometimes thought. Rather, they were the critics and conscience of society. Prophets served as a channel between the divine and human worlds. In many cases, prophets dared to speak truth to power. And they could expect to be met with distrust and occasional violent backlash from those in power for their troubles. Others received a warmer hearing and were able to advise or effect change at the upper levels of society, despite not holding official positions within its formal structures of power.

The prophetic movement associated with John the Baptist appears to have had an influence on Jesus. Our main sources for the historical John include all four canonical Gospels, as well as Josephus (*Antiquities* 18.116-119). The problem for the critical historian, at least in the case of the Gospels, is that they interpreted John through the prism of the Christian proclamation, despite John *not* being a part of the Jesus movement himself. We see this problem come through especially in the birth and infancy of John. If the general chronological, geographical, and familial material in Luke is accurate, then John was born in Judea, shortly before Jesus, to Elizabeth and a priest called Zechariah (Luke 1). These basic pointers may or may not be accurate, but the story of John's birth was written up by Luke to heighten John's importance in the divine plan and cannot be used for any serious reconstruction of his birth and younger years.

As ever, there are still plenty of problems when reconstructing the adult life of John. But what becomes clear is a simple but important point: the theme of John the Baptist as a preacher of repentance, judgment, moral conservatism, and the end times was an early one that predated the Gospels. What is also clear is a theme the Gospel tradition downplayed as Jesus became increasingly important in Christian thinking: John's influence on Jesus. Accordingly, it is worth spending some time on John and the kinds of ideas that would have influenced Jesus and others in the movement.

John as Religious Organizer and Wilderness Man

John's earliest public appearances were in the Judean desert (Mark 1.4-5; Matt. 3.1-6; Luke 3.2-6) and by the river Jordan where he carried out his famous immersions. In addition to his end times preaching and immersions (see below), he was remembered for his asceticism (Matt. 11.18-19; Luke 7.33-34; cf. Mark 2.18-20) and he was not the only person doing this at the time: Josephus mentions another called Bannus who lived in the wilderness, took clothing and food from what grew in the wild, and bathed regularly in cold water to maintain a holy life (*Life* 11).

When in less inhabited areas John's appearance was rugged and masculine: he sported clothing made of camel hair and a leather belt and ate "locusts and wild honey" (Mark 1.6; Matt. 3.4). The English translation of the Greek *meli agrion* as "wild honey" may be too precise. It could mean "honey" akin to how we understand it, but it could also refer to sweetness or syrup from dates, figs, or tree sap. Like Bannus, then, John was remembered for surviving on whatever food he could forage in the wilderness.

Quite why John and Bannus did this is not clear. Either may have been forced into the situation for social or economic reasons, while in the history of asceticism these are not unusual acts. Some have speculated John may have been evoking imagery from the story of the Garden of Eden (Gen. 2.4-3.24) to point to a new Golden Age or that John and Bannus were tying in their austere, manly public self-presentation with notions of repentance. In the case of John, we will see below that there were also probably associations with the anticipated return of the ancient Israelite prophet Elijah at the end times. Elijah was a legendary prophet from the time of kings Ahab and Ahaziah, almost 1000 years before John and Jesus. Four major stories concerning him are found in the Hebrew scriptures (1 Kgs 16.29-19.18; 21.1-29; 2 Kgs 1.2-2.17; 2.1-18) and they were familiar and highly regarded tales among Jews in John's time.

John the Baptist was remembered by his contemporaries as a prophet like Elijah but also as a religious organizer of the sort mentioned in the previous chapter, and one who had a popular authority outside the official channels of the divine. Indeed, one thing we can establish about John was that a social movement formed around him, and he was almost certainly more popular than Jesus was during his lifetime (cf. Mark 11.32), even if we are not able to make numerical guesses. Josephus' account of John's life (*Antiquities* 18.116-18), independent of the Gospels, claims Antipas, Tetrarch of Galilee and Perea, was so concerned by John's popularity that he swiftly had him killed. Josephus added that when Antipas' army was defeated by the Nabateans in 36 CE, some Jews saw this as a justly deserved divine punishment for his rash treatment of John. The Gospel of Mark, with typical exaggeration, claims "people from the whole Judean countryside and all the people of Jerusalem" would go out to see John and get immersed (Mark 1.5; cf. Matt. 3.5; Luke 3.3), but he effectively made the same point as Josephus: John's movement was extremely popular.

The location of John the Baptist in the wilderness is notable too because the remarks made about Jesus and the urbanization projects in Galilee also apply here. As noted in the previous chapter, Herod the Great, Antipas' father, was renowned for his lavish building projects, including in Jerusalem and the region of Judea in the southern part of Palestine. As was evident in Galilee, building projects in Judea also brought changes and not everyone perceived the changes for the better. For starters, the "Romanization" of Judean culture, while enthusiastically embraced by many of the elite in power, made some Jews uncomfortable. But more importantly, these projects would have put greater demands for labor and resources on the peasanty, while increased trade involved more elite demands for luxury goods, and shifting land uses once again meant dislocations for precarious workers and their families.

Herod built or rebuilt distinguished palaces, fortifications, fortresses, and towns, including towns near his estates and the great port of Caesarea Maritima on the Mediterranean coast (see figure 2). These constructions also redirected and intensified trade patterns and water demands. Most famous of all was Herod's dramatic expansion of the Holy Temple in Jerusalem which was not fully completed until decades after his death (see John 2.20). The Temple became known as one of the great buildings of the Roman world, certainly in Jewish circles. As Josephus put it, "The expenditure devoted to this work was incalculable, its magnificence never surpassed" (*War* 1.401).

Figure 2.
Remains of the Roman Amphitheatre of Caesarea Maritima, one of many structures commissioned by Herod the Great. commons.wikimedia.org

But to add to the socio-economic changes, there were further issues concerning the Temple and Jerusalem and the importance of Jewish laws that added to discontents. Indeed, they give us insight into how tense the situation could get and the sensitivities surrounding Jerusalem. Jerusalem and the Holy Temple not only unified Jewish society but were a provincial power base of the *repressive imperial apparatus* in this part of the Roman Empire. Previously, we introduced the concept of the *ideological imperial apparatus* as the "soft power" which replicated the dominant ideas of the ruling elite. The basic social function of the *repressive imperial apparatus*, however, was "hard power" via timely intervention into politics and governance to enforce elite interests on the masses. The repressive imperial apparatus included the military, methods of tax collection, the Sanhedrin and royal courts, other mechanisms and direct methods associated with enforcing laws, and so on. It was backed by violence or coercion through threats of violence in favor of the interests of the ruling class.

Consequently, the Temple regularly featured as a symbolic site of struggle over its ideal function and was the focal point of unrest. Toward the end of his life and the day before a lunar eclipse (13 March 4 BCE), Herod the Great had to deal with Jewish subjects unhappy with his decorations in the Temple precinct (Josephus, *War* 1.648-655; *Antiquities* 17.149-67). Two popular teachers called Judas and Matthias encouraged, to the point of martyrdom (see also chapters 8-10), pulling down everything "idolatrous" in the Temple, including a golden eagle Herod had erected on the Temple gate. When young men managed to attack the golden eagle, they were caught and seized by a sizable guard. Perpetrators and their mentors were, accordingly, burned alive by the repressive imperial apparatus.

Direct Roman rule inevitably generated feats of militant resistance in a land thought to belong to the God of the

Jews and in a major urban center thought especially holy. Josephus gives accounts of events from the time of Pontius Pilate, the prefect of Judea, and so closer still to the time of John's activity. On becoming prefect of Judea in 26 CE, Pilate brought Roman standards into Jerusalem with images of the Roman Emperor (but cf. Philo, *Embassy to Gaius* 299-305). As Josephus points out, this was controversial because making such images contravened Jewish law, and in Jerusalem this was especially insulting. When the standards were discovered, a rambunctious crowd descended on Caesarea to pressure Pilate into removing them. When it was clear the crowd would not relent, Pilate threatened them with violence. According to Josephus, Pilate only relented once he saw how deadly serious they were for their ancestral traditions: they would gladly lay down their lives for the sake of God and country. Nevertheless, sometime after this, Pilate also used Temple money to fund an aqueduct which sparked another popular protest which he suppressed by ordering soldiers to beat the protestors down with menacing clubs rather than deadly swords (*Antiquities* 18.55-62; *War* 2.169-177).

Against this general backdrop, John emerged as a popular prophet of repentance and end times. Given John's popularity among alternative gatherings in the wilderness, we should classify him as an example of the establishment-critical religious organizer outlined in the previous chapter. He is comparable to other such figures who emerged out of prophetic movements and who were often dealt with violently by the repressive state apparatus without too much deliberation. A telling comparison is again Theudas from the mid-40s CE who had a large following, claimed to be a prophet, and took his associates to the river Jordan (*Antiquities* 20.97-98). The Roman procurator certainly saw Theudas as having the wrong sort of authority and so had the group dealt with violently, murdering some followers, capturing others, and decapitating

Theudas himself.

According to Acts of the Apostles, the Pharisaic authority, Gamaliel I, saw the new Jesus movement as comparable to the Theudas movement. What is also notable was another type: the more obviously violent Judas the Galilean who believed the only ruler and lord Jews should recognize was God (*Antiquities* 18.23; *War* 2.118, 433). The ambiguity of divine authority, a theme which turned up in Jesus' conflicts, is clear in Gamaliel's words according to Acts:

> Fellow-Israelites, consider carefully what you propose to do to these men. For some time ago Theudas rose up, claiming to be somebody, and a number of men, about four hundred, joined him; but he was killed, and all who followed him were dispersed and disappeared. After him Judas the Galilean rose up at the time of the census and got people to follow him; he also perished, and all who followed him were scattered. So in the present case, I tell you, keep away from these men and let them alone; because if this plan or this undertaking is of human origin, it will fail; but if it is of God, you will not be able to overthrow them—in that case you may even be found fighting against God! (Acts 5.35-39)

The context of Acts 5 is one where the members of the developing Christian movement were going to be put to death over competing claims to authority, before Gamaliel's intervention. Irrespective of whether Gamaliel said these words or whether the meeting even happened, these were assumptions faced by any new or growing movement claiming divine authority and not sanctioned by Rome or their official representatives in Palestine. For elite Jews like Josephus, the ideal constitution for the Jewish people was theocracy, but understood as rulership by the appointed priests in the Temple, not popular prophets on the margins. Likewise, Antipas had delegated political authority over his territory from Rome. Against this political and cultural backdrop, it is little wonder John was beheaded by Antipas.

John the Baptist's rise on the margins of Israelite society does raise further questions about his class background. Was John formerly a member of the Jerusalem establishment who, due to growing concerns about the direction of the Jewish polity, left to amass oppositional forces in the wilderness? The Gospel accounts simply narrate the Baptist's sudden "appearance" in the wilderness "proclaiming a baptism for the repentance of sins" (Mark 1.4) and provide no explanation of his previous life or what led him to this point. Consequently, the class location of John remains underexplored in historical scholarship.[1] Avoidance of the topic is perhaps, in part, due to the confusing nature of the evidence.

On the one hand, the description of the Baptist as an itinerant and existing off a meager diet and dressed in poor-quality clothing alludes not only to the prophet Elijah, as we shall see in more detail below, but also to material deprivation and extremely modest living conditions. One of the Q traditions concerning the Baptist, conveyed by Luke and Matthew, explicitly contrasts John's clothing with that of the rich and powerful. When Jesus spoke to the crowds about the Baptist, he asked them directly what they went out into the wilderness to look at: "A reed shaken by the wind?... Someone dressed in soft clothing? Look, those who put on fine clothing and live in luxury are in royal palaces" (Luke 7.25; cf. Matt. 11.8). The contrast between the Baptist's "hard" life of poverty and the "soft" clothing of the palace elite quite possibly underscores the contrast between John's modest circumstances and those of his chief opponent, Antipas. Indeed, Antipas himself was the first Herodian ruler to issue coins bearing a reed (see figure 3).

Figure 3.
Coin issued by Herod Antipas featuring an upright reed. Jesus'
rhetorical allusion to "a reed shaken in the wind" (Luke 7.25)
may consequently have been a not-so-veiled reference
to the "soft" Antipas. bibleodyssey.org

On the other hand, Luke's account of the Baptist's priestly descent, through the parentage of Zechariah and Elizabeth (1.5-80; 3.2), would suggest more noble origins for John. For instance, if John was a member of a religious sect like the Essenes, this would have afforded him a level of material privilege as part of a priestly community. While we noted in the previous chapter the details of the infancy narratives are not historically verifiable, John's status as a priest is corroborated by the priestly associations of water immersions. If John was also connected to the Qumran community that produced the Dead Sea Scrolls, as some scholars have suggested, this would further support the case given that community was priestly in origin.

While priestly descent does not automatically entail elite class, it is possible John was located among what scholars label the "retainer class," functionaries of the political and religious elite who were located materially below the upper stratum of the ruling elite, for instance, but above the mass of non-elite peasantry including those forced to join bandit groups, and the majority of Jesus' and John's respective associates. This would make John a class traitor of sorts: driven by millenarian concerns in reaction to the perceived social and economic changes experienced in Judea, he abandoned a relatively secure livelihood to urge repentance and resistance against the ruling elite. Nevertheless, leadership of such movements often came from outside the peasantry (or at least was recruited from their intelligentsia as in the case of Jesus) and in this sense John the Baptist was not unusual.

John, Elijah, and the Great and Terrible Day of the Lord

As far as we know, John's movement was not physically violent in the here and now, and John would not lead a violent insurrection. Instead, John's movement took what was simultaneously a realistic and unrealistic position in a world of massively disproportionate distributions of power: rather than the relative futility of violent insurrection in a largely peasant context, God (or his helpers) would instead mete out violent justice in the imminent future.

We can try and be more precise about how John's movement saw the imminent future. John warned someone more powerful than himself was coming next, who would baptize with the Holy Spirit and (so Matthew and Luke) fire (Mark 1.7-8; Matt. 3.11; Luke 3.16). The Gospels imply the identity of this figure was Jesus. But, importantly, this idea of Jesus as the fulfillment of "the one who is to come" was only inferred and not explicitly mentioned by the Gospel accounts which is the opposite of what we would expect if the prediction was invented by the Gospel authors. This suggests John's prediction of "the one who is to come" was an inherited, pre-Gospel tradition which did not make such a clear identification. We can also detect embellishment by the Gospel authors, such as Luke's addition of people "questioning in their hearts" whether John was the Messiah (Luke 3.15). Here Luke deliberately steers the passage toward identifying Jesus as "the one who is to come" and downplays the importance of John in relation to Jesus, a problem Luke also dealt with in his second book (Acts 19.1-6) and an issue that would not easily go away because of John's ongoing popularity during the first century.

That John predicted someone powerful was coming next is further underscored by Matthew 11.2-6 (cf. Luke 7.18-23; Q) where John sent an associate to ask Jesus directly whether he was, in fact, the one to come. Jesus answered cryptically but implied the affirmative. As there is some indirectness here, it is commonly argued we are dealing with an early tradition that reflects the view of the historical Baptist as the Gospels would be less likely to introduce any doubts given their common agenda to proclaim Jesus as the Jewish Messiah (on "Messiah," see Chapter 5). This is possible, and Matthew 11.2-6//Luke 7.18-23 looks like a further attempt to firm up a known ambiguous prophecy by making it apply to Jesus.

But if this prediction did not, in John's understanding, refer to Jesus, then who was this figure supposed to be? It is most likely a reference to common expectations in some forms of early Judaism to an elevated or supernatural figure who would be integral in the events of end times. It is possible this was coupled with the theme of John as the returned Elijah, prophesied at the end of the book of Malachi: "Lo, I will send you the prophet Elijah before the great and terrible day of the Lord comes" (Mal. 4.5). Although not useful for earlier historical reconstruction, the account of the Baptist in John's Gospel (John 1.19-28) is intriguing. John's Gospel rewrites what is found in Mark, Matthew, and Luke with an emphatic denial that the Baptist was the Messiah or Elijah. Clearly, the author wanted to make sure any competing claims John the Baptist was the Messiah were wrong, presumably so because similar claims had occurred (cf. John 1.6-9). Likewise, John's Gospel sought to counter any claims the Baptist was Elijah returned, not least because that Gospel pushes the end times to a more distant future (see below).

Despite the Gospel of John's theological embellishment, it is apparent these claims go back to an early tradition. A connection between the Baptist's appearance in the wilderness and Elijah is attested in the Synoptics. As noted above, John is described as "clothed with camel's hair, with a leather belt around his waist" (Mark 1.6; Matt. 3.4) which is typically thought an allusion to Elijah who was described as a "hairy man, with a leather belt around his waist" (2 Kgs 1.8). Moreover, in the same Q passage discussed above, contrasting John's rugged appearance with the "soft" clothes of the elite, Jesus is said to have identified John as the fulfillment of prophecy from Jewish scriptures of the messenger who will prepare the way (Matt. 11.7-15; Luke 7.24-30), later identified as Elijah (Mal. 4.5).

Jesus, according to Matthew, made this connection between John and Elijah more explicit still: "if you are willing to accept it, he is Elijah who is to come." Luke did not include this saying despite making the implicit connection between John and Elijah, probably because of discomfort with overliteral identification between two people, or perhaps due to anxiety over the delay of the end times. Luke also did not include Mark 9.11-13 where Elijah, presumably identified with John, is said to have returned and been mistreated. Moreover, Luke omits Mark 1.6 and the reference to John's Elijah-like sartorial inelegance. But Luke is not opposed to a different sort of identification with Elijah and we get an indication of how Luke understood this when he has an angel predict "with the *spirit and power of Elijah* he [John] will go before him, to turn the hearts of parents to their children, and the disobedient to the wisdom of the righteous, to make ready a people prepared for the Lord" (Luke 1.17, emphasis added). The flip side of all this is that the more literal ways of identifying John with Elijah predate Luke and may have been in the source for Matthew 11.7-15 and Luke 7.24-30 which appear independent of Mark's takes on Elijah (Mark 1.6; 9.11-13).

We cannot say definitively whether the historical John readily identified with Elijah, how many of his audience thought he was, or whether Jesus or someone else made the connection. In any case, we must be mindful that our primary sources, the Gospels, have a vested interest in ranking Jesus higher than the Baptist. As such, we ought to be suspicious of features that all-too-neatly fit their agenda such as the identification of John as the returned Elijah preparing a path for the Messiah Jesus. What we can say, however, is the identification appears in the earliest materials we have, and John likely believed he was one of the last figures before judgment would fall. What we can further deduce is that he was remembered as a religious organizer who could employ symbolic gestures grounded in Jewish ancestral traditions to make his point. Political associations of the identification of John with Elijah are suggestive to say the least: Elijah and his disciples are depicted in 1 Kings as bringing pronouncement of divine judgment on king and court. Elijah and Elisha and their followers also foment a popular rebellion against the house of Ahab.

But the "political" associations do not stop with John's connection to Elijah. The motif of "wilderness" had varied connotations within Israel's story, but its primary association was of deliverance from Pharaoh and the conquest of the land. When political or religious conditions became unbearable, pious figures would often withdraw into the wilderness as a symbolic (and also practical) gesture. Such a practice was modeled by the "many who were seeking righteousness and justice" and who sought refuge, along with their families and livestock, in the desert during the infamous rule of Antiochus IV Epiphanes in 168 BCE, only to be hunted down and killed by the king's loyalists (1 Macc. 2.29-38). Josephus disparagingly described the wilderness as a place where people would similarly "delude themselves" into thinking God would show signs of liberation (*War* 2.258-59). We noted above named leaders like Theudas but there were others, such as another we have already seen: the Egyptian, who is also mentioned in the New Testament (Acts 21.38). Theudas is once more a useful comparison for unpacking John's symbolic gestures because parallels with Moses and the escape from Pharaoh's Egypt through the Red Sea are clear enough: Theudas had a large following, claimed to be a prophet, and led people out to the river Jordan where he promised to divide it (*Antiquities* 20.97-98).

Connections between the wilderness and John's "ascetic" characterization in the Gospels also strengthen the idea John was operating as a kind of religious organizer. During the Herodian period, numerous ascetic Jewish groups, from the Essenes (who were possibly responsible for the Dead Sea Scrolls) to the Therapeutae (in Egypt), had some special connection to the wilderness. The first-century apocalypse the *Testament of Moses* referred to a Levite priest named Taxo who, along with his seven sons, fasted 3 days before taking up residence in a cave in the desert (9.1-7). Another pseudepigraphic text, the *Martyrdom and Ascension of Isaiah*, depicted Isaiah retreating to a mountain in the desert. When his disciples arrived, "All of them were clothed in sackcloth...were destitute, and they all lamented bitterly over the going astray of Israel. And they had nothing to eat except wild herbs which they gathered from the mountains" (2.10-11).

Baptism of Repentance

The most well-known thing about John the Baptist is found in his nickname: he was baptizing people. John's baptisms, according to Mark's Gospel, were baptisms "of repentance for the forgiveness of sins" (Mark 1.4b). Themes of "repentance" familiar to John were based on the Jewish concept of *teshuvah* (or the Aramaic equivalent, *tetuvah*). This was the language of turning and returning to God and the commandments. It was a common idea in Jewish literature and collective in its call, in that Israel or Jews as a whole should change their ways. Calls to repentance often had a polemical edge in the sense of turning to a specific interpretation of the Jewish law which was not universally agreed (see Chapter 7). Matthew implies something like this by adding the Pharisees and Sadducees to John's polemics when he has John address them as a "brood of vipers!" (Matt. 3.7-10).

We will return to ideas about repentance and the Jesus movement in Chapter 5, but for now another pivotal aspect of repentance should be noted: judgment. The threat of divine judgment was an interrelated theme, and this threat was enhanced by millenarian beliefs that they were living in or near end times. One such group in the first century was the Qumran community based on the northwestern shore of the Dead Sea, close to where John was active. This group was associated with the Dead Sea Scrolls, discovered sensationally in 1947, which contain numerous discussions of repentance and returning to the commandments as they understood them. As one scroll puts it: "And we are aware that part of the blessings and curses have occurred that are written in the b(ook of Mos)es. And this is the end of days, when they will return in Israel to the L(aw) and not turn bac(k)..." (4Q398 11-13, 3-5).

John's immersions or baptisms were like this collective call for Israel or Jews to return to the commandments as he understood them, though quite what that involved is unclear as we will see. Use of water and transformation of the individual or group appeared in different contexts in early Judaism, such as immersion after contracting impurity (see Chapter 7) or in some circles to symbolize initiation into the Jewish ancestral traditions. In the context of John's immersions, it is more specifically part of the metaphorical language of being cleansed from sin and returning to the correct way of behavior, a concept known from the Jewish scriptures (e.g., Is. 1.16-17; Ps. 51.1-2) but also from the Dead Sea Scrolls. Symbolism of water and the removal of sin in a communal setting appears in a scroll called the Community Rule: "And it is by the holy spirit of the community, in its truth, that he is cleansed of all his iniquities. And by the spirit of uprightness and of humility his sin is atoned. And by the compliance of his soul with all the laws of God his flesh is cleansed by being sprinkled with cleansing water and being made holy with the waters of repentance" (1QS III, 7-9).[2]

These sorts of texts help us understand why the Gospels and Josephus use different language to describe John's immersions. Mark, for instance, has the familiar language of "baptism of repentance for the forgiveness of sins" and people being immersed and "confessing their sins" (Mark 1.4-5). Josephus, on the other hand, frames baptism as "a consecration of the body implying the soul was already thoroughly cleansed by right behavior" (*Antiquities* 18.116-118). Both are approximately saying the same thing as the language of purification and ideas about removal of sin could overlap in early Judaism. There may be one notable difference between these two accounts of John the Baptist. Mark implies baptism was the moment where the sins were forgiven, whereas Josephus suggests it was prior to the act. But irrespective of exactly when the sins were forgiven, both accounts connect the overall process with forgiveness and adherence to moral behavior.

From time to time, a minority of scholars have claimed John's baptism of repentance for the forgiveness of sin was a deliberate challenge to the role of the Jerusalem Temple. This is because the Temple itself had an "official" system of priests and animal sacrifices to deal with sins. This argument is not especially strong. Regulations for sacrifice in Jewish scriptures do not cover all sins and the same collection of scriptures elsewhere suggests forgiveness occurs without the need for sacrifice or the Temple. Jews could simultaneously support the Temple system and not rely on the Temple for forgiveness. To give one relevant example from an early Jewish text: "As water extinguishes a blazing fire, so almsgiving atones for sin" (Sirach 3.30). We should also remember plenty of Jews, including those in close proximity to Jerusalem, were unable to get to the Temple regularly, but this did not mean that, when it came to forgiveness, they rejected the concept of sacrifice.

Similarly, John's baptism and collective repentance with the expectation of divine intervention at the end times could co-exist with the acceptable continuation of animal sacrifice at the Temple. It is possible that John, like the group responsible for some of the Dead Sea Scrolls, believed the Temple system was corrupt and needed replacing, but there is no clear evidence for this unless one reads it into Mark's exaggeration that "all the people of Jerusalem were going out to him" in Mark 1.5. If John was intentionally challenging the very need for the Temple system through his immersions, however, we would require evidence, such as someone explicitly criticizing him for this. It is worth observing that it was only after the Temple was destroyed by the Romans in 70 CE that we have evidence of Christians rejecting the sacrificial or Temple system and its role in administering the forgiveness of sins. For the earlier generation of the Jesus movement, critique was mostly directed at the supposed hypocrisy of its leaders, as we shall explore further in our discussion of the Jesus movement's disruption in the Temple (Chapter 9). It was therefore similarly unlikely that John's immersions invalidated the Temple system's role in the forgiveness of sins.

Baptizing Jesus

One recipient of John's immersions was, of course, Jesus. But, when ordered chronologically, the evolving Gospel tradition does some interesting maneuvering regarding the Baptist's status: it soon detects a potential theological problem with Jesus being immersed for the forgiveness of sins. Indeed, the belief that Jesus was "without sin" had emerged among a number of Christians after his death (2 Cor. 5.21; Heb. 4.15; 1 John 3.5; 1 Pet. 2.22). Jesus undergoing a baptism "of repentance for the forgiveness of sins" thus presented a potential problem for at least some of the Gospel authors. Of what "sin" would Jesus need to repent?

In our earliest Gospel, Mark simply says Jesus came down from Nazareth and was baptized by John in the Jordan (Mark 1.9). Luke also says Jesus was baptized, but there are hints of unease. He adds that Jesus was praying (thereby giving him more agency than Mark did) and does not mention explicitly that the baptism was performed by John, even if it is implied ("Now when all the people were baptized, and when Jesus also had been baptized and was praying, the heaven was opened," Luke 3.21). With Matthew, however, the unease becomes explicit as the text explains *why* Jesus had to be baptized by John:

> Then Jesus came from Galilee to John at the Jordan, to be baptized by him. John would have prevented him, saying, "I need to be baptized by you, and do you come to me?" But Jesus answered him, "Let it be so now; for it is proper for us in this way to fulfil all righteousness." Then he consented. (Matt. 3.13-15)

Matthew recognized the awkwardness of Jesus having sins needing to be forgiven, as well as the implication that John baptizing Jesus inferred John's superiority. "Consent" was required only for the more powerful person, in order that the assumed hierarchy which put Jesus on top was not threatened. John's Gospel goes further still in elevating Jesus. In John 1.19-34, the Baptist testified Jesus as the "Son of God" and "the Lamb of God who takes away the sin of the world," that he himself ranked below Jesus, and through baptism John the Baptist could point to the "one who baptizes with the Holy Spirit."

Remarkably, however, no actual baptism of Jesus by John is narrated by the text.

Clearly, Jesus' baptism by John the Baptist was an embarrassment for some followers, and it was a problem that did not go away. Mark appears not to have found this idea and the implicit inferiority of Jesus embarrassing so we could leave it open as to how early this idea emerged. Nevertheless, it is difficult to see why John baptizing Jesus would have been invented. This would further support the already strong argument (see Chapter 5) that the Jesus movement too thought God would soon intervene in history and hence the requirement for immediate repentance.

Ordinarily, John's Gospel is not of use but there are occasional instances where, however unintentionally, it might have the more accurate framework for what happened in Jesus' lifetime. Incidental details about Jesus' relationship to baptism can be detected in John's Gospel. One is the implication that the Jesus movement carried out their own baptisms. According to John 4.1-2, the Pharisees had heard Jesus was "making and baptizing more disciples than John," though the Gospel adds the explanation it was not Jesus but his associates. That John's Gospel had to make such a qualification may suggest embarrassment and that the opposite was the case: Jesus too baptized people. But it may also be another case of John's Gospel downplaying the Baptist's role in relation to Elijah by having his work subsumed into Jesus' movement. In the absence of any serious supporting evidence, there is not much more to be said.

Another example is perhaps a stronger case, albeit still speculative. It concerns the possibility that Jesus and John's respective movements overlapped. Mark 1.14 claims Jesus became active apart from John after John's arrest. John's Gospel, however, assumes Jesus and the Baptist overlapped (John 1.28-40; 3.22-30; 10.41-42). Even here John uses this information to ensure the Baptist is not identified as Elijah. Nevertheless, it is possible John's Gospel is (however unintentionally) correct.

Corroborating evidence is found in Matthew 11.2-6 and Luke 7.18-23 (Q) and the question from John about whether Jesus was "the one who is to come." As we saw above, because there was doubt in John's question there is less chance the saying was a later invention. But what we can add to this is that Matthew and Luke frame this passage differently which suggests their own editorial hands at play. Matthew claims John heard in prison about Jesus and sent his question via his own associates (Matt. 11.2). Luke does not have this information, even though the author would have assumed John was in prison (Luke 3.10-20). Further, Matthew's claim of a "progressive" Herodian prison with visitor rights, and so on, is unlikely. Josephus tells us John was "brought in chains to Machaerus," Antipas' hilltop fortress in Perea and near the east coast of the Dead Sea. It is difficult to imagine Antipas allowing his prisoners to send out or receive messengers. Accordingly, it is argued, not unreasonably, that the sentiments in John's hesitant saying circulated independently of its framing. The upshot of this argument is that the saying most likely existed when Jesus and John were both active.[3] If this is the case, then presumably Mark did not have the chronological information available or wanted to keep the eras of John and Jesus separate for theological reasons.

Fruits of Repentance

The theme that Jews baptized by John should practice the right sort of ethical behavior is mentioned by Josephus and the Gospels. Josephus claims that John "exhorted the Jews to live righteous lives, to practice justice toward their fellows and piety toward God, and so doing to join in baptism." Matthew 3.8 and Luke 3.8 support this but word John's hope for behavioral change in terms of bearing "fruit worthy of repentance." The general principle is standard enough, but what did John's movement mean exactly by "worthy fruit?"

On first sight, the Gospel of Luke's account of John's ethical teaching and call for repentance appears to provide us with precise examples. According to Luke 3.10-14, John claimed those with two coats should share with those with none, whoever has food should share, tax collectors should not collect more than is owed, and soldiers should be satisfied with their wages. This is not entirely removed from sentiments that would have influenced Jesus and it is possible John said such things, or at least found such ideas agreeable. However, historians should be wary about this passage. It is found only in Luke and aligns with Lukan interests as the text grapples with the only partial success of Jesus' hope that rich people, including tax collectors, would give up their wealth (see Chapter 5). Instead, Luke presents us with the unique story of Zacchaeus: a rich tax collector who gives up not all but half his wealth, and more than compensates those he defrauded (Luke 19.1-10).

A more precise flavor of John's ethical teachings is discernible in his criticism of Antipas. Like other religious organizers in different cultural contexts, John took a dim view of the "loose" morality of the elite. If Mark 6.17-18 is correct, then Antipas was singled out for marrying his brother's wife which John suggested was against the commandments (Lev. 18.16; 20.21). We cannot prove John was saying such things, but it would not necessarily contradict Josephus' general account either. We also have that Q tradition mentioned above (Matt. 11.7-15; Luke 7.24-30) where Jesus brought class to the fore in comparing John and the elites. Recall that Jesus asked the crowds whether they came out to the wilderness to see a "reed shaken by the wind" or "someone dressed in soft robes," pointing out those who live in luxury dwell in royal palaces and not, like the hardened John, in the wilderness. It is difficult enough to know whether Jesus said something like this, so we can only speculate that John himself agreed. Nevertheless, it is a passage independent of Mark 6.17-18 where John is remembered as an antagonist toward Antipas for his criticism of Antipas' nefarious behavior.

A similarity between Jesus' and John's emphasis on strict moral adherence to traditional values was assumed early on. Unfortunately, our sources do not exhibit an interest in the particulars of John's ethical teaching and Luke's attempt to provide some may be more a case of filling the gaps than reliable tradition. We are safest when thinking on the general level about John's ideas of repentance in light of the imminence of end times. What is notable about John is that there is no serious attempt by the Gospel writers to include non-Jews in these stories, one of the defining features of what we otherwise know about the development of first-century Christianity. Repentance in the sense of returning to the commandments only works when the message is reserved for Israelites or Jews. Indeed, in Matthew 3.9-10 and the parallel in Luke 3.8-9 (Q), where John's audience should not presume that because they are Jewish (i.e., that they can claim Abraham as their ancestor) they will be saved, there is no attempt by the authors to relate this to the inclusion of non-Jews. Writing decades before Matthew and Luke, the language of bearing fruits and struggles to incorporate Abraham into the salvation of non-Jews was attempted by Paul (Gal. 4-5), and again there is no indication of such an influence on the presentation of John the Baptist in Matthew 3.9-10 and Luke 3.8-9. Rather, the emphasis is on Jews alone: specifically, if Jews behave correctly then they can expect to be saved. Whether John said even some of the words attributed to him cannot, of course, be proven but the themes associated with him emerged from a context where concern for non-Jews was not an obvious priority, and so are likely from early in the tradition.

The Death of John the Baptist

According to Mark 1.14, John the Baptist was arrested. We find out later he was imprisoned and eventually executed at Antipas' fortress. This happened sometime before Antipas' army was defeated by the Nabateans, which is explained by Josephus as a punishment for Antipas' earlier treatment of John (*Antiquities*

18.116). Mark 6.17-29 has a gossipy account of John's death which may reflect an early attempt by Jews associated with the Baptist movement to account for their innocence. In this story, Mark tells us Herodias (Antipas' wife) and her daughter were ultimately to blame for John's demise whereas Antipas wanted to protect the man he apparently believed was "righteous and holy." The story uses common gendered and sexualized clichés about deceitful women leading unfortunate men astray. In this instance, Herodias' daughter famously danced before Antipas to trick him into what her mother wanted: John the Baptist's head on a platter.

Whatever the origins of the story, it is unlikely it ever took place. Josephus blames Herodias for Antipas' eventual exile but gives no indication that anything swayed Antipas to kill John other than *realpolitik*. Antipas was also in no position to give away half his kingdom to Herodias' daughter as Mark asserts. Indeed, this strange claim is one of the more obvious clues that Mark 6.17-29 is a creative rewriting of the story of Esther (see e.g., Esth. 5.3; 5.6; 7.2) to portray John as an innocent victim who posed no seditious threat.[4] It is unlikely anything other than a standard execution took place after a standard imprisonment. It did not involve John's associates coming and going during visiting hours, and it did not involve John imparting wisdom to a curious Antipas.

Despite its obvious embellishments, one noteworthy theme in the story is that in stark contrast to his rugged reputation as a wilderness man, John's death was understood as emasculating. Not only was the insinuation that John's fate lay with the will of an elite woman and her daughter potentially undermining of his manliness, but the gruesome account of John's severed head paraded around the royal court on a platter was a visible demonstration of his loss of manhood. Indeed, interpreters have sometimes drawn a symbolic link to castration. The Greek term used for "head" (*kephalē*), like its English equivalent, has a double meaning, denoting both the physical head of a person or animal, but also the person of superior rank. To behead John was to castrate the "head" of a threatening movement.[5]

We will see in Chapter 6 how the construction of a hegemonic masculinity in the wider Roman world implicated the Jesus movement in interesting and contradictory ways, and it is relevant to flag here similar things may have been happening to the Baptist movement. By following in its wake, and witnessing the unmanning repercussions of John's execution, the Jesus movement may have taken onboard early ideological lessons. But more on this later.

Like other religious organizers challenging the status quo, John's reaction to a changing Judea was a millenarian one. A divine intervention in human history was at hand, and John's movement thought this would be led by an intermediary figure. Others associated John with Elijah returning before end times. To avoid the great judgment, repentance through immersion and adherence to strict moral behavior rooted in traditional Jewish values was required. John's movement manifested in the wilderness, and it was getting popular. Symbolism of the wilderness in the story of liberation from Pharaoh and the conquest of Canaan by the Israelite tribes would not have been lost on Antipas who acted quickly to suppress the potential threat. John was executed for the cause of "righteousness," emerging from a Judean world marked by Roman imperialism, intensified urbanization, and the interrelated and often deadly tensions between political rulers and religious organizers. We should appreciate Josephus' starkly brutal account here: Antipas thought John was a potential threat and had him killed. Questions could be asked later.

Chapter 4

Becoming a Religious Organizer

Quite when Jesus left John the Baptist and became part of another movement, we do not know. Jesus is presented undertaking his own ascetic practices in the wilderness, but these stories are fantastical (Matt. 4.1-11//Luke 4.1-13) and even the comparatively restrained account in Mark's Gospel claims that Jesus "was in the wilderness for forty days, tempted by Satan; and he was with the wild beasts; and the angels waited on him" (Mark 1.12-13). Whether Jesus withdrew for an extended period of reflection in the wilderness as scholars sometimes suggest we cannot know based on the slim evidence we have.

There are further problems relating to chronology. We do not know how long the Jesus movement was publicly active in Galilee and Judea, because the Gospels do not provide us with any firm evidence. John's Gospel has traditionally been used to claim the movement was publicly active for 2-3 years on the basis that the Gospel mentions three Passovers (John 2.12-25; 6.4; 11-19). Sometimes this is set against the account in Mark's Gospel which mentions only one Passover (Mark 11-15) and thus the possibility for a one-year period of activity. But the Gospels do not make claims about how long Jesus or the movement were active, and they are not necessarily in conflict on this issue: just because Mark mentions one memorable Passover does not mean the author thought Jesus did not celebrate other Passovers in Jerusalem. Rather, Mark's author focused on the Passover that mattered most to telling his story.

What we lack in evidence for the duration of the Jesus movement, however, the Gospels make up for in terms of its structure, the people involved, and its grounding in popular support. These aspects laid the foundations for its brand of revolutionary millenarianism which will be explored in the next chapter. Our concern now is to understand these foundational matters of the movement's constitution, to explain why the Jesus movement could not be easily disregarded by elite society, and why it ultimately emerged as a serious force to be reckoned with.

Building the Vanguard

To begin, we should dispel romantic notions that this movement was proudly egalitarian and progressive in the sense of the "radical liberalism" of today. Certainly, it challenged the ruling elite but in its place was the expectation that there would be a different ruling class reflecting and serving the interests of the peasants, as we will see in the next chapter. The Jesus movement emanated from a peasant culture with internal hierarchies and worked with inherited assumptions about the ideal and often patriarchal[1] function of kings, judges, angels, and an overarching divine ruler. A progressive egalitarianism would have been mostly nonsensical in Jesus' agrarian context given such concerns speak more to cultural and material shifts through late-stage capitalism than the material changes affecting the peasantry in first-century Galilee. Rather, a culturally credible vanguard party cast in recognizable concepts was needed for such a movement to thrive.

The inner vanguard group of the Jesus movement reflected such hierarchies, even if understood as providing a new hierarchy to overthrow existing hierarchies. The Gospels provide names of Jesus' closest male associates known as "the Twelve" who were distinguished from a wider group of supporters with varying levels of attachment and commitment to the movement. The Twelve appears to have been a central committee or politburo with membership sometimes changing. There is early evidence for this. Paul, writing in the mid-first century, recalls events in the period shortly after Jesus' death when associates saw visions of the heavenly Jesus (see Chapter 10). According to Paul, Jesus "appeared to Cephas, then to the twelve. Then he appeared to more than five hundred brothers at one time, most of whom are still alive, though some have died" (1 Cor. 15.5-6). This was the politburo after Judas Iscariot's death and Acts claims Matthias was chosen by lots to replace Judas on the central committee (Acts 1.12-26). The various names of the Twelve listed across the Gospels add up to more than twelve which may again point to changing membership, though it may also point to a lack of knowledge of who was closely involved, to the deliberate placing of favored figures by given Gospel writers (see below), or indeed to any combination of these options.

The label "Twelve" was itself significant. Twelve tribes of Israel descended from the Patriarch Jacob and his sons. By the time of Jesus, the tribes were long scattered and there was an established hope for the restoration of the twelve tribes as part of a larger national restoration of Israel, as can be seen, for instance, in the Dead Sea Scrolls (e.g., 1QM 2.2-3, 7-8; 3.13; 5.1). This is also reflected in material associated with Jesus and inherited by the Gospel writers, including a parallel passage in Matthew 19.28 and Luke 22.29-30 (a likely Q tradition):

Jesus said to them, "Truly I tell you, at the renewal of all things, when the Son of Man is seated on the throne of his glory, you who have followed me will also sit on twelve thrones, judging the twelve tribes of Israel." (Matt. 19.28)
...and I confer on you, just as my Father has conferred on me, a kingdom, so that you may eat and drink at my table in my kingdom, and you will sit on thrones judging the twelve tribes of Israel. (Luke 22.29-30)

Matthew and Luke molded this tradition to suit their interests, but it remains that the idea this politburo would sit on thrones judging the twelve tribes of Israel is common to both and presumably predated both. Moreover, unlike much of what we know about the first-century Christian movement (including Matthew and Luke), this tradition about end times has nothing to say about non-Jews and concerns Israel alone. Already by the time of Paul's letters in the 50s, for example, there was a sense that "the saints," namely all those raised with Christ whether Jewish or not, would "judge the world" (1 Cor. 6.2). What Paul meant exactly by this may be up for debate, but Jesus' more parochial focus on the Twelve as judges of Israel was likely, then, an early theme associated with the movement, coming from a time before its expansion to non-Jews through the work of Paul and others.

As noted above, there was a hierarchy within the Twelve and the closest faction to Jesus consisted of Simon Peter and the brothers James and John (the sons of Zebedee), with Simon Peter and John continuing their positions among the leaders of the movement after Jesus' death. We must be careful here given the Gospel writers or their copyists may have heightened or downplayed the importance of certain members for purposes that reflect power and leadership struggles later. For example, Matthew's Gospel subtly accentuates Peter's prominence when compared to Mark (which is interesting given the traditional but far from certain view that Mark contains Peter's memoirs interpreted by Mark in Rome; Eusebius, *Ecclesiastical History* 3.39.15). For instance, while all three Synoptics include Peter at the top of their respective lists of the Twelve, Matthew explicitly states that Peter is "first" (*protos*) (Matt. 10.2; cf. Mark 3.16).

In any case, these party organizers of Peter (along with his brother Andrew) and the sons of Zebedee (James and John) were given their own origins story in the Gospels, first appearing in Mark 1.16-20 (//Matt. 4.18-22) where they immediately react to Jesus and follow him, while Luke adds an account of a miraculous catch of fish (Luke 5.1-11). These narratives function prototypically given that they provide a model of discipleship for their early readers, but they also provide important early information. Simon bar Jonah (Matt. 16.17) was given the Aramaic epithet *Kepha*, "Rock", which was both transliterated into Greek as *Kēphas* and translated into Greek as *Petros* (from which we get the English "Peter"), as Paul confirms (e.g., 1 Cor. 15.5; Gal. 1.18; 2.7-14). It may have been a nickname to reflect his prominence and position as effective second-in-command, as Matthew would later develop in his own way (Matt. 16.17-19). James and John were not only known as the sons of Zebedee but also the "Sons of Thunder." Mark also refers to this title in an apparently Aramaic form (usually given in English as "Boanerges") which looks like a botched attempt at transliteration, hence it was omitted by Matthew and Luke to avoid further confusion. Why James and John had this title, we do not know. One guess is it relates to their righteous fury and bravery as revolutionary martyrs in the face of violence; this is possible (cf. Mark 10.35-45; Luke 9.51-56) but it remains an educated guess.

In this respect it is worth noting a nickname of another from the Twelve: Simon the Cananaean (Mark 3.18), which Luke explains means "Simon, who was called the Zealot" (Luke 6.15; Acts 1.13). It is popularly claimed that Simon earned this nickname because he belonged to a violent revolutionary party called "the Zealots" but such a party did not exist until the uprising against Rome in 66-73 CE. Instead, at the time of Jesus, the term "zealot" would have referred to militant Jews prepared to defend group boundaries and customs with violence or threats of violence, usually grounded in the example of Phinehas from Jewish scriptures. According to this story (Num. 25), an Israelite man brought a foreign woman into the Israelite assembly and so Phinehas drove a spear through them both which in turn stopped a plague against the Israelites. Phinehas was lauded by God himself who praised Phinehas for his zeal which helped assuage God's wrath, adding "he was zealous for his God, and made atonement for the Israelites" (Num. 25.13). Phinehas became an example of dedication while the language of zeal could refer to aggressive defenses of Jewish customs more generally (Philo, *Special Laws* 2.253) or with occasional reference to the prophet Elijah (e.g., 1 Kgs 19.10; Sirach 48.1-2). This tradition of zeal was mentioned by Paul who wrote of his "zealous" persecution of the Jesus movement shortly after Jesus' death and in defense of his own traditions (Gal. 1.13-14; Phil. 3.6).

The nickname of Simon the Zealot should be understood in this context. It might be countered that the Jesus movement was non-violent, but we should not overstate this. As we will see in Chapter 7, this was a tactical and disciplined non-violence before the end times rather than an absolute rejection of violence in principle (cf. Mark 14.46-47). In any case, it is hard to know whether Simon's nickname was based on a pre-existing reputation or linked to the agenda of the Jesus movement. The coupling of zeal, assuaging God's wrath, and atonement would have certainly found a comfortable home in the Jesus movement. But as we will see, the emphasis may have shifted in Simon's case from violent defense of group boundaries to extolling the virtues of revolutionary martyrdom.

Fishing for (not so Great) Men

Stories of Jesus' first associates also provide information about their class background and how, along with a rural artisan like Jesus, the vanguard emerged with cultural credibility from the world of agrarian workers.

It is crucial here to counter the bourgeois tendency found in some scholarship that regards Peter, Andrew, James, and John as "entrepreneurs" of the Galilean fishing trade. While most economic activity in antiquity was centered on the cultivation of land, and fishing on the Sea of Galilee stands out as an important exception, it would be strange to think that the fishing trade itself operated as an exception outside the larger set of economic relations in Galilee. Fishers and their households were presumably subject to the same excessive taxation, discontent, banditry, warfare, and violent reprisals that implicated the daily life of farmers and other villagers.

Indeed, the idea of a loosely regulated free-market in which entrepreneurial fishing collectives pursued commerce independently of imperial or imperial-backed control speaks past almost everything we know of Rome's embeddedness in the political-economy of its territories. To sustain its military might and extensive infrastructure, and backed by an extensive repressive imperial apparatus, Rome and its client-kingdoms were reliant upon revenue funneled upwards through its taxes and other measures of economic extraction like tariffs, tolls, or tithes (see below). The local aristocracy, though constituting a small minority of the population, lived off a share of any surplus produced to sustain their relatively indulgent lifestyles. Josephus labels Antipas himself as a "lover of luxury" (*Antiquities* 18.245). Such a lifestyle, not to mention the large-scale urbanization projects discussed in Chapter 2, is comprehensible only in terms of Antipas' extraction of Galilean resources. The consumption of fish itself was highly prized by the elite. Given the scarcity of meat in antiquity, fish and fish products were often on the menu at lavish banquets. The Roman diet included the use of fermented fish sauce known as garum which was used to flavor meats and other foods.

Archaeological evidence gives the impression that the lives of Galilean fishermen were mostly ordinary, though the interpretation of some of this evidence is disputed. The notion in some quarters of possibilities for social ascendency has been fueled, in part, by extensive excavations in the fishing port of

Magdala on the Sea of Galilee, which reveal an industrious hive of frenetic activity during the first century. But it would be wrong to assume any surplus of economic production would necessarily "trickle down" to the workers given, again, what we know more generally about the broader patterns of economic distribution in Galilee.[2] Any "investment" in fishing infrastructure was not the result of venturing capitalists but of the ruling Galilean elite, as demonstrated by Herodian involvement in sponsoring building projects in Sepphoris and Tiberias. In any case, the lack of monumental structures and poor-quality housing in the remains of Capernaum, the small lakeside village where the Gospels initially place Jesus' fishermen associates, testifies to a material situation no different from other economically marginalized villages in Galilee.

The famous "Jesus boat" (also known as the Kinneret boat or the Ginosar boat) discovered in the seabed of the lake during the winter of 1985 after an extended drought, speaks more to agrarian resourcefulness than a life of affluence. Archaeologists believe the boat comes from the first century and is likely the type of boat used by the fishermen disciples. (Of course, it is unlikely that this was the actual boat they used which is why the label "Jesus boat" may be misleading.) By the standards of ancient boatbuilding, the timber used in the boat's construction was of poor quality, underscoring the need to keep expenses down. Archaeologist Jonathan L. Reed observes the boat "had to be patched, pegged, and glued together of various kinds of inferior wood and scraps from previous boats, and when it finally gave out, nails and any sturdy wood were removed to use in a subsequent boat."[3] The archaeological evidence, then, when properly contextualized, puts fishers in a similar strata to other agricultural workers, with neither fishing nor farming proving a secure pathway to climbing the social pyramid.

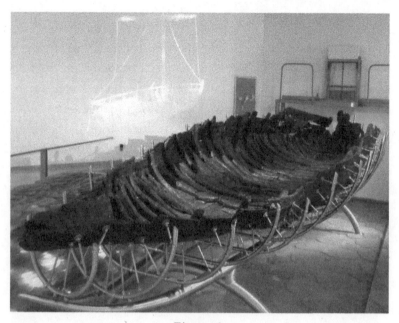

Figure 4.

The "Jesus Boat" on a metal frame in the Yigal Alon Museum in Kibbutz Ginosar, Tiberias, Israel. commons.wikimedia.org

Astute readers of the Gospels have, however, noticed subtle differences between the two sets of brothers: whereas Simon Peter and Andrew leave their nets behind to follow Jesus, James and John also leave "their father in the boat with the hired men" (Mark 1.20). This would suggest the latter household had means to buy their own boat and hire day laborers. As with any social class we can expect small variations in wealth between households, and the peasantry in different social and historical contexts, of course, have their own internal hierarchies and households of higher or lower status. It appears fishing households were no different. But this does not make them aspiring entrepreneurs! It is also a stretch to classify them as part of some distinct or hypothetical "middling" group made up of mostly urban-based artisans, traders, or merchants who carried on commerce between cities to small local dealers.

Rather, fishers collectively came out of, and would to some extent identify with, the exploited classes of agricultural laborers, slaves, and ancillary workers, including artisans like Jesus, building and transport workers, and so on. Members of fishing households were born, lived, and died in rural villages among the peasantry and for all practical purposes can be regarded as peasants themselves.

Most peasants lived at or near subsistence level. Hence, the Q tradition preserved in the Lord's Prayer, to "give us each day our daily bread" (Luke 11.3//Matt. 6.11). A sober reading of several early Christian sources confirms the general impression of hardship for Galilean fishing families, albeit such perceptions are mediated through elite perspectives. In the book of Acts, for example, the Jewish religious leaders regard the fishermen Peter and John as "uneducated" and "ordinary" (Acts 4.13). Moreover, the story of Jesus' miraculous catch of fish (Luke 5.1-11) presupposes the precarious nature of fishing as a labor-intensive but low-reward occupation. In setting up the miracle, Luke has Simon complain to Jesus that the disciples' "have worked all night long but have caught nothing" (5.5). John's possibly repurposed version in John 21.1-14 includes these details but from the voice of the narrator. The description that the disciples "have worked all night" communicates in the Greek a sense of having toiled to the point of fatigue in total darkness.

That the fishermen disciples were associated with relatively meager origins continues into the Patristic period. John Chrysostom, for instance, suggests the detail in Matthew 4.21 (cf. Mark 1.19) that James and John were "mending their nets," alludes to their frugality (John Chrysostom, *Homily 14 on Matt. 14.3*). Elsewhere, Chrysostom elaborates on John's occupation as a marker of "extreme poverty" (John Chrysostom, *Homily 2 on John 1.1*). Similarly, in the so-called "Gnostic" Pseudo-Clementine writings, "Peter" speaks of his own humble origins: "For we, from our childhood, both I and Andrew, my brother, who is also my brother as respects God, not only being brought up in the condition of orphans, but also accustomed to labor through poverty and misfortune, easily bear the discomforts of our present journeys" (Pseudo-Clement, *Homilies 12.6*). While obviously not reliable as specific historical information about the brothers, the assumption that Galilean fishermen were from the lower classes of society is widespread through the various writings of early Christianity. It is only in the modern period that we find people assuming them as part of some lucrative enterprise.

Tax the Rich!

The common view that Jesus' movement was initially or even primarily a movement of the poor, however, is complicated by the inclusion in the Twelve of Levi (or Matthew) the tax collector. Interestingly, Cicero places tax-gatherers alongside other "vulgar" occupations of the lower classes such as manual laborers, artisans, and fishers (Cicero, *De Officiis* 150), though this is likely designed as a slur. Be that as it may, taxation was obviously a major arm of the repressive imperial apparatus and the main method of economic extraction from the peasant classes. It would appear, then, that Levi, son of Alphaeus, was working on behalf of Antipas the tetrarch, to keep the poor poor and the rich rich. Accordingly, Levi should be profiled somewhat differently from the fishermen associates in terms of social history.

Given Jesus called Levi by the Sea of Galilee, we might imagine he had leased the tax rights for fish harvest in Capernaum, and so was directly responsible for exploiting Peter, Andrew, James, and John. Tax collectors in the Roman Empire farmed taxes such as customs and market dues, taxes on inheritances, and slave manumissions. Small tax leaseholders would bid for the rights to collect taxes within a village or district for a distinct period (usually one year). They lived off the surplus revenue collected above the amount bid; however, they bore significant risk if they could not generate the sum that was promised to the royal financiers. While Levi (a Jewish name) was part of the subject population and not a Roman official, tax collectors were not always themselves the holders of tax-farming contracts, but sometimes underlings hired by them. These individuals were generally taken from the native population, but the higher officials to whom they reported were often foreigners.

The first-century Jewish philosopher Philo (20 BCE–50 CE) relays a chilling tale about one such tax collector, and the unusual and violent lengths he went to in order to collect outstanding dues:

Not long ago a certain man who had been appointed a collector of taxes in our country, when some of those who appeared to owe such tribute fled out of poverty, from a fear of intolerable punishment if they remained without paying, carried off their wives, and their children, and their parents, and their whole families by force, beating and insulting them, and heaping every kind of contumely and ill treatment upon them, to make them either give information as to where the fugitives had concealed themselves, or pay the money instead of them, though they could not do either the one thing or the other; in the first place, because they did not know where they were, and secondly, because they were in still greater poverty than the men who had fled.
But this tax-collector did not let them go till he had tortured their bodies with racks and wheels, so as to kill them with newly invented kinds of death, fastening a basket full of sand to their necks with cords, and suspending it there as a very heavy weight, and then placing them in the open air in the middle of the market place, that some of them, being tortured and being overwhelmed by all these afflictions at one, the wind, and the sun, and the mockery of the passers

by, and the shame, and the heavy burden attached to them, might faint miserably; and that the rest, being spectators, might be grieved and take warning by their punishment. (Philo, *Special Laws* 3.159-160)

Whatever the situation for Levi, we flag here what remains an important story concerning him: immediately following his "call," Jesus and others attend a dinner at his house where they are joined by "many tax collectors and sinners" (Mark 2.15). As we will see in the next chapter, the term "sinner" was regularly used to denote exploitative rich people, and this episode will become a pivotal moment for our broader argument that the Jesus movement demanded those with landed properties and personal wealth to give some, if not all, their possessions to the poor and/or to support Jesus' agenda. In becoming a prominent member of the movement, Levi's networks and possible access to wealthy individuals in Galilee would have come in handy. But in joining the Jesus movement, Levi's occupation as a tax collector was also turned on its head: rather than taxing the poor, he would now tax the rich!

Discipleship of Equals? The Vanguard Jesus Party

We will see further demands placed on Levi, the fishermen, and the rest of the Twelve in later chapters. For now, we should also note that the Twelve were part of a vanguard "Jesus party," so to speak, in that there was a wider network of support for the Jesus movement with differing levels of commitment and interest, but also from varying levels of socio-economic backgrounds and differing genders. In addition to stories about individual followers, we should return to Paul's claim that Jesus appeared to "more than five hundred brothers" (1 Cor. 15.6). This recalled events shortly after Jesus' death and, even if the numbers were exaggerated (as they typically were in the ancient world), implies a sympathetic movement of some size was in place by the end of Jesus' lifetime. Whatever the historical accuracy of the story, Luke 10.1-17 mentions a special group of followers numbering around *seventy* which reflects the main point there was a larger following beyond the Twelve.

While the Twelve were all male (and thus reflective of male-dominated power structures) Jesus' associates included women, some of whom were deemed important enough by the Gospel authors to be named. After Jesus' crucifixion, Mark's Gospel notes watching on from a distance were "Mary Magdalene, and Mary the mother of James the younger and of Joses, and Salome. These used to follow him and provided for him when he was in Galilee; and there were many other women who had come up with him to Jerusalem" (Mark 15.40-41; cf. Luke 24.10). Luke 8.1-3 is an independent tradition which provides a similar review of the role of women, noting that (in addition to the Twelve) Jesus was accompanied on his preaching by "some women who had been cured of evil spirits and infirmities: Mary, called Magdalene, from whom seven demons had gone out, and Joanna, the wife of Herod's steward Chuza, and Susanna, and many others, who provided for them out of their resources."

The fact that these women had a surplus of "resources" to sustain Jesus and the Twelve would suggest they were of a higher social status than your typical fishermen, farmers, or artisans. Women with resources appear elsewhere, such as the woman labeled a "sinner" in Luke 7.36-50. It is still common to regard this woman as a prostitute despite the text never saying she was. As noted above, the term "sinner" refers to exploitative rich people, and this may be the use in Luke 7.36-50 where the woman has an alabaster jar of ointment (Luke 7.37) which we know from a similar story was an indication of wealth (Mark 14.3). However, Luke 7.36-50 may be a development of Mark 14.3-9 which limits its use in reconstruction of the earliest Jesus movement.

We will return to the significance of Mary Magdalene and the women who had undergone exorcisms below. For now, the elite or relatively elite status of the women is worth stressing because their social status meant they had the finances to support the Jesus movement. Elite women in the ancient world sometimes found themselves with time and space to study philosophies and ideas while women running households (who also played an important part in the spread of the movement after Jesus' death) were also in a position to offer resources and support.

And the Jesus movement would have needed financial support. Itinerancy (whether forced or otherwise) was a feature of the movement (see Chapter 6), combined with localized bases of support or a local connection (e.g., Mark 1.29-31; 2.1, 15; 3.19-20; 7.24; 11.11-12; 14.3, 12-15; Luke 11.37). An itinerant movement without its agricultural workers working could not sustain itself. Most lived at subsistence level, and manna did not always fall from heaven. Resources needed to come from somewhere. As we will see, it is striking that a primary target for the Jesus movement's teachings were wealthy people. There were several reasons for this, but one is regularly overlooked in scholarship: to fund and sustain the movement. And it appears certain women in positions of relative influence were able to do so.

Contrary to the reception of the Last Supper intensified by Da Vinci's painting, the account of Jesus' last Passover in Mark's Gospel assumed a variety of people were present beyond the famous thirteen of popular memory. Not only was it assumed the Jesus movement had the resources and networks to have a "large room upstairs" (Mark 14.15) in a crowded Jerusalem at festival time, but also there was a range of followers present (14.12-26). The account mentions there were the Twelve and there were disciples but assumes these groups should be distinguished, hence Jesus narrows down the defector from the Jesus movement to "one of the twelve, one who is dipping bread into the bowl with me" (14.20).[4] As we have seen, Mark's Gospel later adds Galilean women accompanied him (Mark 15.40-41), and so they were assumed present at the meal and perhaps among the more prominent members. Whatever happened at Jesus' last Passover, and we return to this issue in Chapter 9, it is notable that it was simply assumed a range of supporters accompanied him to Jerusalem.

Crowds and Peasant Unrest

Further information about the range of supporters and popular sympathy underpinning the Jesus movement is found by looking at the presence of crowds (cf. Mark 10.46). The Gospels make over a hundred references to crowds in connection to Jesus during his ministry and execution. Scholars often regard the crowds in the Gospel tradition as a useful literary invention which provide a narrative foil and thus intensify Jesus' individual exceptionalism. On the contrary, rather than minimizing the role of crowds in history, we find their frequent participation in events particularly illuminating. Instead of isolating Jesus and the vanguard from the crowds, we seek to take them seriously as participants and even agents of historical change. While the details of their conflicting portrayal within the Gospels cannot be trusted in every respect, their dominating presence gives expression to disenchantment with the material changes affecting Galilee and Judea. Indeed, as with many social movements, crowds imply underlying economic antagonisms that anchor their *raison d'être*.

The Greek term for crowd (*ochlos*) carried strong political connotations within the broader Greco-Roman and Jewish traditions. On the one hand, for instance, the term applied to the "lower classes" or "commoners," thereby underscoring its usefulness as an articulation of distinctive economic group interests. For example, Xenophon explicitly used the term in a contemptuous manner to distinguish between the views of the lower classes and the rulers (*Cyropaedia* 2.2.21). Similarly, the aristocratic Nicias (an Athenian politician and general during the Peloponnesian war) expressed worry that his emissaries to

Athens would not "report the truth" but instead opt "to please the mob" (*Thucydides* 7.8).

On the other hand, the use of *ochlos* in the Septuagint (that is, the Greek translation of the Hebrew Bible) was often connected to military affairs. In Isaiah 43.17, for instance, the "capacity" or "power" that brings out "chariot and horse, army and warrior" is rendered a "strong crowd." Similarly, through much of the Prophets and Maccabean literature, the crowd designates a militarized mob (e.g., Ezek. 16.40; 17.17; 23.24, 46, 47; Dan. 11.13, 25, 43; 1 Macc. 1.17, 20, 29; 9.35; 2 Macc. 4.40; 11.6; 14.23, 43–46; 3 Macc. 1.28; 2.7). In the New Testament, the book of Acts uses *ochlos* repeatedly in connection to riots (17.13; 21.27, 34–5; 24.12, 18), and, as will be explored in chapters 9 and 10, some events surrounding the Passover and death of Jesus can be informed from such a perspective. Such perspectives should also convey the forceful, burly, unpredictable, and vigorously robust qualities of crowds, as opposed to more passive, backgrounded, or subdued characterizations that sometimes accompany bourgeois historiography.

Indeed, as suggested in Chapter 1, in moving away from the Great Man approach to life of Jesus research, we regard Jesus as not the singular "genius" behind the movement, but rather as someone who emerges more plausibly as a religious organizer from within the amorphous collective of the peasantry. Typical approaches to the crowds in historical Jesus research either ignore them completely or see them as radiating outward from an overly-charismatic Jesus and thus providing a ready-made audience for Jesus' novel teachings, healings, and spectacles.[5] It should be warned: the notion that crowds erupt due to the actions of singular individuals, however, is the stuff of bourgeois fantasy, not sociological reality. A certain amount of blurring and messiness, in combination with their shared relation to underlying social and economic forces, makes better sense of their role in the initial expansion of the movement.

Indeed, a careful reading of the Gospels does not uniformly show the crowds initially radiating outward from Jesus at all. In fact, it is only Matthew's Gospel wherein a link between Jesus and the formation of crowds is clearly initiated. For Matthew, Jesus' call of the two pairs of fishermen into his vanguard party leads ultimately to the formation of a crowd. The call narrative in Matthew 4.18–22, for instance, directly precedes the first eruption of crowds in verses 23–25: "And great crowds followed him [Jesus] from Galilee, the Decapolis, Jerusalem, Judea, and from beyond the Jordan."

The other Gospels lack Matthew's stylized presentation, and the crowds appear to already "exist" prior to Jesus' arrival. For our earliest Gospel, Mark, the crowd first appears abruptly in Capernaum as a physical barrier between Jesus and four people carrying a man unable to use his limbs (Mark 2.4). Mark's crowd exhibits a density that suggests it had already reached a life of its own, independent of Jesus. For Luke, the crowd appears even earlier in the Synoptic sequence, during John the Baptist's appearance in the desert (Luke 3.7), and so, once again, precedes Jesus. A conversation between the Baptist and the crowds, who speak with a unified voice, ensues with John challenging them to "bear fruits worthy of repentance" (3.8). The crowds do not re-emerge until 4.42, where they appear before (and not after) Jesus' call of the fishermen in 5.1–11.

In contrast to the Synoptics, John's crowd first appears in 5.13 during a festival in Jerusalem. As a feast crowd, the mass of people is already "in that place" prior to Jesus' arrival. According to John, rather than being the reason for the crowd's composition, Jesus disguises himself within it to slip away from "the Jews" in a shroud of anonymity. Obviously, John's text is not to be privileged in historical reconstruction (especially, as we noted in Chapter 1, for its problematic portrayal of "the Jews"), but the idea of pre-formed crowds existing both independently and inter-dependently of the movement will be an important one going forward.

What these conflicting accounts from all four Gospels gesture toward is a general pattern of crowd formations in Galilee and Judea occurring both as a response to certain fixed events (i.e., Passover), but also organically and unpredictably and so presumably also in response to material changes that were disrupting the regular rhythms of everyday peasant life. For the purposes of the rest of this book, the crowds ought to be understood as historical subjects, with many leaning in as sympathizers or even active participants in the broader movement and with some even signing on as card-carrying members of the Jesus party.

Healings, Exorcisms, and Miracles

Another recurring feature of the Synoptic Gospels, alongside the presence of crowds, is that Jesus and the Jesus movement were known as miracle-workers, healers, and exorcists, and this likewise helps us understand how the movement gained popular support and authority in a Galilean peasant context.

Joan E. Taylor reasons a driving factor behind what made Jesus and the movement "good news" in Galilee was that it was in the middle of a chronic and ongoing health crisis.[6] Health crises were, of course, not unusual among the peasantry in the ancient world. Before the advent of modern medicine, hardship in health issues, including high rates of infant mortality, were normal and expected. It is also worth pointing out that the idea of Jesus as a healer and exorcist would not have been culturally unusual as stories about healers and exorcists were popular in the region roughly around this time.[7]

That Mary Magdalene was mentioned among the associates and among other women understood to have undergone exorcisms is important for understanding the network of support for the Jesus movement.[8] Indeed, Taylor has elsewhere argued that "Magdalene" could be a nickname referring to "Tower," and thus in line with nicknames given to other core associates, as well as a nod to her association with the fishing port, which would make further sense given the sorts of connections we have already seen.[9]

Acts of exorcism or healing made such recipients personally reliant on the exorcist or healer, as well as on a wider support group for such people. A tradition in Matthew and Luke (and thus a possible Q tradition) is from a world understood in terms of spirits and demons but clearly illuminates the importance of social reintegration, support networks, and ancient welfare provision in the face of more extreme forms of possession:

> When the unclean spirit has gone out of a person, it wanders through waterless regions looking for a resting-place, but it finds none. Then it says, "I will return to my house from which I came." When it comes, it finds it empty, swept, and put in order. Then it goes and brings along seven other spirits more evil than itself, and they enter and live there; and the last state of that person is worse than the first. (Matt. 12.43-45//Luke 11.24-26)

A core task of the Twelve was casting out demons and stemming the influence of malign spirits (Mark 3.14-15; 6.7, 13; Luke 10.17) which likewise points to an awareness of the need to embed associates within the community and provide necessary support or after-care for the exorcized. This in turn formed a source of credibility for its popular authority.

For some readers, the idea of exorcisms and healings without the assistance of modern medicine may appear far-fetched. It may be one thing to accept certain cultural contexts interpret the world in terms of demons and spirits, but surely the critical historian cannot accept people were going around miraculously curing diseases! First, it is, of course, possible that a figure or movement could have the reputation of carrying out miraculous deeds, irrespective of whether they happened. Second, not all such deeds have to be categorized as "miraculous" by the historian. To understand this point, it is heuristically useful to distinguish "healings" from the category of "miracle." If by miracle we mean supernatural intervention overcoming laws of nature, such as walking on water or turning water into wine, then this is not the sort of thing critical historians readily accept in reconstructing the details of lives past or present. Miracle stories are well attested across the Gospel tradition and, while serious historians will not accept them as reflective of actual events, it can be argued that Jesus was understood as having supernatural abilities and authority from an early stage. Nevertheless, using the distinct categories of "healer" and "exorcist" nuances our understanding of ideas about authority and the Jesus movement because these are actions that may well have occurred.

As anthropological and medical studies of psychosomatic illness have shown, "healings," such as a person being able to move their limbs or talk after previously being unable to do so (e.g., Mark 2.1-12), are attested across cultures and do not necessarily require a supernatural explanation, though some in the Gospels clearly do (e.g., John 11.1-44). Of course, a given cultural setting (such as Jesus') could interpret causes and effects in terms of the supernatural, and such belief systems are an important aspect of the process.[10]

Likewise, people believed to be possessed by a spirit and an exorcist able to "exorcize" the spirit are recurring cross-cultural phenomena which do not demand that the historian necessarily accepts a supernatural cause. The issue is, of course, far more complicated than this and more could be said about the precise nature of the "illness" or "possession," but the point is that in the case of the historical Jesus, some healings and exorcisms that are cross-culturally recognizable can be assessed in terms of their accuracy as much as a parable or a legal dispute.

While proving that the Jesus movement carried out such acts is as difficult as ever, stories of a man with restricted hand use (Mark 3.1-6), a girl unable to wake (Mark 5.21-24, 35-43; cf. Luke 7.11-17), a woman bleeding for 12 years (Mark 5.25-34), a man unable to see, hear or speak (Mark 7.31-37; 8.22-25; 10.46-52), a woman unable to straighten up (Luke 13.10-17), and so on, could potentially reflect something of the early reputation and activities of the movement (cf. Matt. 11.2-6; Luke 7.17-23), even if healings (and exorcisms) were temporary fixes.

There are more indications, and thus an argument of collective weight, that Jesus the healer and exorcist was an early theme in the development of the Jesus movement. In one case, we have the assumption of a world where Sabbath observance would have been normative and unchallenged and given without explanation: "That evening, at sunset, they brought to him all who were sick or possessed with demons" (Mark 1.32; cf. Mark 1.21). This story assumes people knew Jews waited until after the Sabbath was over (i.e., after sunset) before assisting others. This is the sort of passage that may well have emerged in a setting away from a movement dominated by the issue of non-Jewish inclusion and from a time before the Gospel of Mark, which included in its audience enough non-Jews lacking in such knowledge of Jewish law and who required explanations (e.g., Mark 7.1-5) (see further, Chapter 7). But we can also look at these stories from a specific angle where healings and exorcisms provide information about the divine authority behind the Jesus movement and, conversely, how the movement would justify clashes with other sources of authority.

In Mark 2.1-12, we have that story set in Capernaum about Jesus healing a man unable to use his limbs who had been lowered into the crowded house by way of a hole dug through the roof (the structurally weak, makeshift roof was a feature of homes in the region, and Luke 5.19 changes this to a tiled roof to suit Luke's own audience elsewhere). The ability to (re-)use the limbs is part of a healing story that has the classic traits of reports of psychosomatic and trauma cases across cultures. Similarly, trust in the authoritative healer (cf. Mark 5.27-29; 9.24-25) and a large expectant crowd is an integral part of the process of healing and once this is established, Jesus is said to have responded, "Son, your sins are forgiven/released" (Mark 2.5). This then provoked a response from "teachers of the law" sitting nearby who were "questioning in their hearts" (Mark 2.6) whether Jesus had authority to speak in such a "blasphemous" manner. Jesus was said to have noticed and thus responded with the claim "the son of man has authority on earth to forgive/release sins" (2.10), before the healed man stood up and walked off with his mat.

We have kept the translation of the Greek verb *aphiēmi* deliberately ambiguous as it can be used in the sense of both "forgive" and "release," as can the equivalent Aramaic words. This is also important for understanding the passage as a whole. The healed man is described as a *paralytikos*, traditionally translated "paralytic." The term denotes an inability to use limbs or speak and is associated with punishment for sins, hence the idea sins can be both forgiven and (if we visualize the state of man before and after) released.

There may also be another layer of meaning here: as healings, exorcisms, disease, and sin were understood in interconnected ways, there was probably an assumption the healing released the man from the bondage of Satan. While not identical, this concept is found in Luke 13.10-17. This is a story about a woman who was "bent over and was quite unable to stand up straight," a condition blamed on "spirit." According to Luke's Gospel, Jesus claimed, "ought not this woman, a daughter of Abraham whom Satan bound for eighteen long years, be set free from this bondage on the Sabbath day?" (Luke 13.16). Similarly, Mark has another story about "teachers of the law" accusing Jesus of exorcising spirits with satanic authority. However,

Jesus reverses the allegation back on them by accusing them of "blasphemy" (Mark 3.22-30). This too is what the conflict in Mark 2.1-12 is about: the source of authority for this non-scribal leader of a lower order movement. For Jesus it is godly; for his opponents it is demonic.

There are problems with claims that the healing in Mark 2.1-12 specifically reflects an event in the life of Jesus. That the "teachers of the law" question Jesus "in their hearts" should immediately make us suspicious as Mark has a tendency to frame such conflicts in terms of an overarching motif about Jesus' authority and blasphemy (cf. Mark 14.62-64). But that there is a general theme of controversy over authority to heal and exorcize, and claims to divine authority in healings and exorcisms, in independent sources (e.g., Mark 2.1-12; 3.20-30; Matt. 12.22-32//Luke 11.14-23; 12.10; Luke 13.10-17; Luke 14.1-6), would point to this being an early theme possibly going back to the Jesus movement.

This argument is strengthened when other points are noted: the term "son of man" does not look like the elevated quasi-messianic term Mark uses later in the Gospel in contexts which show signs of creative fiction (e.g., Mark 13.27-28; 14.61-66; see chapters 8 and 9). Rather, it looks like a literal translation of the idiomatic Aramaic term meaning "man" or "human being" which was used with reference to the speaker and a wider group of people. The term was understood in the sense of "a man in my position has authority on earth to forgive/release sins," and thus related to the idea that a wider group of people were authorized to carry out healings and exorcisms (Mark 3.14-16; 6.7, 13; 9.38-40; Luke 10.17) (see further Chapter 7).

Stories pointing to divine authority are important for our analysis because they are simultaneously an *indication* and *justification* of popular authority (cf. Acts 5.33-39). For a grassroots peasant movement with leadership lacking in scribal authority, claims to divine authority required cultural credibility among the broader population. This factional authority did not come from official or pre-existing sources of divine channels (themselves grounded in their own public support), such as the priesthood associated with the Holy Temple, or the popular Pharisees, and so the Jesus movement would need its own mass support to thrive. The reputation of Jesus and his associates as successful healers and exorcists added to the cultural credibility of the vanguard party of the movement.

As we will see in Chapter 7, the Jesus movement promoted serious interpretations of the Jewish scriptures, often grounded in the concerns of the peasantry, which would have also generated wider, popular authority with which to carry out such acts. But before getting there, we must first turn our attention to a fuller explanation of their revolutionary and millenarian manifesto for a new world order in a changing Galilee and Judea.

Chapter 5

Revolutionary Millenarianism

The Jesus movement believed in the coming of an idealized Golden Age with accompanying divine judgment. While there are precise technical uses of the term "millenarianism" in Christian theology, we use this label generally to refer to this sort of millenarianism as a cross-cultural phenomenon. Millenarianism was widespread in early Judaism and involved culturally specific concepts such as hopes for Israel's dominance over all the nations of the earth and a Davidic king or messianic figure. We have further qualified the concept throughout this book as "revolutionary millenarianism." The Jesus movement's millenarianism was revolutionary in that it envisaged a new social and political order that would wipe away the old one and replace it with a new hierarchy to serve the interests of the peasantry.

What was remarkable about the movement's early manifesto was its insistence that the rich, those perceived largely responsible for the material changes affecting Galilee and Judea, needed to surrender their wealth or face divine wrath at the coming judgment. Of course, the point of championing the interests of the peasantry was not about romanticizing "the poor"; it was about reversing the material hierarchies in Galilean and Judean society. And while the millenarianism of the Jesus movement was revolutionary in a social and political sense, it was not completely revolutionary: it sought to right perceived socio-economic wrongs through the installation of a new kingdom, with different kings and lords in charge, a form of utopianism, and not a developed blueprint for a tectonic shift in the mode of production. In envisaging a new world order where the last would be first and the first would be last, the movement was, ultimately, unable to conceive of a world beyond autocratic (or agrarian) models of leadership.

"Millenarianism" as a recurring, cross-cultural phenomenon is related to the concept of "apocalypticism" which describes similar phenomena consisting of expectations of impending destruction, judgment, and a cataclysmic transformation of the social and political orders. When we use such language in this chapter, we are typically referring to these sorts of ideas.

Popular knowledge of apocalypticism owes much to the New Testament book of Revelation (otherwise known by its title, the "Apocalypse"). The Greek word *apokalypsis* used at the beginning of Revelation (Rev. 1.1-3) points to further ideas of "disclosure," "unveiling," and visions. *Apokalypsis* may also denote the genre of Revelation and, while the term was not used in this way prior to the second century CE, it has been argued that there was a style of writing in early Jewish literature that was "apocalyptic." Such literature (including texts such as Daniel, 1 Enoch, and 4 Ezra) typically involves a human recipient of a divine revelation and a narrative full of symbolic and fantastical language. These texts contain "apocalyptic" ideas about end times, collective salvation, transformation of the world order, promised messianic or supernatural assistance, and judgment on perceived wrongdoers, alongside speculations about cosmology and meteorology.[1]

Apocalyptic discourse is not restricted to such texts, however, and apocalyptic visions of the end times, judgment, transformation, and so on are found across a wide variety of ancient Jewish sources, including the Gospels. This is why we can also describe the Jesus movement (and the movement that became Christianity) as an "apocalyptic" (and likewise a "millenarian") movement, whether or not they wrote a literary "apocalypse" before Revelation. As part of our understanding of the details of the revolutionary millenarianism of the Jesus movement, we first need to address a challenge to the very possibility of such ideas emerging from the peasantry.

Apokalypsis: for the Oppressed Masses, the Displaced Elites, or Both?

A tendency in recent scholarship is to challenge the notion that ancient Jewish apocalypticism reflected the interests of oppressed lower-class groups and instead was the product of a displaced scribal elite.[2] If we restrict the concept of apocalypticism to the production of texts then there is some truth to this. After all, it was functionaries from the ideological imperial apparatus of Judean society who were responsible for producing the texts we now label "apocalyptic," and so this constitutes our primary evidence for such views existing in the first century.

Some, however, have taken this argument further and suggest both apocalyptic texts *and* the system of apocalyptic thought reflects displaced elite interests. Randall W. Reed has developed this case at length and, if he is right, his arguments would have serious ramifications for materialist understandings of revolutionary millenarianism. For Reed, the social function of "the apocalyptic system" is an "ideological tool of power" and, when it is combined with the threat of divine judgment, "apocalyptic is bent on exercising power to control the behaviors and beliefs of its audience...apocalyptic depends on a short-term solution for enforcing behavioral norms and theological beliefs."[3]

On the class location of apocalypticism, Reed is emphatic:

> It is not the struggling under-classes who rebel against the imperial boot; rather, apocalypticism is an elite response to political displacement...[B]y situating the class of the apocalypticists in the tradition of the learned scribes, we are forced to abandon notions of apocalyptic as an expression of proletarian protest...Apocalyptic is a move of the powerful who have encountered a world which no longer works with

the categories which have secured their power in the past.[4]

What we can take from Reed's argument is that he has isolated *some* tendencies involved in apocalypticism. However, his understanding is too rigid or vulgar as the evidence we have suggests a far more nuanced situation around the time of the Jesus movement.

For instance, Reed's claim about enforcing behavioral or theological norms is too general to be analytically useful: no doubt this happened but the same point applies to any number of literary forms or ideologies which have been used to influence, mold, or control behaviors. Other points Reed raises have their analytical uses but a reductive presentation of them gives almost no scope for complex social realities and the contradictions constantly at play in people's lives. Certainly, the notion of displaced and disgruntled elites is important for understanding early Jewish apocalypticism, but this does not mean it is *consistently* a phenomenon from above. Irrespective of where such ideas originate, the cross-cultural and recurring phenomenon of peasant myths and hopes of an ideal king and the hatred of evil, manipulative, or self-serving royal advisors suggests the realities are more complex.

It is a basic point about the nature of ideology that elite ideas filter out and get modified, adopted, or even transformed among different classes and social groups. Production of ancient apocalyptic *writings* may well have been the scribal enterprises of a displaced elite, but to restrict apocalyptic *beliefs* and *ideas* to such circles does not follow, and nor does restricting the influence of apocalyptic books in their reception. Given agrarian workers did not have the means or infrastructure to produce texts reflecting their own ideas of the day, we are restricted to using texts produced and preserved by a scribal elite to reconstruct what best approximates their views (see Chapter 1). And while this is obviously a limitation in attempting a history from below, the methodological disposition that we can only make historical determinations about those classes responsible for producing the texts we have is much worse: it runs the risk of erasing the perspectives of the lower classes from history altogether.

It is telling, therefore, that Reed barely touches on the possibility of apocalypticism from below in the first century, and where he does, he tries to downplay its significance or even deny its existence.[5] But it is this sort of evidence that undermines his vulgar understanding of apocalypticism as an exclusively elite phenomenon. As we have seen, movements like the one associated with John the Baptist (Mark 1.4-11; Matt. 3.1-17; Luke 3.1-22) were remembered for sizable urban *and* rural followings, which suggests apocalyptic views were taken up more popularly by farmers and fishers, even if size was typically exaggerated ("And people from the whole Judean countryside and all the people of Jerusalem were going out to him," Mark 1.5; *Antiquities* 18.118; cf. Mark 11.27-32). We might compare Josephus' disparaging discussion of the followers of wilderness leaders with popular hopes for transformation and supernatural intervention: "Deceivers and imposters, under the pretense of divine inspiration fostering revolutionary changes, *they persuaded the multitude to act like madmen,* and led them out into the desert under the belief that God would there give them tokens of deliverance." Recall, the authorities saw these popular movements as threats to the social order and sent troops out to "put *a large number* to the sword" (*War* 2.258-59; our italics).

We can again point to the popularity among the masses of figures like Theudas (*Antiquities* 20.97-98; Acts 5.35-39; cf. *War* 2.261-262; Acts 21.38). Remember that, according to Acts, Gamaliel saw the Jesus movement as comparable in type to the one led by Theudas (see Chapter 3) and the point underpinning the Acts passage was that these movements were popular ("Theudas rose up, claiming to be somebody, and a *number of men, about four hundred*, joined him" [our italics]). Leadership may have sometimes come from displaced elites or the local intelligentsia (cf. Luke 1.5-80; 3.2), but the perception that these figures were associated with high numbers meant, presumably, that there was broad interest in apocalyptic ideas. Whatever the historical realities behind these accounts of popular movements from around the time of Jesus, no one thought it unusual that they were immersed in apocalyptic thought.

But are these *movements* comparable with the writers of apocalyptic *texts* like Daniel or 4 Ezra? Certainly, there are shared apocalyptic themes about divine intervention and societal change. And, for all their differences of nuance and content, this is not a neat either/or situation. Some of the early Jewish apocalyptic texts held authoritative status for people beyond the writers' immediate social circles. The book of Daniel, written around 160 years before Jesus' birth, was the product of a displaced scribal elite, but it was also a popular book consumed beyond these circles. Daniel itself suggests the "wise among the people shall give understanding to many" (Dan. 11.33). This could be read as a power play in Reed's terms, but this would only enhance our argument that this was part of the standard process of ideological dissemination *beyond* the scribal elite. Daniel was read and heard in new and different ways as it moved from its original context. In Jesus' time, for instance, it was interpreted to look for the fall of the Roman Empire with the replacement by a new, divinely backed one.

Indeed, the application of apocalyptic texts like Daniel to current events in the first century was unlikely to predict a favorable future for Rome. For a start, readers and hearers would have known Israel would replace the Roman Empire when confronted by a passage like this: "And in the days of those kings the God of heaven will set up a kingdom that shall never be destroyed, nor shall this kingdom be left to another people. It shall crush all these kingdoms and bring them to an end, and it shall stand for ever" (Dan. 2.44). Josephus, writing for a Roman audience, also shows how dangerous this text could be when he explains some of the symbolic language in Daniel concerning the history and fate of the world empires. Josephus knew this involved good news for Israel and bad news for foreign empires like Rome, and so he conveniently cut off his explanation when it came to the critical point:

> I have not thought it proper to relate this, since I am expected to write of what is past and done and not of what is to be; if, however, there is anyone who has so keen a desire for exact information that he will not stop short of inquiring more closely but wishes to learn about the hidden things that are to come, let him take the trouble to read the Book of Daniel, which he will find among the sacred writings. (*Antiquities* 10.209-10)

Despite our quibbles, Reed's claim that apocalypticism was not for "the struggling under-classes who rebel against the imperial boot" is not completely without merit and reflects a healthy reaction against rose-tinted suggestions that the Jesus movement were one-dimensionally anti-imperial. Against anti-imperial readings, it is sometimes countered that Galilee was not under direct Roman control during the lifetime of Jesus. But we should not throw out the baby with the bath water. Antipas may have ruled Galilee, but he was, ultimately, answerable to Rome and everyone knew who, ultimately, ruled their world. (Recall that Tiberias in Galilee was named in honor of the Roman Emperor.)

The problem with the reaction against anti-imperial scholarship is that it often does not go far enough: rather than expressing indifference toward empire, the early Jesus movement appears to have been ardently in favor of it. As with Daniel above, however, the trouble was that the wrong "empire" was currently ruling the world. Thus, when the Jesus movement spoke of the coming "kingdom of God," as we shall see below, it came with the accompanying assumption that present-day rulers would be not abolished, but rather replaced by another set of divinely appointed rulers.

No doubt, apocalyptic literature could and did come from the displaced scribal elite. But if we only focus on scribal and genre issues surrounding apocalypticism, then the conclusion that apocalyptic ideas in antiquity did not circulate among the lower classes is a near inevitability. If, however, we think of apocalypticism as both a cross-cultural phenomenon involving predictions of dramatic political and social change, and which employs a cluster of shared ideas that cuts across class and status, then we can see apocalypticism was not an exclusively scribal phenomenon. It was (and is) a shared discourse that could be used, reused, appropriated, transformed, modified, and so on in new and varied social contexts. Among the peasantry, apocalypticism would take on new and varied, and even contradictory, meanings. It is therefore essential we contextualize such language in its appropriate class settings. And, as we will see, in the case of the Jesus movement, a movement largely grounded in the peasantry, fantastical and transformational millenarian language was utilized to envisage a new world order and punishment for those overlords deemed responsible for the upheavals in Galilee and Judea.

A Regime Change from the Heavens:
The Dictatorship of the Peasantry

The Jesus movement envisaged a regime change coming down from the heavens: authority of the kingdoms of Herod and Rome would be handed over to the peasantry. The central phrase that the Jesus movement used to describe this coming revolution was the "kingdom of God." The meaning of the phrase was that the Jewish God had always technically ruled the universe (e.g.,

Dan. 4.34) but would dramatically intervene in world history to right wrongs and restore Israel to a place of ongoing pre-eminence (Dan. 2.44).

In the first century, the kingdom of God referred to an actual kingdom, ruled by God's anointed (see below), not a heavenly afterlife or ethereal vision as it has sometimes come to be understood through the Christian tradition. Matthew's Gospel uses the similar sounding "kingdom of Heaven," but the two are basically synonymous. Matthew's version does have the advantage of communicating both a spatial sense of God's kingdom in the heavens and from heaven as well as a qualitative sense that God's kingdom is heavenly. But the point remains that the kingdom of God or Heaven was for *this* earth and was breaking-in through the actions of members of the Jesus movement. Thus, sayings about the present and future kingdom can be found side-by-side in the Synoptic Gospels, and this does not have to be seen as a contradiction in light of how God's kingdom was understood in early Judaism (cf. Mark 4.26-32).

Precisely how audiences were supposed to envisage this future transformation taking place is not always clear in our sources. Nevertheless, we can make some general comments on the structure of this new world order. The language of "kingdom" also implied notions of territory and rulership of territory. The expectation of this kingdom and kingship on earth would also involve a human king (cf. 1 Chr. 28.5) in addition to God-the-king and was, as ever, grounded in long-established ideas of empires and kingdoms in the ancient world, including dominion over other lands but now with Israel to be the final dominant, everlasting kingdom or empire (Obad. 19-21; Zech. 14.9; Ps. 47.2-3; Dan. 7.27; *Antiquities* 10.209-10; cf. *Antiquities* 10.268, 272-77). As Dale Allison has shown in detail, the language of "inheriting the kingdom" in the Gospel tradition would have evoked "taking possession of the land."[6] Mark 11.10 gives some flavor of this sentiment when Jesus arrived in Jerusalem and the

Jerusalemite crowd erupted, "Blessed is the coming kingdom of our ancestor David! Hosanna in the highest heaven!"

Indeed, the English translation "kingdom" may not encapsulate the enormity of what the Jesus movement and other millenarians were expecting. Some scholars have argued that "Empire of God" may better reflect their own expectations given the Greek word for kingdom, *basileia*, was also used when referring to Rome's Empire.[7] Another possibility is "Dictatorship of God" or, to de-mystify the term, "Dictatorship of the Peasantry," both in the sense of whose interests this new order would serve (the peasantry) and in the sense of a theocratic system of governance with extreme punishment for dissenters. By recasting the overly familiar language of "kingdom" as "dictatorship," we emphasize the properly political content of the phrase to which modern readers have become desensitized. As a movement for and of the peasantry, the kingdom was both a rallying cry but also a promise to share in the tangible power and glory of the age to come.

Predictions about the imminent kingdom are found across the Gospel tradition and here we follow a dominant strand of critical scholarship in acknowledging this is among the material most likely to go back to the earliest Jesus movement.[8] The Gospel of Matthew has John the Baptist as the first one to announce the coming "kingdom of Heaven" (Matt. 3.2), but this was added later by the author and may have been done to imply greater consistency between the Baptist and Jesus movements. In any case, the idea of a divine kingdom was not unique to the Jesus movement but part of a broader millenarian tendency in early Judaism (cf. Dan. 12.11-12; 1QpHab 8, 1-14; 4 Ezra 4.26; 2 Bar. 82.20; 85.10). Several prophets of ancient Israel, for instance, fantasized over a future time when God's rule or reign would be established (e.g., Obad. 21; Hag. 2.21-23; Zech. 14.9) and Israel would no longer suffer oppression at the hands of other nations. The specific phrase "kingdom of God" itself appears in early Jewish sources by the time of the writing of the Gospels (e.g., Wisdom 10.10).

Enthusiasm about end times escalated after Jesus' willful martyrdom (e.g., Rom. 13.11-12; 16.20; 1 Cor. 7.29; 1 Cor. 10.11; 1 Cor. 15.51-52; Phil. 4.5), including a concern that the end should already have come by the mid-first century (1 Thess. 4-5). By the turn of the second century, however, headaches had set in about the end not taking place as expected, and early Christian texts had to account for the delay in creative ways (John 21.20-23; 2 Pet. 3.3-10).

This, we recall, is one of the reasons why the Gospel of John is a problem for reconstructing the historical Jesus: John removes virtually all references to the kingdom of God and instead mentions the phrase only in John 3.3, 5, where the discussion has shifted toward being "born again" (or "from above"). In contrast to Mark and Matthew, John's Gospel significantly tones down the imminent millenarianism of the Jesus movement. Rather than pointing forward to the life of an age to come, in which the material hierarchies of the world will be turned on their head, John's Gospel treats "eternal life" as something to be accessed in *this* life right now (e.g., John 11.25-26). John downplays the movement's earlier revolutionary millenarian plea to repent in the face of coming judgment, and instead reformulates the movement's primary message as an appeal to "believe" or have faith in the one sent from heaven (i.e., Jesus).

Whatever embellishments exist within the Synoptic Gospel tradition, the earliest Jesus movement expected imminent end times and the most straightforward conclusion is that this was reinterpreted later by John and others when expectations failed to materialize.

The Damned Rich!

The millenarianism associated with the Jesus movement was partly a product of urbanization projects taking place in Galilee and Judea. While we should not expect reactions to socio-economic changes to be always expressed in socio-economic language, in the case of ideas about the kingdom in the Jesus movement it clearly was. As mentioned above, the Jesus movement's millenarianism was revolutionary in the sense that it envisaged an overthrowing of the existing order and hit hard at class exploitation in the present. Indeed, one of the striking features about their millenarianism was that it attacked wealth and looked forward to a time of economic role-reversal on earth.[9] A mission to the poor would not go far enough, or perhaps was not even required. What was called for was a mission to the rich, and the Jesus movement had lots to say about how the wealthy should either relinquish their wealth, preferably to fund the movement, or expect God's wrath in the coming judgment. This was unmistakably class warfare at its purest.

For example, in Mark 10.17-31 we have a story about a rich man who has observed a list of commandments but is now expected to sell his many possessions or properties, give the proceeds to the poor, and become part of the Jesus movement. The commandments listed (Mark 10.17-22) are based on the Ten Commandments from the Jewish scriptures, but Mark's Gospel has an additional commandment not found there: "You shall not defraud" (Mark 10.19). This language concerned (not) exploiting workers or withholding their wages (see, e.g., Deut. 24.14-15; Mal. 3.5; Sir. 4.1; 1QapGen 20.11). But even this commandment the rich man had apparently observed; instead, for the rich man, giving away his possessions was the problem.

Mark 10.17-31 appears to function as a critique of an established idea about wealth and possessions indicating blessing and reward, hence why Jesus is presented as saying how hard it is for the rich to enter the kingdom of God by comparing it to the impossibility of a camel passing through the eye of a needle (Mark 10.23-25). There is no ancient evidence to support the conjecture sometimes floated that this was a reference to a narrow gate in Jerusalem which a camel might struggle to get through. This sort of convenient thinking is common in the later reception history of Mark 10.23-25, which sometimes tries to dull the sharp edge of the message: it is *impossible* for a rich man to enter the kingdom of God. Some later manuscripts also take the edge off by adding phrases like "how hard it is for those who trust in riches" or changing "camel" to "rope" (a similar sounding term in Greek). Rather, it is precisely because wealth was rejected as a reward for observing commandments that the disciples were amazed (Mark 10.26). Wealth as a moral reward was, after all, a long-established tradition.[10]

Peter was also shocked and expected a reward for what the close associates of Jesus had done ("Look, we have left everything and followed you," Mark 10.28) and Jesus' words in 10.29-31 explain this. They would be dramatically rewarded with households in the age to come, or so the argument goes. This reflects other Jewish traditions promoting eschatological reward for those who suffered for observing the commandments (e.g., 1 Enoch 96.4; 103.5-8; Dan. 12; 2 Macc. 7) and a damning of the rich who claimed to have been rewarded in the present. Indeed, the passage, like other Jewish texts,[11] goes as far as equating wealth with wickedness, and sin would inevitably follow from being wealthy in the present day. As Jesus was remembered saying elsewhere, you cannot serve God and Mammon (Luke 16.13//Matt. 6.24).

Accordingly, what this revolutionary millenarianism did was promise to turn the world upside down, punish those who benefited from the world as it was, give all the trappings of wealth to those who had suffered, and urge the rich to mend their ways before it was too late. As Mark 10.31 put it, "many who are first will be last, and the last will be first." There is no way of knowing if the story in Mark 10.17-31 took place, though there were already signs of embellishments added to a pre-existing story. For example, the addition of "persecutions" to

111

a list of blessings (10.30) which suggests things had not turned out quite as hoped.

In any case, there are several other prominent examples of this reversal in the Synoptic Gospels. The Magnificat in Luke 1.46-55, for instance, a hymn of praise and thanksgiving and often recited in the context of Christian worship, also clearly transmits this theme of the first being last, and the lowly being "lifted up." Verses 51-53 in particular crystalize the reversal envisaged by the revolutionary millenarianism of the Jesus movement:

> He [God] has shown strength with his arm;
> he has scattered the proud in the thoughts of their hearts.
> He has brought down the powerful from their thrones,
> and lifted up the lowly;
> he has filled the hungry with good things,
> and sent the rich away empty.

Although unique to Luke, it is possible that the Magnificat, or at least the general thrust of it, went back to the earliest tradition and/or was continuing earlier concerns of the movement.[12]

The Gospels of Matthew and Luke also contain those well-known and intriguing lists of blessings, the "beatitudes" (Matt. 5.3-12//Luke 6.20-26), where the theme of economic reversal is once again made plain as day. In the ancient world, to be "blessed" referred to the freedom of the wealthy from normal cares and worries. The beatitudes, however, turn such notions on their head: they express a vision of life in the kingdom that included divine favor or reward not for the rich and secure, but for the poor, the mourning, the hungry, and the meek.

In the Gospel of Matthew, the beatitudes appear in the equally recognizable Sermon on the Mount (Matt. 5-7). Scholars have long recognized the Sermon is a literary construct used by Matthew to compile disparate sayings into a coherent narrative frame. Luke's version of the beatitudes also appears to shape material to suit the author's interests. Luke's Gospel alternates blessings, including for the hungry and the hated, excluded, and reviled, with several "woes" against the rich and satisfied, which further cements the promise the earthly status of those addressed would be reversed in the kingdom (Luke 6.20-26). Recipients were thus "blessed" in the sense they would be the privileged recipients of divine favor through God's imminent reign. Although we cannot confirm the historical veracity of each beatitude, they do appear to reflect a common Q tradition which presumably predated the Gospels. But there are additional arguments which suggest at least some of them must have belonged to the early Jesus movement.

Indeed, directly contrasting wealth and poverty, God and Mammon, is common across the Synoptic tradition and found in numerous independent sources and subgenres (e.g., Mark 10.17-31; Matt. 6.24//Luke 16.13; Luke 14.12-24//Matt. 22.1-14; Luke 4.18; 12.13-21; cf. *Thom.* 64). Common too are related themes such as debt (e.g., Luke 12.57-59//Matt. 5.25; Luke 6.35; 16.1-8; Matt. 5.40-42; 6.12; 18.23-35), lack of sustenance and shelter (Matt. 25.31-46; Luke. 6.20-21), and hostility to the trappings of wealth (e.g., Matt. 11.8//Luke 7.25; Matt. 6.25-34//Luke 12.22-31; Luke 6.24-25). It is sometimes argued that hostility to wealth was clichéd and used among elite writers for their own purposes. However, the frequency of the theme across the Gospel tradition suggests it was a major one inherited by the Gospel writers, and though they developed it in their own ways, the best explanation is that it emerged earlier with the Jesus movement in its reaction against the socio-economic changes taking place in Galilee.

We can see the same sentiment plainly expressed in a different tradition independent from the texts mentioned above: the Parable of the Rich Man and Lazarus (Luke 16.19-31). The parable, unique to Luke, points to the fate of the poor man Lazarus and a tellingly unnamed rich man. The rich man had the usual trappings of wealth, dressed in purple (the color of wealth and power) and fine linen (cf. Luke 7.25). He ate well, did not pray for his daily bread, and, as part of his assumed blessings, was buried honorably (cf. Deut. 28.26; Jer. 8.1-2; 16.1-4; Ezek. 29.5; Tob. 1.16-2.10; Josephus, *Apion* 2.211).

By way of contrast, Lazarus was not only poverty stricken at the rich man's gate but was covered in sores, which were understood by some as a sign of divine punishment or disfavor (Ex. 9.10-11; Deut. 28.35; Rev. 16.2). Lazarus was forced to satisfy his hunger with what fell from the rich man's table, and his sores were licked by dogs (whose saliva was thought to have therapeutic properties). The text is silent on his burial, and so this possibly featured as another marker of disfavor (e.g., Jer. 7.33; 22.19; Ezek. 29.5; 1 *Enoch* 98.13; *War* 4.317, 331-332, 359-360, 381-382).

This stark disparity of socio-economic status was, however, dramatically reversed in the afterlife. Lazarus "died and was carried away by the angels to be with Abraham," an important and authoritative patriarch from the Jewish ancestral traditions. By contrast, the dead rich man was in agony, tormented by flames in Hades. He "saw Abraham far away with Lazarus in his bosom." To be at someone's bosom meant to recline to the right of the host (the place of honor) at a meal (cf. John 13.23). The text thus visualizes the socio-economic disparity between the two men in spatial terms of relative closeness to the ancestral patriarch, and Abraham speaks vividly of a "great" and untraversable "chasm" that now separates them (Luke 16.26).

It is notable that there are no moral reasons given for the respective fates of Lazarus and the rich man, not even a hint that the rich man had misused his wealth.[13] Instead, the patriarch Abraham offers a straightforward explanation: "Child, remember that during your lifetime you received your good things, and Lazarus in like manner evil things; but now he is comforted here, and you are in agony" (Luke 16.25). Only when it was too late did the rich man realize his dilemma. He asked Abraham to send Lazarus back from beyond the grave to warn the rich man's brothers so they could avoid torment. However, Abraham responds, surprisingly, that they already have the Jewish scriptures ("Moses and the Prophets") but have not taken them seriously enough. Even someone coming back from the grave to warn them, he suggests, would make no difference. The implication, of course, was the idea that the scriptures, "correctly" interpreted, viewed wealth disparity itself as inherently evil.

We will observe in Chapter 7 how the Jesus movement had regular debates with their detractors over the "correct" interpretation of the scriptures. For the Jesus movement, this typically meant credible interpretations aligned with the interests of the peasantry. And while Luke has a vested interest in promoting stories about wealth and poverty, there is yet another indication that this parable was inherited from earlier tradition: there is no concern for non-Jews in the story, just Jews who should repent and return to observing the Jewish scriptures. As we saw in Chapter 3, inclusion of non-Jews was not an aspect of the movement during the time of Jesus.

Against the idea of an early tradition, however, it has been argued that the final verses of the parable reflect editing in light of Jesus' resurrection:

> Abraham replied, "They have Moses and the prophets; they should listen to them." [The rich man] said, "No, father Abraham; but if someone goes to them from the dead, they will repent." He said to him, "If they do not listen to Moses and the prophets, neither will they be convinced even if someone rises from the dead." (Luke 16.29-31)

Luke's Gospel does elsewhere show interest in relating the resurrection of Jesus to the Jewish scriptures (Luke 24.27, 44) but that is not what is happening here, and it is striking that the Gospel does not take the opportunity to add such an argument to the parable. On the contrary, Lazarus' fate in the afterlife was not contingent upon Jesus' sacrificial death. Moreover, the only person who is hoped to return from beyond the grave is Lazarus so that the rich man can warn his brothers.

As we have seen above, calling the rich to change their ways and repent in the face of divine judgment underlies several parables, sayings, and epithets of the early Jesus movement. It is a common cliché that Jesus had a "mission to the poor." We prefer to turn the cliché on its head: the Jesus movement had a "mission to the rich." We do not deny the Jesus movement was concerned with poverty. That is obvious. Indeed, the movement readily encouraged the underclass and those lacking riches not to worry about the coming judgment when they would receive their reward a hundredfold. However, the sharp end of the Jesus movement's demands was directed toward the rich. And this was not just about moral behavior, it was about them giving up their wealth.

Ideological Re-education: Wealthy "Sinners"

The Jesus movement's "mission to the rich" was also associated with another key theme from early in the tradition: Jesus' association with "sinners." Indeed, Luke's Jesus made plain what was assumed in Mark, "I have not come to call the righteous, but sinners to repentance" (Luke 5.32//Mark 2.17// Matt. 9.13). The common perception that Jesus' association with "sinners" was controversial because they were downtrodden, societal outcasts is wrong. Sober analysis of a wide range of Jewish literature from over a millennium, including Jewish Scriptures through to rabbinic literature, shows the term "sinners" had a relatively stable meaning which actually points in the opposite direction.[14]

"Sinners" were lawbreakers who acted as if there was no

God and were due punishment. Revealingly, whenever their socio-economic status is mentioned, it is *always* to designate oppressive rich people. As one early Jewish text put it: "Now I tell you, sinners, you have satiated yourselves with food and drink, robbing and sin, impoverishing people and gaining property, and seeing good days. Have you seen the righteous, how their end comes about, for no injustice is found upon them until their death?" (*1 Enoch* 102. 9-11). This equating of "sinners" with the exploitative rich is typical of any number of early Jewish texts.

By the time of the Jesus movement, the term could also be used in several interrelated ways. For instance, accusing "sinners" of being "lawbreakers" could function as a polemic against people who did not observe a specific sectarian interpretation of the law. The hostility toward those acting lawlessly meant that non-Jews (and particularly powerful nations) could be also labeled "sinners," which as we will see in the final chapter has important ramifications for the spread of Christianity after Jesus' death. This range of uses of "sinners" is found or implied across the Gospel tradition (Mark 2.15-17; 14.41; Matt. 11.19// Luke 7.34; Luke 7.37; 18.13; 19.1-9).

In terms of the uses of the phrase with reference to oppressive wealth, we should note that Jesus was understood as associating or eating with tax collectors and "sinners" (Matt. 11.19//Luke 7.34; Luke 18.13; 19.2, 7-8). Recall that Levi, one of the Twelve, is specifically identified as a tax collector, as we saw in the previous chapter. Immediately following his own "call," Jesus and others attend a dinner at his house where they are joined by "many tax collectors and sinners" (Mark 2.15-17). As the Gospel texts indicate, however, a tax collector was the hated occupation of wealthy, corrupt individuals (Cicero, *De Officiis* 1.150; Josephus, *War* 2.287, 292; m. *Nedarim.* 3.4; b. *Sanhedrin* 25b). Or, as Jesus threw back a criticism of his behavior in a possible Q tradition, "you say, 'Look, a glutton and a drunkard, a friend of

117

tax-collectors and sinners!'" (Matt. 11.19//Luke 7.34). In Levi's case, as we observed, in joining the revolutionary vanguard, he would no longer tax the poor on behalf of Antipas, but tax the rich on behalf of the movement.

So why was the Jesus movement associating with "sinners" and tax collectors, the types of people deemed responsible for Galilean discontents? One reason could be a straightforward material one raised in the previous chapter: rich "sinners" and tax collectors had the resources to keep the movement going. But while association with sinners was fraught, and their eventual punishment expected, the themes associated with the Jesus movement (e.g., Mark 2.15-17; Luke 15; 19.1-10) reflect an early Jewish tradition (perhaps a minority one) which hoped wealthy sinners might be able to change their ways.

In general terms, this hope was part of a long-established Jewish tradition of repentance which was conceptualized in the language of turning or returning known as *teshuvah* in Hebrew (*tetuvah* in Aramaic), i.e., Israel returning to God's commandments (see Chapter 3). This meant there was some hope for "sinners" and the key scripture was Ezekiel 33:

So you, son of man, I have made a sentinel for the house of Israel; whenever you hear a word from my mouth, you shall give them a warning from me. If I say to the sinner, "O sinner, you shall surely die," and you do not speak to warn the sinner to turn from their ways, the sinner shall die in their iniquity, but their blood I will require at your hand. But if you warn the sinner to turn from their ways, and they do not turn from their ways, they shall die in their iniquity, but you will have saved your life...Say to them, And I live, says the Lord God, I have no pleasure in the death of the sinner, but that the sinner turn from their ways and live; turn back, turn back from your evil ways; for why you will die, O house of Israel?...And when the sinner turns from their wickedness, and do what is lawful and right they shall live by them (Ezek. 33.7-9, 11, 19; translation modified for ease of comparison)

Because of the importance of a text like Ezekiel 33, others in early Judaism may have agreed with the Jesus movement that "sinners" may eventually repent.[15] However, the dominant opinion from the evidence we have is that it was fruitless trying to convince the powerful to give up their possessions. And, not only that, it was also dangerous. As one saying put it: "Who pities a snake charmer when he is bitten, or all those who go near wild animals? So no one pities a person who associates with a sinner and becomes involved in other's sins" (Sirach 12.13-14).

The theme of repentance is found across the Gospel tradition in independent sources (e.g., Mark 1.14-15, 40-45; 6.12; Matt. 11.20; Matt. 11.21//Luke 10.13; Matt. 12.41//Luke 11.32; Matt. 18.12-14//Luke 15.3-7; Matt. 5.23; Luke 13.1-5; 15; 19.1-9). This suggests the theme was associated with the Jesus movement well before the Gospels were written. The theme of repentance is also found in independent passages which reflect a time when animal sacrifices and the Holy Temple were assumed to be crucial in the process of restoration, something not typical of the movement as it spread beyond Judea and Galilee after Jesus' death and thus once again pointing to an early theme.

Assumptions of intra-Jewish *teshuvah*-repentance with no concern for the salvation of non-Jews was found in a famous parable also framed by ideas of repentance and Jesus' association with tax collectors and sinners: the Parable of the Prodigal Son (Luke 15.11-32; cf. 15.1-2). The parable works with Jewish assumptions in that it discusses how the rebellious son leaves the household and associates with unclean pigs before returning home for a kosher meal with the family (a clear parallel is found in rabbinic literature [*Deut. Rabbah* 2.24]). But the parable also justifies Jesus' association with tax collectors and sinners in the face of criticisms, notably through the character of the older brother who grumbles at the blessings his younger brother receives. To this the father replies: "Son, you are always with me, and all that is mine is yours. But we had to celebrate and rejoice, because this brother of yours was dead and has come to life; he was lost and has been found" (Luke 15.31-32). This reflects another independent tradition where Jesus tells the Twelve, "Go nowhere among the Gentiles, and enter no town of the Samaritans, but go rather to the lost sheep of the house of Israel" (Matt. 10.5-6). Again, note how there is no interest in non-Jews here. The emphasis is on bringing those who were lost back into the fold (cf. Matt. 18.12-14//Luke 15.3-7).

There is one passage which may well be a post-Jesus creation, but which speaks to this demand that wealthy sinners need to repent: the story of Zacchaeus, the chief tax collector and "sinner" (Luke 19.1-9). When Jesus was said to have passed through Jericho, the wealthy and diminutive Zacchaeus wanted to get sight of him but could not see over the crowd because he was too short. He climbed a tree and captured Jesus' attention and they went back to Zacchaeus' house, much to the displeasure of onlookers who cared little for such "sinners."

But there is a telling detail when Jesus pronounces salvation on Zacchaeus' house. While the rich man of Mark 10.17-31 was expected to give up everything, Zacchaeus only gave up half his possessions to the poor, in addition to repaying those he had defrauded (Luke 19.8). This may be Luke explaining away the problem that Jesus was not wholly successful in getting the rich to part *completely* with their wealth. E. P. Sanders once claimed in his critique of the idea that repentance was a major theme for Jesus, "no one would have objected if Jesus persuaded tax collectors to leave the ranks of the wicked: everybody else would have benefited. If he were a successful reformer of dishonest tax collectors, Jesus would not have drawn criticism. But in fact he was criticized for associating with them."[16] Sanders may have unintentionally pointed to the correct historical interpretation here: if Jesus was not an especially successful reformer of the rich who wanted to keep their privileges, wealth, and interests, then we can understand why he was criticized for associating with such disreputable people with a malign influence.

Be that as it may, there is evidence the Jesus movement had moderate success in its "mission to the rich." In addition to several wealthy women who traveled with the poorer associates and funded their activities (see Chapter 4), the (possibly legendary) story of Joseph of Arimathea, as we will see in Chapter 10, signals they may have indeed convinced at least a few high-ranking elites to part with prized resources for the sake of the cause.

A New King of Kings and Lord of Lords?

To recapitulate: the Jesus movement would act as a vanguard political party in this new kingdom, and its politburo would be installed through God's decisive intervention as the custodians of new theocracy on earth, ruled in the interests of the broader peasantry. To meet the material demands of the lower classes, the rich would have to give up their wealth and/or hand over their possessions or face torment in the coming judgment. The Jesus movement thus sought to reach out to these people and convince them to repent before it was too late.

But what was Jesus' anticipated role in this coming kingdom? While later Christians certainly proclaimed Jesus as the rightful king of kings and lord of lords, did this idea originate from the earliest period of the Jesus movement?

The Gospels confess Jesus as the "Christ" (Greek: *christos*), a term otherwise known as "Messiah" from the Hebrew *mashiach* (with the same root used in Aramaic). A common understanding of "Messiah" at the time of Jesus was a figure expected to lead Israel to global dominance and who would be wrapped up in expectations of kingship and military leadership. The book of Revelation appears to understand Messianic identity in this way when it fantasizes about Jesus the Messiah ruling "all the nations with a rod of iron" (Rev. 12.5).

The basic meaning of the term, however, is "Anointed One," i.e., someone anointed to carry out a task. This could involve anointing a prophet, a priest, or a king, including foreign kings such as the Persian Cyrus who was anointed by God to subdue the nations according to Isaiah 45.1. Around the time of Jesus, there was an expectation of a king, in the line of David, anointed to bring about Israel's victory. However, it is still debated whether there was a title *the* Messiah, and it appears qualifications (e.g., kingly, priestly, or prophetic) were needed for the term to make sense.

Whether "Messiah" was a title used by the historical Jesus himself during his lifetime is doubtful. It is revealing that the title was never put on the lips of Jesus in Mark, our earliest Gospel, and it is also strikingly absent from Q traditions. The classic explanation for why Jesus commands people to silence about his Messianic identity in Mark was that it functioned as a narrative explanation for why Jesus was not confessed as the Messiah during his lifetime but came to be afterward. This theory is known, in scholarly circles at least, as the "Messianic Secret."[17] While there is much discussion about the theory, including whether it applied in Mark as a broader concept about Jesus' "true" identity, the basic point is an important one and we can see it at work in Mark 8.27-30:

> Jesus went on with his disciples to the villages of Caesarea Philippi; and on the way he asked his disciples, "Who do people say that I am?" And they answered him, "John the Baptist; and others, Elijah; and still others, one of the prophets." He asked them, "But who do you say that I am?" Peter answered him, "You are the Messiah/Christ." And he sternly ordered them not to tell anyone about him.

We should note here the related confession of Jesus as the "Son of David" is a Matthean favorite (e.g., Matt. 1.1-17). In Mark, however, there is little if any interest in confessing Jesus as the "Son of David," and the idea is either ambiguous (Mark 12.35-37) or used by Jews in and around Jerusalem to describe fellow Jews including Jesus (Mark 10.46-52; 11.9-10). "Christ" and "Son of David" became popular titles for Jesus soon after his martyrdom. It is likely this was because of the rapid elevation of Jesus among the emerging Christian movement who used the title "Christ" or "Messiah" in an absolute form to eliminate the possibility of other contenders, whether kingly, priestly, or prophetic.

More to the point, however, we should avoid making overly confident determinations about a long dead person's *self-understanding*. Not only can they not be asked directly, but it is a basic point of historiographical method that, if we have no materials coming directly from that person (literary or otherwise) then we have no way of getting back to *their* self-understanding beyond external and subjective impressions of how others came to think of them; others who, as we have seen, were not averse to shaping their portraits in line with pre-existing theological and literary agendas. Even if Jesus did not think of himself as the "Messiah" or "Son of David" during his lifetime, the Jesus movement nonetheless took on related elevated "messianic" and kingly rhetoric from which the titles could later surface. As discussed previously, for the Jesus movement this would have involved the enthroned Twelve judging those included and excluded, on behalf of the vanguard (Matt. 19.28//Luke 22.29-30).

We have also seen claims to "divine authority" (e.g., Mark 2.1-12) and there was a similar emphasis on custodianship of the kingdom in the present in the Gospel tradition (e.g., Mark 3.22-30; 4.26-32; Matt. 12.28//Luke 11.20; Luke 13.20-21//Matt. 13.33; Matt. 13.44; Matt. 16.19; Luke 17.20-21; Luke 22.29-

30; *Thom.* 113). Some of these sayings were embellishments and inventions but given the theme appears in independent traditions then it is likely early. One even includes the memory of Jesus associated with satanic dominion (e.g., Mark 3.22-30), which presumably would have been potentially embarrassing for the early Christians, and so it may be an early one.

As Matthew 19.28//Luke 22.29-30 implies, Jesus' emergence as the leader of the vanguard also involved notions of his own enthronement, in addition to divine authorization of the movement as a whole. Of course, there were plenty of "kingly" and "messianic" claims attributed to Jesus but the rapid and early speculations about Jesus' exalted status after his death make it difficult to be sure the extent to which they were present during his lifetime. It *might* be that the label "king of the Jews" shortly before Jesus' crucifixion in Mark 15 and inscription on his cross in Mark 15.26 accurately record the humiliation and parody of his ideas by his executioners. We will also see in Chapter 8 that claims to enthronement in the context of revolutionary martyrdom (Mark 10.35-45) could reflect early themes of the Jesus movement and possibly go back to a time *before* Jesus' death.

Certainly, elevated claims of such leaders are hardly unusual in the history of millenarianism. There were also related models available to the Jesus movement from the world of banditry where bandits and bandit leaders mimicked the world of kings and kingship (*War* 2.57-62; *Antiquities* 17.273-278; Tacitus, *Hist.* 5.9). While the Jesus movement did not ultimately take the route of large-scale human force in the here and now (at least not for a few centuries), there were notable similarities with bandit groups in that banditry was also a product of social upheaval (e.g., *Antiquities* 17.270-284; *Antiquities* 18.269-275; *War* 2.57-65; *War* 2.585-88; *Life* 35, 66). Further, like the Jesus movement, bandits too attacked power, wealth, and Roman power (*War* 2.427-248; *Antiquities* 18.269-275; *War* 2.228-231; *Antiquities*

20.113-117; *Life* 126-127). But not even the most successful bandit leader could mete out the coming punishment that the Jesus movement was promising.

Agrarian Realism: Is There No Alternative?

It has sometimes been said of our age that it is easier to imagine the end of the world than the end of capitalism. Something like this may have been present in first-century Galilee where it was, apparently, easier to imagine a millenarian Golden Age with different rulers in charge than the end of agrarianism: a peasant utopia on earth with all the trappings of the old world. Indeed, for the ancients, what we today call "empire" and "imperialism" was just the basic reality, the zero-sum level of ideology, and any rethinking of the world would inevitably need to be expressed through such concepts, just as appeals to "universal rights" or "democracy" are common sense language in which to ground grassroots struggles today.

If the present world order was ruled in the interests of a wealthy urban elite whose authority was ultimately grounded in the power of the Roman Empire, then the expected kingdom of God would require greater power still. The language of empire was the only language of power the Jesus movement knew to carry out such a challenge. As the labels "kingdom of God" and "kingdom of Heaven" imply, even the divine realm in the ancient world was modeled on known earthly societies. The old structures of domination, authority, and power would remain in the coming kingdom but with a notable coup d'état of its leadership who would now rule in the interests of the peasantry. A top-end revolution. Just as the movement was unable to conceive of a world without kings and lords, slavery, or patriarchy, it did not imagine a world without poverty (recall the much-abused saying "you will always have the poor with you" Mark 14.7//Matt. 26.11).

Anointing Jesus as a king among the peasantry ready to take

his place in the coming transformation of the world was among the most obvious cultural options for an emergent millenarian movement in rural Galilee without access to established sources of authority. There were also broader intellectual traditions to draw upon which had significant appeal in Galilee and Judea at the time. As we know from other Jewish apocalyptic texts, the expectation was God and his eschatological judges, kings, and representatives of vanguards would not only purge Israel of wealthy sinners and make non-Jewish nations subservient but would also bring about the promised justice of the scriptures, and end hunger and disease with abundant blessings.[18]

The Jesus movement knew their great leap forward could not be achieved without supernatural intervention. While this hope was fantastical, it was simultaneously realistic and understandable in its ancient cultural context because there was no other way the world could be changed so dramatically and so quickly. Rethinking the work of Mark Fisher on "capitalist realism" and the dominant inability of contemporary culture to think of a world beyond capitalism,[19] we might even say the Jesus movement was embedded in a world of "agrarian realism." When they did imagine the end, it was still cast in the familiar language of kingdoms and empires ruled by a benevolent lord or king in the name of the common good.

Chapter 6

Family Troubles

Rejection in Galilee

The Jesus movement emerged from the peasantry with a support base, but it did not enjoy universal support. Ideology has historically played its part in keeping the peasantry in place and it was not going to disappear overnight with yet another millenarian movement. We should remember the revolutionary potential of millenarian groups was often contained by the deep-rooted parochialism of village life. This included internal economic dependencies and the conservatism of village power structures.

Mark's Gospel, as we recall, tells of an occasion when Jesus returned to his hometown and started teaching in the synagogue but was criticized because of his artisanal status ("Is this not the carpenter?" Mark 6.3). Mark adds an intriguing summary statement: "And he could do no deed of power there. Except that he laid his hands on a few sick people and cured them. And he was amazed at their unbelief" (Mark 6.5-6). The hostile reception Jesus received in Nazareth quite possibly points to a historical event in his lifetime because the account goes against the rapidly elevated ideas about Jesus after his death. Matthew's Gospel shows how problematic this presentation could be and changed it to clarify that Jesus was not personally lacking in power: "And he *did not do* many deeds of power there, because of their unbelief" (Matt. 13.58). As ever, this does not mean the version in Mark's Gospel automatically takes us back to the historical Jesus. Jesus' apparent lack of power was not too theologically problematic for the author, which means, theoretically, someone could have created such a story without much embarrassment. Nevertheless, the tendency in Mark's

Gospel to present Jesus in elevated terms wherever possible would suggest this story is an inherited theme rather than invented from scratch.

Mark's Jesus also remarked that this hometown rejection included people close to him: "Prophets are not without honor, except in their hometown, and among their own kin, and in their own household" (Mark 6.4). This was not the first occasion family members had voiced concerns. The Gospel of Mark earlier describes how Jesus' closest kin reacted when he was obstructed by a blockading crowd: "Then he went into the household; and the crowd came together again, so that they could not even eat. When his family heard it, they went out to restrain him, for people were saying, 'He has gone out of his mind'" (Mark 3.19b-21). A similar point to that made about Jesus' rejection in Nazareth also applies here: Mark's Gospel does not reveal any embarrassment about Jesus' family assuming he was "out of his mind," but this likely reflects inherited and known criticisms of Jesus. In this case, Mark's Gospel tried to counter such known allegations by collecting them and their refutations together (Mark 3.21-35).

But family troubles do not concern Jesus alone in the Gospel tradition. It appears they were also impacting on others in the movement. In Chapter 5, we saw in passing that the close associates of Jesus had left households, families, and fields "for the sake of the good news" and were, accordingly, promised eternal reward (Mark 10.29-30). Other independent Q traditions talk about a son leaving his dead father to be buried by others (Luke 9.59-60) and Jesus' awareness that the movement would pit family members against one another (Matt. 10.34-36//Luke 12.51-53//*Thom*. 16.1-4). Another Q passage provides a further clue that this theme derives from early tradition:

> Whoever loves father or mother more than me is not worthy of me; and whoever loves son or daughter more than me is not worthy of me. (Matt. 10.37)

Whoever comes to me and does not hate father and mother, wife and children, brothers and sisters, yes, and even life itself, cannot be my disciple. (Luke 14.26)

The differences between Matthew's and Luke's versions are not as strong as they appear in translation. Differences can be accounted for by the likely Aramaic word (from the root *sn'*) underpinning the Greek texts of Matthew and Luke, which had a wide enough semantic area to account for both Matthew's "loves...more" and Luke's "hate." The same root is found in Hebrew and in discussions of who is loved more or preferred (Gen. 29.31-35; Deut. 21.15-17), concepts which the English "hate" does not quite capture.

Given there is no other indication that the Jesus movement actively, deliberately, or provocatively broke commandments about honoring parents and family members (cf. Mark 7.9-13) and given there is no criticism of him doing so, we should understand Matthew 10.37//Luke 14.26 as promoting primary loyalty, in this case to the party. We will see in the next chapter how the pragmatic ethics of the Jesus movement were grounded in agrarian concerns and a preference for what would sustain rather than undermine the conventional norms of peasant life. Even so, social and economic tensions underlying the changes in Galilee could sometimes lead to a breaking point in familial ties, and in such cases, membership required such dedication that it took priority even above the socially valued household. This would also lead to some interesting and creative negotiations with ancient constructions of gender, as will concern us for much of this chapter.

Collectively, what this suggests is the fragmentation of households was an early theme inherited by the Gospel writers. Moreover, the theme often appeared alongside notions of the itinerancy of Jesus and the Jesus movement. By "itinerancy," we simply mean Jesus' traveling from one place to the next and the lack of a permanent or stable home place. Jesus' itinerancy is underscored by the Q tradition preserved in Matthew 8.20// Luke 9.58: "And Jesus said to him, 'Foxes have holes, and birds of the air have nests; but the Son of Man has nowhere to lay his head.'" Itinerancy is generally recognized by scholars as the modus operandi of the historical Jesus' ministry.

Both the itinerancy of Jesus and the Jesus movement and the fragmentation of households were thus interrelated themes and likely to have emerged from the changes taking place in Galilee as Jesus was growing up. Traditional household patterns were shaken up by the building of Tiberias and the rebuilding of Sepphoris. These changes brought about shifts in village production patterns and crucially, as we saw in Chapter 2, they also brought about forced dislocation from lands (e.g., *Antiquities* 18.36-38). As an itinerant, Jesus and some members of the movement suddenly found themselves outside of the dominant kinship structures of the wider Roman world. This is why understanding the socio-economic background to the emergence of the Jesus movement is crucial; it allows the historian to avoid the common pitfalls of anachronism and avoid overemphasizing the early Jesus movement's itinerancy as entirely voluntary.

Homelessness, Itinerancy, and the Jesus Movement

Indeed, another curious tendency in modern scholarship is the assumption that Jesus' itinerancy was a "chosen lifestyle," a descriptor that dovetails comfortably with the neoliberal ethos of late capitalism. In commenting on Matthew 8.20, for instance, R. T. France explains Jesus' "chosen way of life is one of homelessness and insecurity...and his disciples were called to share his style of life. This was a matter of choice, not of necessity, as Jesus' family was probably a comfortable, if not affluent, 'middle-class' one."[1] While the whole concept of a burgeoning "middle class" is anachronistic to the economic profiling of pre-capitalist societies,

France's words also reverberate contemporary obsessions with framing homelessness as a "chosen lifestyle" and reducing the complex struggles of homeless people to the level of individual decision-making and personal responsibility.[2]

This tendency to regard Jesus' itinerancy as a "lifestyle" and thus not requiring much social or economic explanation is widespread. Rather than Jesus' itinerancy emerging from the material conditions of real life, as a consequence of the social structures of his time and place, it magically descends upon him from the heavens, quite literally, as the dove descends on him at his baptism (Mark 1.10). From there Jesus was driven by the spirit "out into the wilderness" and later, coming to Galilee, began an itinerant ministry, roaming from village to village, proclaiming the kingdom of God and a message of repentance (Mark 1.12-15).

This "short-circuiting" of the material reasons undergirding Jesus' itinerancy can be detected, for instance, in the following quote of the historical Jesus scholar John P. Meier, who writes:

> To a certain degree, Jesus first marginalized himself. At the age of roughly thirty, Jesus was an ordinary carpenter in an ordinary hill town of lower Galilee, enjoying at least the minimum of economic necessities and social respectability required for a decent life. For whatever reason, he abandoned his livelihood and hometown, became "jobless" and itinerant in order to undertake a prophetic ministry, and not surprisingly met with disbelief and rejection when he returned to his hometown to teach in the synagogue.[3]

Meier's inclusion of the phrase "for whatever reason" implies the actual reasons that generated Jesus' abandonment of work, hometown, and supposed "decent life" were not as important as the fact that he himself *chose* to pursue it. Elsewhere Meier suggests, "Relying basically on the goodwill, support, and economic contributions of his followers, Jesus intentionally became marginal in the eyes of ordinary working Jews in Palestine." This romantic characterization of Jesus' supposedly intentional actions, however, is premature and overstated. It reflects a worldview rooted in modern, capitalist assumptions about the human subject as *homo economicus*, an autonomous individual agent who behaves in accordance with rational self-interest and whose decisions and motivations are isolated from broader social, political, and economic forces.

A minor, although largely discredited, scholarly trend that does attempt to explain Jesus' itinerancy situates it against the background of Greco-Roman Cynics. The philosophical school known as Cynicism had its own anti-society undercurrent that encouraged people to repudiate civilization and live as beggars and ascetics. While there are some informative parallels with the early Jesus movement (such as wandering around without possessions other than a cloak and a stick, cf. Mark 6.8), we should be suspicious of pushing the analogy too far because of the attraction for contemporary audiences who find the idea of a culturally "subversive" Jesus appealing. In seizing on the Cynic-like Jesus hypothesis, a minority of scholars and their "radical liberal" audiences were able to indulge in the witty, seemingly countercultural aphorisms attributed to Jesus, while marginalizing the hard-hitting apocalyptic themes of divine wrath and judgment, which, as we have seen, were integral to the revolutionary millenarianism of the early movement. Another potent criticism of the Cynic-like Jesus hypothesis is that the Cynics' poverty was a *chosen* way of life typically (but not in all instances) adopted by the educated Greco-Roman elite, and not one they were necessarily born into, as were peasants.

Given the precariousness of rural, non-elite life in Galilee, it is unhelpful to suppose the Jesus movement's emergence, including its itinerancy, was unrelated to the material changes affecting the region. The idea that the movement was enthusiastically soaking up elite offerings of Greco-Roman philosophies, for example, is more plausibly positioned as its exact opposite: the peasantry were in part reacting *against* the gentrification of Galilee as they perceived it to be impinging on their lives. Even if Jesus had enjoyed stable tenure as a *tektōn* in the building projects in Sepphoris, a comfortable leisured existence required significant land ownership, and this does not apply in the case of Jesus. Similarly, as we observed in Chapter 4, Galilean fishers themselves endured a chaotic existence. Recall the miracle in Luke 5.1-11 where the disciples complained they "have worked all night" but caught nothing. It is not difficult to imagine scenarios in which hardship eventually provoked them to abandon work and seek out alternative options available for survival. One option was banditry. Another was investing in millenarian hopes and dreams of a new age when their troubles would be set right, and the elite perceived to be responsible for the changes would be justly punished.

As is obvious from the Gospels' accounts of the supernatural commissioning of Jesus' ministry (such as the dove descending upon him at his baptism in Mark), the extent to which the historical Jesus and the movement's itinerancy was generated by wider social and economic forces remains clouded by our primary sources. The paradigmatic framing of the "call to discipleship" narrative in Mark 1.16-20, for instance, implies their abandonment of family ties was entirely voluntary, and so requires a careful reading against the grain of the text.[4] The priority in these texts was to underscore the movement's immediate needs to recruit loyal members and to convince them to give up whatever they had.

The verses surrounding Jesus' famous lament that he had "nowhere to lay his head" also exhibit this paradigmatic quality: in Luke's version in 9.57-62, three persons approached Jesus while he was "going along the road." The first said: "I will follow you wherever you go," to which Jesus responded with his appeal to foxes' holes and birds' nests. Jesus requested a second person join him, but the man gave the excuse that he needed to return to bury his dead father, i.e., deal with existing familial obligations. A third person declared he would join the movement but asks permission to first "say farewell to those at my home." Jesus responds with the epithet: "No one who puts his hand to the plough and looks back is fit for the kingdom of God." There was a strong and uncompromising message in this passage for new recruits: the revolutionary millenarianism of the movement demanded complete dedication to the cause. Collective and immediate needs of the movement were to be ranked above existing familial and economic obligations. Single-minded allegiance thus exacerbated the disintegration of family ties.

It is important to recognize these stylized "discipleship" stories have a didactic function and appear uninterested in portraying the actual messiness of the various pushing and pulling factors involved. Whatever the reality behind these accounts, we can be sure more complex social and economic forces were at play. Indeed, peasants generally do not take such drastic actions like abandoning their livelihoods unless conditions have become such that they can no longer pursue traditional patterns of life (cf. *War* 4.84; *Antiquities* 16.271-272; 18.269-275).

In any case, Jesus and his associates' experiences of itinerancy and hardship were idealized by later generations of Christians, such as the authors of the Gospels, as models for imitation. Toward the end of the first century, when Matthew and Luke were likely written, the itinerancy and "life of poverty" experienced by some in the movement as a consequence of material conditions had become formalized (see e.g., Matt. 10.5-15) and, in some cases, was being abused (*Didache* 11). In subsequent decades and centuries, monasticism and the ascetic and solitary ideal exerted a powerful influence on the way Jesus was collectively remembered and understood.

The neoliberal tendency to regard the itinerancy of Jesus as a "lifestyle choice," however, needs to be resisted. For the earliest members of the Jesus movement, itinerancy was a gritty reality and more of a matter of survival than the performance of a particular religious identity. Going forward in this chapter, it should be assumed that the realities behind household fragmentations were more complex than their highly stylized portrayal within the Gospels.

The Jesus Party as Family

The dislocations in Galilee likely put strains on existing family ties. Uprooting in some cases led to more fluid households, especially when heads of household could no longer adequately provide for their families. Accordingly, the very concept of family emerged as a particular site of struggle within the early Jesus movement. For many members, the Jesus party itself came to function as a surrogate place of kinship and identity, a "Jesus family," so to speak, that could provide for their needs. But this was not without controversy in the beginning. The following passage in Mark, in which members of Jesus' own biological family were left outside of this new household, underscores the renegotiation of family ties that was taking place:

> Then his mother and his brothers came; and standing outside, they sent to him and called him. A crowd was sitting around him; and they said to him, "Your mother and your brothers and sisters are outside, asking for you." And he replied, "Who are my mother and my brothers?" And looking at those who sat around him, he said, "Here are my mother and my brothers! Whoever does the will of God is my brother and sister and mother." (Mark 3.31-35)

In addition to re-drawing the boundary lines of who is "inside" and who is "outside," the text also accounts for the perceived social deviancy of those left behind by the changes in Galilee. Kinship was to be redefined first and foremost in terms of alignment to "the will of God." Rather than attempting to restore familial ties broken due to the upheavals in Galilee, the faithful were encouraged to enthusiastically embrace their new situation.

Halvor Moxnes argues passages like Mark 3.31-35 point to the Jesus movement "queering" standard assumptions of households. Moxnes uses "queer" not in a limited sense referring exclusively to sexual identity, but rather to mean "a questioning of settled or fixed categories of identity, not accepting the given orders or structures of the places that people inhabit."[5] According to Moxnes, this non-normative family around Jesus appears to have been fatherless, despite including women in roles such as a "mother" and in a context mimicking Jesus' own household. In the paradigmatic "call to discipleship" narratives (Mark 1.16-20), for instance, the act of moving away from secure familial attachments involved surrendering to widespread ideas in the Roman world asserting the importance of male headship and the relative impotence of falling outside these conventional institutions. Moxnes argues these narratives should be read from a *spatial* perspective rather than a *temporal* perspective. From a temporal perspective, interpretations are centered on "conversion," which are influenced by a modern construction of history-based progress and change (i.e., "before" and "after"). From a spatial perspective, however, the stories depict a transition from conventional to unconventional space, thereby exposing the perceived "queer" consequences of becoming card-carrying members of the Jesus family.[6]

Space itself is socially regulated according to generally assumed gender norms, and the proximity of men bonded together as bandits or other "untamed" millenarian groupings could be perceived in the wider Roman world as dangerous and threatening to the stability of the social order. To take one cross-cultural example, Christopher Hill has observed that, within seventeenth-century England, the increasing numbers of vagabonds and "masterless men" who resided outside of the dominant feudal relationship of landholder and peasant, were regarded by traditional elites as a dangerous, disaffected, and rebellious supplement to society.[7] Back in the first-century, the household (*oikos/oikia*) was promoted through the ideological imperial apparatus as an essential microcosm of society. Every household was under the authority of the Roman emperor who was the "Father of the Fatherland" or head of the household of Rome (see figure 5). The father or *pater* exercised dominance and protection in return for obedience and submissive devotion. Fragmenting households in rural Galilee thus gestured toward the fragmentation of the entire Empire. For this reason, the movement could expect to be discredited and attacked by elites.

Figure 5.
A Roman coin minted in 14 CE. The inscription on the left reads CAESAR AVGVSTVS DIVI F PATER PATRIAE (Caesar Augustus, Son of God, Father of the Fatherland). On the right appears TI CAESAR (Tiberius Caesar), who is standing in triumphal quadriga.
commons.wikimedia.org

Moxnes suggests we have indications the Jesus movement were ridiculed due to not meeting expectations of gender roles: men like Jesus were not carrying out stereotypical male tasks such as providing for their households but were instead wandering around the countryside with an assorted surrogate family and supported financially by possibly semi-elite women (Luke 8.3). One instance of potential ridicule that Moxnes observes concerns eunuchs:

> His disciples said to him, "If such is the case of a man with his wife, it is better not to marry." But he said to them, "Not everyone can accept this teaching, but only those to whom it is given. For there are eunuchs who have been so from birth, and there are eunuchs who have been made eunuchs by others, and there are eunuchs who have made themselves eunuchs for the sake of the kingdom of heaven. Let anyone accept this who can." (Matt. 19.10-12; cf. Mark 12.18-27; Luke 20.34-36)

Eunuchs were understood in ambiguous ways in the ancient world, sometimes construed as "womanly," "half-men," or "effeminate," and sometimes ridiculed accordingly (cf. Apuleius, *Metamorphoses* 8.24-31; Lucian, *Eunuch* 8-9; Lucian, *Syrian Goddess* 20, 26-27, 51). Indeed, these sorts of understandings of eunuchs may have been known in the region from traveling cultic groups (cf. Justin, *Apology* 1.29). Moxnes thus claims that the Jesus movement ironically embraced the polemics aimed at them (e.g., "eunuchs for the sake of the kingdom of heaven") to describe their socially castrated movement not living up to conventional gender stereotypes.[8] While we cannot show with any certainty that a passage like Matthew 19.10-12 quoted above reflects an earlier polemic aimed at the Jesus movement, Moxnes has provided an important contribution to our understanding of the fragmentation of households in relation to ancient understandings of gender.

In broader perspective, providing a controversial alternative to traditional expectations of familial roles is a common feature of millenarian movements.[9] Settings of social upheaval, uprisings, and revolution can lead to assumptions about gender and sexuality being shaken up, including imagining new possibilities for women and men. Plenty of other cross-cultural examples could be given but a pertinent parallel comes from the Jewish uprising against Rome in 66-73 CE. Josephus claims that the leading violent revolutionary Simon bar Giora had a notable following of women, including his wife (*War* 4.538). When Simon bar Giora joined other revolutionaries who had seized the fortress at Masada, they "regarded him with suspicion, and permitted him and his following of women access only to the lower part of the fortress, occupying the upper quarters themselves; but afterwards, as a man of congenial and trustworthy disposition, he was allowed to accompany them on their raids upon the surrounding district" (*War* 4.505-6). Again, the presentation of women is limited as we might expect in elite sources from the ancient world but that women could be imagined in such a setting and alongside challenges to class power is an important analogy for what was happening a few decades earlier with the Jesus movement.

Men of Contradiction

To summarize the chapter so far: the upheavals caused by the urbanization projects in Galilee resulted in itinerancy and in some cases the fragmentation or disintegration of traditional households. Some members of the early Jesus movement suddenly found themselves cast adrift socially and economically ("eunuchs for the sake of the kingdom of heaven") and this had destabilizing ramifications for their understanding of traditional gender roles, relations, and expectations. In response, and so as not to appear politically castrated, the Jesus movement developed ideas to recast their predicament as a necessary and even virtuous part of their millenarian undertaking.

At this point, a word of caution is necessary. We should not get too carried away with the idea that the Jesus movement was especially progressive or egalitarian in its negotiation of gender, especially not in any modern liberal or genderfluid sense. The fact that even ancient Christians are "queer" these days, according to Maia Kotrosis, has the effect of "solidifying queer's trendiness and intellectual cachet." She further warns "what often follows is a description of the unique position of these subjects in history, a claim about their very atypical deployment of discourse, or a contention that these subjects are peak innovators or distinctly transgressive."[10]

Indeed, despite the social deviancy of the Jesus family, so-called subversive ideas could sit rather comfortably alongside unsubversive ones. Thus, the romantic claim that the historical Jesus radically shattered patriarchal or gendered expectations is a misguided anachronism. Jesus was a man of his time, not an exception, and the point made about "agrarian realism" in Chapter 5 also applies here: the Jesus movement experienced gender through culturally appropriate and available socio-sexual concepts, and such concepts, whether from early Judaism or the wider Greco-Roman world, were patriarchal and came with their own inherited hierarchies and dynamics. Despite their inclusion and occasional prominence, for instance, women were still remembered as serving the Jesus movement in traditional household roles (e.g., Mark 1.29-31).

We should also avoid the specious argument that Jesus' bachelorhood and celibacy was against the expectations of his time and so made him unique or different. Alternatively, it is sometimes argued Jesus *was* married, and this was not mentioned simply because it was assumed. These arguments are speculative, and the truth is we have scarce evidence to make firm conclusions. There were Jewish people who remained unmarried and they (and others who were married) were presented, like the Jesus movement, as prioritizing dedication to God, their movement, and the Jewish law over family and household commitments (*Antiquities* 3.87; *War* 2.119-61//*Antiquities* 18.18-22; b. *Yebamot* 63b). The only proper answer we can give to the question of Jesus' marital status is that we do not know because the Gospels are not interested in the question. After all, if Paul had not mentioned in passing that the associate Peter later traveled with his wife (1 Cor. 9.5), we would never know whether he was married.

Dominant ideologies of power in the ancient world were often reflected in patriarchal constructions of gender and sexuality, including *within* the Jesus movement, even if it reversed certain hierarchies, as we will see below. Gender and power were packaged together, and the protocols of masculinity cut across economic class, ethnicity, culture, and geographical location. The higher one's status, the more masculine one was, and vice versa. True men were positioned above all others, and the social hierarchy that undergirded such ideas extended into the heavens with the equation of perfect masculinity with divinity. The hierarchical structure of the Roman Empire was itself regarded as especially masculine and dominant over foreign nations (such as Judea) that were deemed soft and effeminate. At the individual level, emperors and elite men could be more assured in their masculinity, but others would have to earn it through feats or strength, the ability to have influence over others, or even to have influence or mastery over themselves. Thus, just as conquered nations were humiliated and effeminate, slaves, under the control of others, were regarded as non-masculine, irrespective of their biological sex.

Figure 6.
*Emperor Claudius subjugates Britannia personified as a woman,
with inscribed base. The inscription reads: Tiberios Klaudios
Kaisar – Bretannia. The invasion of Britain in 43 CE was
the signature conquest of Claudius' regime.*
commons.wikimedia.org

Scholars of gender have described such ideas as constituting
a "hegemonic masculinity" in the ancient world. The key to
understanding this comes from the Marxist theory of Antonio
Gramsci, who broadened the concept of class struggle to include
daily battles of cultural dominance and subjugation. "Hegemony,"
in this sense, refers to the way dominant ideologies of the elite
become normalized and widespread, in part through the efforts

of the ideological imperial apparatus. The propagation of manly and muscular Roman dominance was asserted and reasserted through artifacts like statues, monuments, and coins. Reliefs from the Sebasteion at Aphrodisias, a first-century Temple dedicated to Aphrodite and the divine household of Caesar Augustus, for instance, depict a series of Roman emperors physically subjugating the various nations they had conquered with imperial (and indeed masculine) power. The nations themselves were personified as women subdued beneath conquering male emperors who towered over them (see figure 6). Another example comes from the aftermath of the conquest of Judea and the destruction of the Jerusalem Temple in 70 CE. To celebrate his conquest of Judea, and perhaps to crush any lingering rebellious spirits, the Emperor Vespasian issued a series of commemorative coins. The reverse of these coins once again depicted a female figure, postured in mourning, with the unambiguous letters "IUDEA CAPTA": Judea conquered (figure 7).

Figure 7.

A "Judea Capta" coin issued in 71 CE by the Emperor Vespasian.
The front side features Emperor Vespasian looking rather pleased
with all his manly accomplishments. The reverse side shows a Jewess
in attitude of mourning, and a captive man with bound hands behind
his back. commons.wikimedia.org

These broad understandings of gender and sexuality were negotiated by people across the Greco-Roman world in different and seemingly contradictory ways. Certainly, as noted above, unconventional behavior with regards to gender could be perceived as veering toward the feminine. Equally, however, acts such as celibacy could be regarded as masculine acts of self-control and discipline, if need be. The Latin *virtus*, from which the English word "virtue" derives, meant both manliness and moral excellence. To be virtuous was to be manly. And to be manly was to be great. These competing possibilities and differing external and internal perceptions of gendered behaviors are important for understanding how the Jesus movement constructed a changed world in gendered ideas and how others may have perceived them.[11]

Despite being on the margins of the Roman Empire, masculinity also mattered to Jews in Jesus' time, and we should qualify ancient gender with reference to localized settings. An elite Jewish perspective can be found in the writings of the first-century philosopher Philo, who regularly expressed anxiety about retaining or losing his manhood. For example, Philo suggests being positioned as a "receiver" in the act of sexual intercourse would effectively turn one into a woman and thus emasculate him (*On Abraham* 135-6). Moreover, cross-dressing could lead to a similar loss of manliness. As he puts it, "So earnestly and carefully does the law desire to train and exercise the soul to manly courage...that it strictly forbids a man to assume a woman's garb, in order that no trace, no mere shadow of the female, should attach to him to spoil his masculinity" (*On the Virtues* 18). Obviously, such perspectives were themselves clothed in misogynistic assumptions about the world, such as the idea that men were naturally configured to be "active" and woman "passive."

And we can imagine similar assumptions were being applied at the level of the ideological construction of the world to the "passive" dislocations as a consequence of the upheavals in Galilee, under the "active" authority of Herod Antipas. Such ideas are at least implied by Josephus' discussion of the forced movement of people and lands in the building of Tiberias. Recall that, according to Josephus, many inhabitants were "necessitated by Herod to come thither out of the country belonging to him and were by force compelled to be its inhabitants" (*Antiquities* 18.36-38).

Such settings of significant socio-economic upheaval would have generated challenges to expectations concerning gender, but which were then negotiated within the constraints of a patriarchal world. By negotiating these issues, they utilized common gendered stereotypes to promote their own agendas, but in ways that often ironically reinforced existing norms. A good example of this from the Gospel tradition is found in Mark's Gospel, whose Twelve male disciples are often depicted as flawed followers of Jesus who misunderstand Jesus' true identity and purpose. Anxieties about their own masculine performance appear to bubble to the surface in Mark 9.33-37 when the Twelve are said to have "argued with one another who was the greatest." Such a question assumes their being ranked on a social scale that, as we saw above, went hand-in-hand with ideas of gender and power, but also the ways in which masculinity and greatness aligned with the glory and majesty of God. Perfect masculinity would form the apex of this social and, indeed, cosmic hierarchy; and the higher ranking one achieved, the more masculine one was.

According to Mark's Gospel, Jesus sat down and instructed them: "Whoever wants to be first must be last of all and servant of all." He then took a child and, putting it among them, declared: "Whoever welcomes one such child in my name welcomes me, and whoever welcomes me welcomes not me but the one who sent me." A child symbolized not innocence but a lack of status, as someone dependent on others. Indeed, the Aramaic word *ṭalyā'*, which may have appeared in an earlier form of the tradition, meant both child and servant. The point, in any case, was that to achieve true greatness, true manliness, one should embrace weakness. Jesus had taken the hegemonic masculinity of the wider Roman world and turned it on his head. Or had he?

While on its surface the teaching appears to undermine prevailing imperial discourses that regard "greatness" as central to any worthy masculine identity, it does not ultimately undermine the dominant idea that winning the masculinity contest was a crucial task. Rather than abolishing the social hierarchy itself, the ladder would simply be reversed, with men lower on the social scale now at the top and the elite at the bottom. The rules of the game had simply shifted. Put otherwise, Jesus' teaching to his disciples, although often using the language of submission and subservience, was intended to *heighten* their masculinity, perhaps through an ironic redefinition of terms. But there was no sense that masculine power itself would be jettisoned. Such ideological constraints are apparent within the notion of "servant leadership" which ironically doubles-down on the necessity for hierarchy, but reflexively justifies the unequal relationship through its appeal to a sense of duty and altruism. Likewise, when the material hierarchies of Galilean and Judean society were reversed, and the first would become last and the last become first, the social ladder would most assuredly remain in place, just with different rulers at its apex.

We should note that the Jesus movement's negotiations with these overarching patriarchal and ideological constraints would have presented even more acutely following Jesus' humiliating death on the cross. While recent attempts to promote Jesus as a victim of sexual abuse (in some cases, a poster boy for the #metoo movement) have the potential to decenter women as the predominant victims of abuse, the point remains that within antiquity crucifixion was intended as a shameful, emasculating death. The intention was not only to conquer but to completely discredit the victim, and visual displays of gendered violence, such as reliefs of Roman emperors conquering the nations, coins commemorating suppressed rebellions, but also crucifixions orchestrated as public spectacles, reinscribed Roman hyper-masculine dominance over their defeated, emasculated combatants. As with other displays of power, such constructions were understood through the prism of gender and sexuality. After all, crucifixion involved being stripped naked and exposed. We will return to this idea in Chapter 10 when we look at Jesus' crucifixion in more detail, but it is worth observing that, given the humiliating nature of Jesus' death, the Gospels appear especially attuned to this question of masculinity: how to present a debased victim of crucifixion as a Great Man?

As we have seen, these gender troubles cannot be restricted to the movement after Jesus' death and were likely emerging during the lifetime of the historical Jesus as well. This could be seen not only in the various household fragmentations experienced by the movement. Women such as Mary Magdalene had prominence in the party and the Jesus movement may have accepted how odd they looked to outsiders. The prominence of some women would become a problem that never really went away. Some streams within the emerging Christian movement after Jesus' death inevitably struggled with women occupying so-called manly roles, ensuring a massive rethinking of gender was not on the agenda (or would have to wait until the end times), and sometimes attacked non-masculine or effeminate behavior (e.g., 1 Cor. 6.9-11; 11.14-15).[12]

But the earliest Jesus movement, despite its inclusion of women, was by no means feminist or proto-feminist and could likewise engage in polemics grounded in gendered expectations, such as when it attacked the masculine credentials of its opponents. In Chapter 3 we saw how Jesus asking the crowds in the wilderness who they expected to see ("A reed shaken by the wind?... Someone dressed in soft clothing? Look, those who put

on fine clothing and live in luxury are in royal palaces," Luke
7.25//Matt. 11.8) was likely an allusion to Antipas and a contrast
between John the Baptist's "hard" life and the "soft" clothing
of the palace elite. This reference to "soft" clothing probably
also functioned as an attack on Antipas' masculinity in contrast
to the masculine ascetic John. The Greek *malakos* is used here
and translated as "soft," but it is a curious word with a wider
semantic area which could also mean "effeminate" behavior and
possibly male prostitution. It is the same word used by Paul to
denote people who would not enter the kingdom of God (1 Cor.
6.9-11), which has also led to controversial and anachronistic
translations, such as by Bishop Tom Wright who combines it
with another Greek word to come up with the novel translation
"practising homosexuals of whichever sort."[13] This translation
obviously owes more to contemporary evangelical obsessions
with regulating sexual behavior than to sober scholarship, but
whatever the best translation may be, there is no doubt that a
certain type of behavior deemed "unmanly" was being attacked
by Paul and this in turn sheds light on the gendered labeling of
Antipas in Luke 7.25//Matthew 11.8.

Fatherly Masculinity

What we would add to Moxnes' argument above, then, is that the
Jesus movement simultaneously defined themselves in relation
to traditional notions of masculinity as well as being aware of
how their alternative Jesus family could be mocked as effeminate.
The clearest example of this is how the members of the Jesus
movement, many of them estranged from traditional household
structures, invested heavily in the idea of a paternal God.

Jesus' frequent use of the term "father" for God has been
romanticized by claims it denoted a special kind of intimacy
between Jesus and God. An exorbitant version of this argument
suggests that when Jesus used the Aramaic term *'Abba* it was a
child-like designation for "daddy." Such claims have been long

discredited. The concept of God as father was a conventional way of discussing and addressing God in early Judaism. In the Hebrew scriptures, the language of father and son or offspring could refer to the relationship between God and the king or God and Israel (e.g., 2 Sam. 7.13-14; Is. 63.16; Jer. 31.9). Jewish texts continued this theme where father was regularly employed as an uncontroversial, respectful, and familiar way of addressing God (e.g., 1QH 17.33-36; 4Q372 1.16-18; m. *Berakhot* 5.1; b. *Taanit* 23b). Psalm 68, for example, praises a paternal God who comes to the aid of Israel in times of need:

> Father of orphans and protector of widows
> is God in his holy habitation.
> God gives the desolate a home to live in;
> he leads out the prisoners to prosperity,
> but the rebellious live in a parched land. (Ps. 68.5-6)

Such ideas must have resonated with many among the early Jesus movement in their own time of need. The Synoptic tradition regularly presents Jesus addressing God as father while God also takes on an idealized paternal role with ultimate authority for the Jesus movement. The famous "Lord's Prayer," a version of which is still frequently recited by Christians today, vividly communicates this sense of divine paternalism and ties it to the revolutionary millenarianism of the movement. Matthew's version has a strong focus on anticipation of the coming kingdom and meeting basic material needs in the meantime:

> Our Father in heaven
> hallowed be your name.
> Your kingdom come.
> Your will be done,
> on earth as it is in heaven.
> Give us this day our daily bread.

And forgive us our debts,
as we have forgiven our debtors.
And do not bring us to the time of trial,
but rescue us from the evil one. (Matt. 6.9-13; cf. Luke 11.2-4)

God the powerful father thus provided for his children's needs (which is, tellingly, basic sustenance). He also forgave his children when they had returned to the fold, acted as a role model, rewarded them, and even knew in advance what his children wanted. That these traditions about addressing God as father occur in independent streams (e.g., Mark 11.25; 14.36; Matt. 6.31-32//Luke 12.29-31; Matt. 6.7-8; Matt. 7.9-11//Luke 11.11-13; Luke 15.11-32) points to the likelihood that the early Jesus movement addressed God as "father." And so too does the fact that the Aramaic *'Abba* is transliterated both in the Gospels (Mark 14.36) as an individual declaration and in Paul's letters as a communal declaration (Rom. 8.15; Gal. 4.6). This suggests the paternal form of address used by the early Jesus movement was maintained as the movement spread beyond Galilee and Judea and among non-Jews.

The rhetoric associated with the fatherhood of God was also tied in with Jesus, members of the Jesus family, and Jews generally who were understood as a son, sons, or children of God (see also, Mark 3.11; 5.7; 12.1-12; cf. *Thomas* 65). This was likewise nothing unusual in Jewish thought where such language could refer to Israelites or be used to praise especially good Jews.[14] These are the sort of uses of "son" and "father" that appear in the earliest Gospel tradition and were utilized by the Jesus movement in their alternative family. As outlined in Chapter 1, however, we should not use John's Gospel here because it suggests Jesus used "Son" or "Son of God" as a highly elevated title to speak of himself, implying controversial equality with God the Father (e.g., John 5.17-18; 10.29-33). If such dramatic claims were made by the historical Jesus, then they would have been included in the earlier Gospels.

Indeed, we can observe how "the Son" as an absolute title for Jesus evolved after his death: Jesus uses the title "the Son" of himself only once in Q (Matt. 11.27/Luke 10.22) and directly and explicitly of himself only once in Mark (13.32). In redacting Mark's Gospel, Matthew often heightened or added the title. For example, after Jesus performed his famous "walking on water" miracle, a story intended to demonstrate Jesus' harnessing of divine power over nature, the associates in Mark's account reacted with utter astonishment and even misunderstanding. For Matthew, however, they "worshiped him, saying 'Truly you are the Son of God.'" (Mark 6.52//Matt. 14.33; cf. Mark 8.29// Matt. 16.16; Mark 15.30//Matt. 27.40; Mark 15.32//Matt. 27.43). By the time we get to John's Gospel, Jesus uses "the Son" as a title for himself 23 times and in a highly elevated manner. Clearly, then, this unique titular use of "the Son" or the "Son of God" was a tradition that grew after Jesus' death.[15]

Whatever the usage and development of "father" and "son" language in respect of the Jesus movement, we should not lose sight of the specific context of the historical movement as an alternative family with allotted roles where God took on the role of the ultimate father figure. In addition to the breakdown of households in Galilee driving this construction of the Jesus family, we should also recall a basic point often missed in scholarship: many people like Jesus lost their fathers at an early age and sometime before their mothers died because it was common in the ancient world for older men to marry younger women (cf. Xenophon, *Oeconomicus* 3.14-16).[16] The Jesus movement, led by a bereft son, filled this gap in their alternative family with the most obvious older man available to them: God (cf. Dan. 7.13).

Butch Millenarianism

The Jesus movement's presentation of a masculine identity can be detected in other Gospel traditions beyond fatherhood and redefinitions of greatness. Certainly, the situation in Galilee may have forced some members of the Jesus movement to commit to a life active in the wilderness and countryside like John the Baptist, but this too could draw on recognizable ancient stereotypes about men being active outside and away from domestic space. Similarly, the discussion about resurrection and marriage in the time to come (Mark 12.18-27) may have involved a critique of patriarchal norms in that when people "rise from the dead, they neither marry nor are given in marriage." Drawing on millenarian themes, the verse implies the resurrected ones would be like those masculinized warriors otherwise known as "angels in heaven."

As we will see in Chapter 8, the Jesus movement would, in time, come to embrace the life and death of a martyr with a preferential option for death. This sort of language was an equally important way of contesting gender in the ancient world and allows us to make further connections still between the revolutionary millenarianism of the early Jesus movement and notions of gender and greatness. As noted above, from the perspective of Roman power, military and physical dominance could be cast in masculine language while the dominated victims were cast in passive and emasculated language. This language was not always accepted by the recipients, and martyrdom could instead be framed as heroic and an extreme form of manliness with the would-be martyr having the ability to take the severest of beatings before death. As we will see, this was one approach taken up by the Jesus movement and the subsequent Christian movement in understanding Jesus' death. And if the potential for martyrdom was a live issue in Galilee, this was only going to be accentuated as the Jesus party headed to a crowded and tense Jerusalem for what would be Jesus' final Passover (see Chapter 9).

Before we come to such issues, we first need to turn to another pivotal and early theme of the Jesus movement: their approach to community discipline, violence, and, most importantly, to their rigorous upholding of the Jewish law. As we will see, their serious approach to these issues provided not only further avenues for them to assert their "butch" millenarian credentials, but facilitated cultural credibility among the Jewish peasantry, as they were responding to the material shifts in Galilean society.

Chapter 7

Discipline and Community

Was Jesus a Violent Subversive?

While Jesus the violent revolutionary as a scholarly tradition has enjoyed staying power over the past 2 centuries, it is far more common these days to claim that Jesus advocated non-violence or even that he was a pacifist against all violence in principle. For example, while Bishop Tom Wright regularly charges his historical reconstruction of Jesus as "dangerous" and "revolutionary," his Jesus was most assuredly *not* a violent conquering Messiah: "The way forward for Israel [according to Wright's Jesus] is not the way of violent resistance," he cautions, "but the different, oblique way of creative non-violent resistance."[1] And yet, despite asserting that Jesus was not "militantly revolutionary," Wright simultaneously claims he was "'doubly subversive' nonetheless." As he puts it: "I have argued throughout that Jesus did not...take the normal option of the military revolutionary...Rather, he announced the end of the present evil age; the real, doubly subversive, revolution."[2] It appears that precisely because Jesus eluded more conventional revolutionary options like taking up arms, this somehow made him even more ("doubly") subversive and radical!

The reality on violence in the early Jesus movement is not so clear cut, and we would suggest party members mostly exhibited a pragmatic and strictly disciplined approach to violence. Bloodshed was to be left to the appropriate moment when God would dramatically intervene to make things right. In the meantime, violence was to be avoided as much as possible, and such views were grounded in popular Jewish traditions about non-violent retaliation.[3] While the movement's message of revolutionary millenarianism was fantastical, it was oddly practical too: there was no way a movement from Galilee had the power or resources to overthrow local elites and certainly not the entire Roman Empire. (Something like this would have to wait a few centuries.)

There was another logic to the Jesus movement's pragmatic approach to violence. Given their call for the rich to repent and support the movement, violently attacking them as other bandits might would have been counterproductive. Non-retaliation and disciplined reactions to provocation, alongside the avoidance of rash oaths, public presentation of strict ethical behavior, male sexual restraint, and maintenance of community relations through material assistance and forgiveness all constitute part of a general theme inherited by the Gospel writers, and are backed up with the end-time threat of an extreme version of gulag called Gehenna (e.g., Mark 9.43-48; 11.25-26; Matt. 5.22, 23-24, 27-29; 33-37, 38-41; Matt. 5.25-26//Luke 12.58-59; Matt. 5.40//Luke 6.29; Matt. 5.42//Luke 6.30, Matt. 5.43-47//Luke 6.27-28, 32-35; Matt. 6.9-13//Luke 11.2-4).

This preference for behavior that would sustain rather than undermine the norms of peasant life contradicts a cliché in modern Jesus research: post-1960s scholarly and popular fetishes for a playful, subversive, ethically provocative, or even quasi-hippy Jesus.[4] While this trend is apparent in the rhetoric of some evangelical scholars like Wright, it also permeates the work of scholars deemed "liberal" and whose Great Man reconstructions of Jesus appear to uniquely subvert the cultural wisdom of his day (and, by implication, ours too).

Jesus being typically imagined as long-haired, bearded, and scruffy, however, should not blind us to the obvious point that comes through strongly in the Gospel tradition: to belong to the Jesus movement required dedication, respectability, seriousness, self-respect, and the maintenance of collective discipline in the face of difficult and changing times in Galilee. If such behaviors seem at odds with some of the "queer" characteristics of the movement identified in the previous chapter, then once again we would do well to remember such contradictions are ultimately manifestations of the contradictions inherent to the social and economic dynamics of their first-century agrarian world. Members of the Jesus party could, on the one hand, embrace accusations of not conforming to typical notions of gender, while, on the other hand, enthusiastically maintain "traditional" social fixtures of rural, peasant life, including rigorous adherence to the Jewish law, as we shall see.

Besides, as we have also observed, the Jesus movement reacted to allegations of "effeminate" behavior with a game of one-upmanship by claiming a degree of hardened "servant" masculinity for themselves as an example to the world. The teaching on disciplined behavior may partly fit into this tendency. Belonging to the movement was not so much about indulging in supposed "subversive" activity for the sake of it, and engagement with perceived frivolous activities was done only for tactical reasons, i.e., as part of the "mission to the rich" (Matt. 11.19//Luke 7.34). If we must use twentieth-century analogies, the Jesus movement was perhaps closer to the serious-minded, morally conservative pre-1960s Communists than the playful post-1960s radical liberals.

Serious Literature

To be respected among the Galilean peasantry, the Jesus movement needed a credible approach toward the Jewish law or Torah. The law was effectively the first five books of the Bible or the Pentateuch (Genesis-Deuteronomy) which further grounded aspects of Jewish identity that were flagged up in the ancient world, such as avoidance of pork or resting on the Sabbath. Modern scholars have somewhat complicated theories behind the origins of the Pentateuch.[5] In Jesus' day, however, its originator was assumed to be the prophet Moses who passed on what he had in turn received from Yahweh, the Jewish deity.

This idea of Moses as originator comes through in the Gospels when Jesus occasionally opens a retort to his opponents with the question "have you not read in the book of Moses...?" (e.g., Mark 12.26). For this reason, the law or Torah is sometimes referred to as the Mosaic law.

Crucially, the law belonged to all Jews. Although factions were divided on the status of various writings, the Pentateuch was important to all. This wide appeal also cut across class lines. From those administering the Temple to those plowing the fields, its relevance was self-evident. Josephus provides one account indicating just how sensitive issues around the law could be for ordinary villagers. He tells of an episode in the mid-first century when Caesar's slave Stephen was robbed on the road to Beth-horon. When soldiers struggled to find those responsible, one of them tore up and burned a copy of the law. The reaction among the Jewish villagers to this provocative act against their god and sacred law was so visceral, so intense that the Roman procurator ordered the execution of the solider, a first-century "bad apple" so to speak, to satiate the crowd and restore order (*War* 2.228-231; cf. *Antiquities* 20.113-15).

What did the law mean for Jesus and the early Jesus movement? Emerging from the Jewish populace we would expect the movement to be just as intense in its devotion. As part of a shift toward emphasizing Jesus' Jewish identity over the past half-century, scholarship now rightly recognizes the historical Jesus accepted the ongoing validity of the law. We would add that the ongoing relevance of the law was simply taken for granted by the early Jesus movement. Contrary to some popular presentations, Jesus' frequent clashes over the law and its interpretation were not intended as subversive, playful, or provocative performances. Rather, debate was conventional, expected, and deadly serious, especially for men wanting to assert themselves (and their masculine credentials) through public competition. Laws contained in the Pentateuch were interpreted and expanded in a range of ways by vastly divergent groups, from dedicated legal experts to violent revolutionaries (e.g., *Life* 70-76, 134-35). As is now increasingly accepted in scholarship, the Jesus party's own understanding of the law should be regarded as one competing strand among others in early Judaism.

Disagreements over the interpretation of the law were occasionally so serious they resulted in deadly conflict among competing groups (e.g., *Antiquities* 13.296-298; 4Q171 4:8-9; 1QpHab 11:2-8; Gal. 1.13-15; cf. Phil. 3.6). It is even possible that, as Mark 3.6 claims, some of Jesus' Pharisaic opponents tried to work with the authorities to have Jesus killed for his interpretation of Sabbath law. As this attempt was unsuccessful (Jesus was instead killed for other reasons, as we will see in subsequent chapters), we can leave open the possibility that it was indeed discussed. Nevertheless, the important point is that the Jesus movement engaged in debates over the correct interpretation of the law rather than outright rejecting its commandments. If the movement was known to be openly breaking such commandments, then they would have had no credibility among the Galilean peasantry. For the Jesus movement to have credibility, it would also need to genuinely represent the prevailing concerns of the peasantry in its legal interpretations.

In any case, a decade or two after Jesus' death, when the movement had managed to recruit large numbers of non-Jews, questions about the Mosaic law's ongoing relevance did begin to surface, as is evident in Paul's letter to the Galatians (e.g., Gal. 2.1-21; cf. Acts 15.1-35). By the mid-first century, a full spectrum of views in the Christian movement is evident, from those who insisted non-Jewish followers of Jesus were subject to full observance of the Mosaic law, including circumcision, to those who saw no abiding significance in the law or even in the Jewish cult and feasts. We must stress, then, that debates over the *relevance* of the law reflect a late development intended to address changing demographics. They do not come from the time of the early Jesus movement.

While much of the Gospel tradition was being written up during this later stage of development, the Synoptic Gospels nonetheless appear to have utilized earlier memories of Jesus as someone vigorously engaged in debates over the law to push their own perspective on its enduring relevance (or not). For example, in building on and developing Mark's own presentation, Jesus is characterized in Matthew's Gospel as possessing supreme authority on the interpretation of the law over and above rival teachers, such as the scribes of Jerusalem (Matt. 7.28-29; 13.52; cf. 15.1-20). As was mentioned in Chapter 2, Matthew also engages artistic license to interpret Jesus through the typology of the Hebrew prophet and lawgiver Moses.[6] Jesus delivered his authoritative interpretation of the law during the Sermon on the Mount, with obvious allusions to the law originating with Moses on Mount Sinai.

Matthew's Gospel also has Jesus say outright: "Do not think that I have come to abolish the law or the prophets; I have come not to abolish but to fulfil. For truly I tell you, until heaven and earth pass away, not one letter, not one stroke of a letter, will pass from the law until all is accomplished" (Matt. 5.17-18). While it is unlikely that this saying goes back to the historical Jesus and belongs to a later reaction against non-law observant forms of Christianity, it may nevertheless represent a genuine attempt to recover earlier memories of Jesus as one for whom the relevance of the law was never in question. Such an argument is strengthened by the association in Matthew's Gospel of the law's ongoing relevance with apocalyptic concerns ("until heaven and earth pass away"). As we will see in detail through the rest of this chapter, what mattered most for the Jesus movement was for the Mosaic law to be mobilized in support of the primary objectives of its revolutionary millenarianism, and this meant culturally credible legal interpretations aligned with the dictatorship of the peasantry.

Disciplined Exegesis

A good illustration of the movement's interpretation of the law in light of the broad concerns of the peasantry is found in Mark 2.23-28. Here we find an argument between Jesus and the Pharisees over whether it is lawful for Jesus' associates to pluck grain on the Sabbath. The Pharisees, who Mark casts as Jesus' chief antagonists,[7] saw this as unlawful, whereas Jesus defended his associates' actions with reference to a story from the scriptures about David and his associates eating bread that was put aside for the priests (1 Sam. 21.1-6). The logic here was as follows: if even a celebrated Great Man like David, who would subsequently become King of Israel, was prepared to commit such an act when hungry, it should be far more acceptable for Jesus' associates to pluck grain under similar circumstances.

This was fundamentally a technical dispute over the interpretation of agrarian rights and obligations during the Sabbath. For Jews, the "Sabbath" refers to a day of observance and abstinence from work kept from Friday evening until Saturday evening. It should not be confused with the "Lord's Day," which in Christian circles is observed on Sundays in memorial of the day of the week Jesus was raised from the dead. Given the regulation of agrarian labor, including time off for religious observance, was of direct concern to the peasantry in Galilee, it is no wonder that the Sabbath emerged as a site of ideological conflict for the Jesus movement. The Pentateuch forbids "work" on the Sabbath (Ex. 20.8; Deut. 5.12) and provides some explanation about the kinds of activities "work" involved, including harvesting (Ex. 34.21). Plucking grain, however, is not mentioned. By the time of Jesus, what constituted "work" was interpreted differently by different Jewish factions, and the issues were regularly discussed in detail. Some interpreters prohibited plucking fruit, allowing only what had fallen on the ground or food that had been prepared in advance to be eaten (CD 10.22-23; Philo, *Life of Moses* 2.22; *Jubilees* 2.29-30; 50.9).

Rabbinic literature gives an example of a similar dispute which is of obvious relevance: when the rabbis disagreed with the "men of Jericho" who "ate Sabbath fruit that had fallen under the tree" (m. *Pesahim* 4.8). Mark's Jesus would have sided with the decision of those from Jericho, and against the rabbis, and there were pragmatic reasons for doing so. Food was readily available in fields and the Pentateuch allowed those poor enough to eat from the edges of fields (Lev. 19.9; cf. Lev. 23.22) which is likely what Jesus' poorer associates were doing in Mark 2.23. In Mark, Jesus justified his position with reference to standard Jewish Sabbath theology with the claim "the Sabbath was made for humankind not humankind for the Sabbath" (Mark 2.27-28; cf. Ex. 16.29). Other rabbis would have agreed with the Jesus movement's interpretation, such as the author of a parallel saying found in a rabbinic commentary on Exodus 31.14: "the sabbath is delivered unto you, and you are not delivered to the sabbath" (*Mekhilta Ex.* 31.12-17). Jewish tradition generally understood the Sabbath as God's gift to Israel, an outworking of the idea the world was created for the benefits of humankind (Gen. 1.26, 28; Ps. 8.4-9; 4 Ezra 6.54-59; 7.11; 2 Bar. 14.18; 15.7; 21.24; *Assumption of Moses* 1.12).[8] From the perspective of the Jesus movement, then, the food had indeed been prepared in advance of the Sabbath by creation itself.

Whether this particular dispute took place cannot be known with any certainty, but we are likely dealing with a pre-Gospel tradition. The dispute is different to what we know was happening in the emerging Christian movement in the decades after Jesus' death. For an increasingly non-Jewish movement, the question of whether to observe the Sabbath at all was the live issue (Rom. 14.1-6; Gal. 4.10; Col. 2.16; John 5.1-18) rather than specific details of Sabbath interpretation and application.

Furthermore, the passage contains cultural assumptions about the Sabbath that add to its likely emergence within a Jewish setting: in addition to the standard Jewish Sabbath theology noted above, the actions of David and his companions were understood to have taken place on the Sabbath, the day when the holy bread was changed.

There is a further argument we can add that suggests this tradition is early. An issue worth developing here (see also Chapter 4) will be of recurring importance in the chapters to follow: the inclusion of the phrase "son of man," which occurs in Mark 2.28. Depending on its usage and surrounding context, what would later become a title for Jesus can also potentially point to early traditions associated with the Jesus movement. Mark 2.28 has one of the most obvious examples of a Greek translation of the Aramaic idiom "son of man" having reference to the speaker and a wider group of people (e.g., "a man in my position") rather than as a unique title for Jesus. This is established by a general framework in Mark 2.27 which Matthew and Luke, copying from Mark, both omit to make "Son of Man" a title for Jesus alone:

> Then he said to them, "The sabbath was made for humankind, and not humankind for the sabbath; so the son of man (/"man in my position") is lord even of the sabbath." (Mark 2.27-28)
> Then he said to them, "The Son of Man is lord of the sabbath." (Luke 6.5)
> "For the Son of Man is lord of the sabbath." (Matt. 12.8)

This would point to an earlier Aramaic version of the saying behind Mark's Greek text which, when combined with the other points, makes an argument of collective weight for this passage emerging from earlier tradition associated with Galilean culture. Unlike the later versions in Matthew and Luke, Mark's version of the "son of man" saying underscores a more collective understanding of the term as it applied to a wider group of people entitled to enjoy on the Sabbath the benefits of creation for basic sustenance.

The legal interpretation advocated by the Jesus movement in Mark 2.23-28 reflects the interests and concerns of peasant farmers, rural poor, and possibly even the landed rich who also would have fields from which the poorer Galileans should be allowed to eat. This message, aimed at a mixed audience, fits with what we saw in Chapter 5 about the "mission to the rich" while obviously also reflecting the broader class concerns of the dictatorship of the peasantry. And this dual focus seems to be a recurring feature of the Jesus movement's interpretation of the law, as we shall see in further examples below.

Divorce and Decadency

This dual focus continues with the Jesus movement's hard stance against divorce. As we saw in the previous chapter, gender would become another ideological site of struggle for the early Jesus movement. No doubt, the rupture of family ties presented challenges and concerns as to the legal complications of matrimonial separation. Here we examine one altercation between Jesus and his Pharisaic opponents on divorce, considering the broader disputes over the correct interpretation of the law.

In Mark 10.1-12, we are told some Pharisees asked Jesus whether it was lawful for a man to divorce his wife, noting "Moses allowed a man to write a certificate of dismissal and to divorce her." Jesus replied that this commandment was given "because of your hardness of heart" and that what "God has joined together" no one should separate. Jesus then reinforced his view with the following line directed at his own associates: "Whoever divorces his wife and marries another commits adultery against her; and if she divorces her husband and marries another, she commits adultery" (Mark 10.11-12).

There is some debate in scholarship about whether Mark 10.2-9 commands an absolute prohibition of divorce or whether the passage assumes divorce would simply have to happen in cases of infidelity or those deemed to have acted in a sexually deviant manner away from home. If this is the case, the two divorce sayings in Matthew would make explicit what Mark assumed. As Matthew 19.9 put it, "whoever divorces his wife, except for unchastity, and marries another commits adultery" (cf. Matt. 5.32). Whatever the precise nuance of Mark's version, the interpretation opposes casual divorce for the sake of remarriage. One strand of thinking in Jewish thought around the time of Jesus allowed the husband to divorce the wife for practically any reason (cf. Matt. 19.10-11), whereas the views attributed to Jesus put him in another strand which placed restrictions on the grounds for divorce (m. *Gittin*. 9.10; cf. *Sifre* Deut. 269; y. *Sota* 1.2, 16b). It also may be significant that Matthew adds divorce is acceptable in cases of "unchastity" (Matt. 5.32; 19.9). The Greek word here is *porneia* which denotes a range of behaviors deemed sexually immoral or deviant and is also the word used to describe behaviors that were causing problems for Paul in the assembly in Corinth in the mid-50s (1 Cor. 5-6). It may be that the author of Matthew believed such "moral degeneracy" had no place in the movement.

There are indications this teaching on divorce predates the Gospels and possibly goes back to the early Jesus movement. The tradition appears to have circulated independently, hence Paul references a version of it in the aforementioned letter (1 Cor. 7.10-15; cf. Matt. 5.32; Luke 16.18). Paul's subtle qualifications reveal the kinds of difficulties this restrictive teaching on divorce was already causing for his assemblies: "if she does separate, let her remain unmarried or else be reconciled to her husband...But if the unbelieving partner separates, let it be so; in such a case the brother or sister is not bound" (1 Cor. 7.11, 15). Several decades later, Matthew's redaction of Mark 10.1-12 also reveals problems putting restrictions on divorce might cause by having the associates of Jesus react with incredulity in response ("If such is the case of a man with his wife, it is better not to marry"). Despite pushing the hardline, Matthew even has Jesus acknowledge the difficulties: "Not everyone can accept this teaching, but only those to whom it is given" (Matt. 19.10-11).

In revealing the problems later associates had with such restrictive teaching on divorce, both Matthew and Paul assumed such teaching was already in existence in the movement, was authoritative, and could not simply be ignored or changed wholesale. By contrast, it is striking that Mark's passage gives no hint at anxieties about the strictness of this teaching. Whatever we make of Mark's narrative framework, the teaching on divorce looks like one of the best cases we have for a specific teaching emerging from the earliest Jesus movement.[9]

The emphasis on restricting divorce in the earliest teaching suggests a preference for traditional ideals of kinship in rural Galilee, despite the pressures discussed in the previous chapter that were breaking some families apart. It counts as corroborating evidence that the dissolution of family ties was not always voluntary, and could be, at least in part, a consequence of the social and economic changes in Galilee. Rather than men being encouraged to wantonly abandon their households, it points in the opposite direction, namely, toward the sustenance of a traditional social fixture of village life.

But there may have been another audience for this teaching: elite women, who we saw were part of the support network for the Jesus movement (Chapter 4). Mark's claim that Jesus pronounced a woman divorcing her husband and remarrying commits adultery is sometimes thought to reflect Roman law because Jewish law (so it is argued) did not allow women to initiate a divorce. This argument does not hold up. A woman could certainly apply pressure for the husband to divorce but there are also examples of elite or semi-elite women initiating divorce, even if some elite men like Josephus did not like it (*Antiquities* 15.259-260; *Papyrus Se'elim* 13.4-7). In any case, the teaching may have had an additional function of protecting women in Galilee from being casually cast out of households on the flimsiest of pretexts which, alongside the logical outworking of a strict restriction on divorce, may account for the untypical emphasis on divorce and remarriage leading to adultery against the wife rather than just the husband (Mark 10.11-12).

Jesus' teaching on divorce is akin to the other strict and "conservative" ethical teachings of the movement. But it also perhaps functioned as a not-so-veiled criticism of the loose morals of the elite. Recall Antipas had married his brother's wife Herodias and was criticized by John the Baptist for doing so (Mark 6.17-29; see Chapter 3). Josephus tells us she separated from her first husband to marry Antipas (*Antiquities* 18.109-136; cf. *Antiquities* 20.141-47) and so we can further see the teaching of the Jesus movement as continuing its antagonism toward the chief representatives of the ruling class, who it deemed responsible for the unsettling changes in Galilee.

Pure and Impure Living

The Jesus movement's presentation of a subset of the Mosaic law, known as the purity laws, was also tailored to the needs of the agrarian populace. "Purity" was the condition of being free from any physical, moral, or ritual contamination. "Impurity" was regarded by the broader population as a kind of unseen contamination contracted and transmitted by people and objects. Impurity was removed where possible through following prescribed rites of purification (e.g., through immersion), though the specific process depended on the type of impurity.

Jewish concepts of pure and impure (or clean and unclean) were grounded in the contrast between holy and common (Lev. 10.10). Physical signs of impurity were regarded as symptoms of a moral or religious imperfection, or demonic possession. In antiquity, temples were understood as literally the dwelling places of the gods. Jewish purity laws were therefore often (though not exclusively) related to their Temple and the closer to the heart of the Temple, the greater the expectation for Jews to be scrupulous about keeping themselves in a state of purity. The process of purification itself usually involved several steps and could occasionally include the offering of a sacrifice at the Temple.

By the time of the first century, there were discussions about the extent to which purity laws should be extended to everyday life, with groups such as the Pharisees and those responsible for the Dead Sea Scrolls having greater interest in maintaining a state of purity as much as possible. For others, such as rural workers, this was less of a concern. But nonetheless ordinary villagers strove to keep the purity laws outlined in the Pentateuch to the best of their ability and made themselves pure when required.

With the language of impure or unclean spirits running through the accounts of the Jesus movement's healings and exorcisms, we should note the intriguing argument that their healings imparted purity and aggressively attacked impurity, including through the removal of impure or unclean spirits.[10] Mark 1.40-45 provides an account of Jesus healing a man with skin disease (usually wrongly attributed to "leprosy") where Jesus touched the man, healed him, made him clean, and sent the man off to be declared clean by the priests (as Lev. 13-14 commands). Whatever the historical accuracy of this story, it gives an indication of how the Jesus movement may have carried out their own understanding of maintaining a state of purity.

The most extensive discussion of purity in the Gospel tradition is found in Mark 7.1-23 (//Matt. 15.1-20). It involves a polemical debate between Jesus and Pharisees and some scribes who asked Jesus why his associates ate without first washing their hands for the purposes of purity law. The dispute was framed in terms of a contrast between "tradition" or "tradition of the elders" (here meaning the interpretation of the law associated with the Pharisees) and the Mosaic commandments, a contrast which is mentioned six times in Mark 7.1-13. Verses 1-5 explains this was primarily related to the interpretation of purity laws and particularly the Pharisaic tradition of washing hands before a meal, a practice which was likely designed to keep the insides pure. Thus, Mark explained to his audience (which presumably included non-Jews) the specific way hands were washed and the immersion of cups, pitchers, and bronze kettles, i.e., implements associated with eating. A variation appearing in some early manuscripts, and most likely the original reading, also includes "dining couches" which is a precise term and the direct equivalent of the Hebrew term used in discussions of the immersion of dining couches in later discussions of Jewish purity law (m. *Miqwaot* 7.7; m. *Kelim* 19.1). Indeed, all the practices Mark labels as "tradition" were discussed in later interpretations of the law; whatever else this text was doing, it accurately reflects the specifics of Pharisaic interpretation which was subsequently codified by the rabbis from the end of the second century CE onward.

Furthermore, Mark 7.4 adds when the Pharisees and "all the Jews" "come from the marketplace, they do not eat unless they purify themselves." This is a conventional translation of the Greek and reflects a widely known Jewish purity practice of bodily immersion. The alternative translation ("and they do not eat anything from the market unless they wash it") requires an unusual understanding of Mark's Greek and the practice of Jews immersing food on return from the marketplace was not a known practice. Certainly, the claim that "all the Jews" practiced these purity laws was an exaggeration, but it nevertheless described the Pharisaic practice precisely. The likely logic behind the Pharisaic purity practice of washing hands before a meal was that it stopped the transmission of impurity passing from hands to food (by way of a liquid such as water or oil) to eater. Bodily immersion was an important part of this process which also involved waiting until sunset to become fully pure again. But during this period, hands could become separately impure and make other things impure.

This context, and Mark's continued emphasis on "tradition" versus commandments, is crucial for understanding the saying in Mark 7.15 that "there is nothing outside a person that by going in can defile, but the things that come out are what defile" and the editorial comment in Mark 7.19 (not entirely clear in Greek) that Jesus "declared all foods clean." Scholars once saw these remarks as indications that Mark's Gospel and, sometimes, the historical Jesus overrode purity laws and even the famous Jewish food laws. However, a sober reading of Mark 7.1-23 shows the opposite is true. In 7.15, 19, Jesus disagreed with the Pharisaic tradition of the necessity of washing hands before a meal. As Mark's Jesus crudely put it: "whatever goes into a person from outside cannot defile, since it enters, not the heart but the stomach, and goes out into the sewer" (Mark 7.18-19).

Furthermore, the claim in Mark's Gospel about "all foods" being clean (assuming the English translation is correct; the Greek is unclear) continues this logic: the foods Jews were permitted to eat were pure irrespective of handwashing. Matthew's Gospel correctly understood Mark 7.19 when including the paraphrase, "to eat with unwashed hands does not defile" (Matt. 15.20). Rather, as Mark and Matthew infer, it is things that come from within, i.e., "immoral" behaviors, which defile and, from their perspective, take priority over Pharisaic interpretation, listed by Mark as "fornication, theft, murder, adultery, avarice, wickedness, deceit, licentiousness, envy/evil eye, slander, pride, folly" (Mark 7.21-22). This is a typical "vice list" found in early Judaism and Christianity used to maintain group boundaries and provide a disciplined presentation of the group to the outside world (see, e.g., 1QS IV.10-11; Wisd. 14.25-26; Gal. 5.19-21; 1 Cor. 6.9-11; 1 Pet. 4.3-6; Rev. 9.20-21; cf. 2 Cor. 12.20-21; Rev. 21.8).

While an editorial hand is clear in Mark 7.1-23, this also indicates the author inherited an earlier tradition. That Mark explains this dispute and the complicated practices for a non-Jewish audience (Mark 7.3-4), rather than disregard it altogether, suggests it was not something the author invented. Indeed, if we take away Mark's editing then we are left with a dispute that really only works in provincial settings like Galilee or Judea where strict adherence to these purity practices was kept. In other words, this points to an early intra-Jewish theme quite different from the cosmopolitan world of the emerging Christian movement, and so the dispute possibly originates from the time of the early Jesus movement.

Indeed, there are also indications of a different version of the same saying about insides and outsides in Mark 7.14-23:

> Then he called the crowd again and said to them, "Listen to me, all of you, and understand: there is nothing outside a person that by going in can defile, but the things that come out are what defile."
> When he had left the crowd and entered the house, his disciples asked him about the parable. He said to them, "Then do you also fail to understand? Do you not see that whatever goes into a person from outside cannot defile, since it enters, not the heart but the stomach, and goes out into the sewer?" (Thus he declared all foods clean.) And he said, "It is what comes out of a person that defiles. For it is from within, from the human heart, that evil intentions come: fornication, theft, murder, adultery, avarice, wickedness, deceit, licentiousness, envy, slander, pride, folly. All these evil things come from within, and they defile a person."

This has led some scholars to suppose Mark inherited the saying in Mark 7.15 and then added a further explanation in Mark 7.17-23.

Irrespective of whether Mark 7.1-23 reflects an actual

episode in the life of the historical Jesus, that it is likely an inherited theme is given further support from independent but related disputes over the interpretation of purity laws and the prioritizing of morality cast in the language of insides and outsides (e.g., Matt. 23.25-28//Luke 11.39-44). Similar concerns are raised in an independent Q tradition where Jesus criticizes the interpretation and expansion of tithing laws at the expense of morality (Luke 11.42//Matt. 23.23), while the theme of insides and outsides in relation to moral purity is one also found elsewhere in the Gospel tradition (e.g., Matt. 5.27-28; 6.16-18).

It is worth noting, too, the ethical lists and injunctions associated with the Jesus movement's teaching on pure and impure, inside and outside, were focused on the types of behavior associated with rich sinners who were likely perceived as decadent exploiters and thus required to radically change their ways. Certainly, some of the references to ethical ideas are general behaviors expected of a disciplined outward-facing movement and accompanying attacks on general wickedness. Others, though, describe the kinds of behavior that could be associated with rich sinners (avarice, murder, pride, greed, plunder, hypocrisy, lawlessness) and promote instead the importance of justice and mercy.[11] We saw in the previous chapter, too, that contestation over some gendered or even sexual predilections may have had connotations to the perceived loose morals of the elite: "Fornicators, idolaters, adulterers, male prostitutes, sodomites, thieves, the greedy, drunkards, revilers, robbers"[12] will not "inherit the kingdom of God," according to Paul in 1 Corinthians 6.9b-10. Such vice lists show how early Christians could indiscriminately mix strict moral and sexual ethics with socio-economic critique.

As ever, then, the various teachings associated with the Jesus movement were tailored to their diverse members and sympathizers, whether group members generally or potential sympathizers from a wealthy background. As we have stressed throughout, this emphasis on strict moral purity was crucial for maintaining party discipline and provided a dignified alternative to both outsiders and potential sympathizers in Galilee. Some of these very people had found their households and traditional ways of life under attack from forces beyond their control.

We will see below how the approach to purity in the Jesus movement was further reflective of typical peasant interests in Galilee, making the connection between ethics and purity a rhetorically powerful combination. First, however, we provide another example of an independent tradition covering the same theme. This story is worth examining in detail because it offers nuance to our discussion and is found only in Luke's Gospel. This is significant because Luke tends to steer away from parochial purity issues to mold the Gospel to a wider and predominantly non-Jewish audience (e.g., Luke 11.39-41//Matt. 23.25-26; Luke 11.42//Matt. 23.23). Indeed, Luke omits Mark 7.1-23 altogether. It is noteworthy, then, that Luke includes this well-known passage grounded in assumptions about purity: the Parable of the Good Samaritan (Luke 10.29-37).

Purity and the Good Samaritan

Parables were simple stories used to illustrate a moral lesson or truth. Jesus' parable about the "Good Samaritan" is familiar to many today, even those who have never graced the insides of a church. This is because a "good Samaritan" has become another way of referring to a person who offers selfless deeds. In the first century, however, this colloquial meaning had yet not taken effect, and a Samaritan was simply a person from the region of Samaria, geographically located between Judea and Galilee, and the religious tradition with a similar (though contested) heritage to Judaism. The parable involves a short story about a hypothetical man attacked, stripped, and beaten by "bandits" when "going down" from Jerusalem to Jericho and left "half-dead" on the side of the road. When a priest and then a Levite (a Temple worker) were going down the same road they avoided the half-dead man and passed by on the other side. The Samaritan, however, took care of the half-dead man and paid for his recovery. The parable once again advocated the kinds of charitable practices expected of the Jesus movement in the context of undisciplined and indiscriminate bandits.

While purity issues may appear unimportant or largely irrelevant to modern readers and so are easily overlooked, the parable is explicitly framed in legal terms (e.g., Luke 10.25-29). This framing involved a question put to Jesus by a legal expert on how to inherit eternal life to which Jesus provided the standard answer for any Torah-observant Jew: love God and love the neighbor. The legal expert followed up with another question on defining "neighbor," and the parable was Jesus' extended response. Jesus and the legal expert both agreed the Samaritan character who showed mercy on the half-dead man fulfilled the role of being neighborly.

The text gives several additional indications of the importance of purity issues. The priest avoiding the "half-dead" man is a crucial detail because priests were not to come into contact with a corpse (the most defiling object in purity law), except in the case of the death of an immediate family member (Lev. 21.1-3). Of course, while the reader knows the victim is only half-dead and thus still alive, the assumption is this would not have been overly obvious to passers-by and so the priest reasonably enacts a policy of caution by putting distance between himself and a potential source of impurity. As corpse impurity was said to contaminate people by rising upward, so the priest avoids the possibility by walking on the other side of the road. The reason for this avoidance of potential corpse impurity was the priest's central role in the service of the Holy Temple in Jerusalem and if a priest was impure then they would not be able to serve there (cf. Ezek. 44.25-27).

Legal traditions accounted for the possibilities of Jews unwittingly contracting impurity from a corpse (cf. Lev. 5.3; Luke 11.44//Matt. 23.27) and the subsequent interpretation of Jewish scriptures involved discussions about what to do with an abandoned corpse. One controversial legal interpreter, who presumably would have agreed with Luke's Jesus, even thought that the High Priest himself should contract corpse impurity in the case of an abandoned corpse (m. *Nazir* 7.1; cf. Num. 6.1-12; Lev. 21.11-12; Philo, *Special Laws* 1.113-115, 250). Indeed, the parable gives a further reason why the priest and Levite *should* risk contracting corpse impurity from a possibly abandoned corpse: they were traveling in a downward direction, away from Jerusalem toward Jericho. In other words, they had finished their shifts in the Temple. This detail is important given we know some contemporary Jewish groups were interpreting purity laws to apply more extensively to everyday life and avoided a state of impurity as much as possible. Against this, the parable advocates a moral action overriding expansions and interpretations of the law (rather than anything in Mosaic law itself), just as Jesus did according to Mark 7.1-23.

This is the reason why the Samaritan is singled out as the moral hero of the parable: the people of Samaria had historical and religious connections with Jews and were known for valuing the Pentateuch. Samaritans were sometimes paralleled with the Jewish group the Sadducees.[13] The Sadducean party was known for its rejection of expansions and developments of the Pentateuch associated with the Pharisees, even if the realities were more complicated. We should avoid liberal romanticizing of this parable which typically claims Samaritans were despised by Jews, and that Jesus was shocking his audience and advocating radical ethnic and/or religious inclusivity by using the foil of a Samaritan Other. Instead, when placed in its ancient cultural context, the parable reveals once more that the Jesus movement engaged in detailed debates over the interpretation of the law.

Indeed, the parable communicates a preference for prioritizing first and foremost the scriptural commandments over expansions of the law, as we see in this text and its explanation of loving the neighbor (Lev. 19.18). Many stories within the broader Jewish literature give voice to similar perspectives which would have cultural credibility in a changing Galilee. One famous account in the Talmud (*Shabbat* 31a), for instance, tells of a non-Jewish man who approached the great sage Hillel and said he would accept Judaism only if the rabbi could teach him the entire Torah while standing on one foot. Accepting the challenge, Hillel, perched on one leg, recited: "What is hateful to you, do not do to your neighbor. That is the whole Torah; the rest is commentary—go and study it!"

As ever, we cannot prove whether it was Jesus or someone else who first spoke this parable, but the fact that the Gospel of Luke contains a story grounded in the details of Jewish purity law (something this Gospel typically avoids doing) would suggest the author was working with a pre-existing tradition. Moreover, what emerges through this, and other legal interpretations put forward by the Jesus movement, is an emphasis on maintenance of community relations through material assistance and care. Such interpretations provided a culturally credible alternative for the peasantry impacted by a changing Galilee.

Pure and Impure Support

The main purity discussions in the Gospel tradition were of the sort associated with Jewish people in Galilee and Judea,[14] had minimal concern for non-Jews and those outside Palestine, and so presumably belong among the earliest independent traditions of the Jesus movement. There is also archaeological evidence pointing to the prominence of discussions supporting the interpretation and in some cases expansion of purity laws around the time of the Jesus movement. For instance, immersion pools for purity have been found throughout the region of

Galilee while stone vessels, understood to be insusceptible to impurity (m. *Kelim* 10.1-3; cf. m. *Parah* 3:2; m. *Kelim* 5.11; 6.2-4; 22.10), have also been found. It is also possible that this recurring critique of expanded purity laws in the Gospel tradition helps us understand another aspect of the supposed controversy of Jesus eating with tax collectors and (wealthy) sinners (Mark 2.15-17): Jesus' behavior might have looked like an open rejection of Pharisaic interpretations of purity law.

But the Jesus movement's understanding of purity law would have wider ramifications for a Galilean audience. In Josephus' description of the forced settlement of Tiberias, he adds it was controversially "built on the site of tombs that had been obliterated, of which there were many there" and that "our law declares that such settlers are unclean for seven days" (*Antiquities* 18.36-38). This resettlement may have caused problems for those more dedicated to maintaining states of ritual purity, but for groups like the Jesus movement this would mean that the necessary social interactions were less problematic.

A helpful analogy for the movement's social interactions with rural workers comes from later rabbinic literature which again collects and develops Pharisaic views on such matters in discussions of the "people of the land." Contrary to some romantic views, the "people of the land" is not a label to designate "the poor" because the category included slaveowners and landowners as well as agricultural workers (e.g., t. *Demai* 3.5; t. *Abodah Zarah* 3.9; cf. m. *Tohorot* 7.6).[15] Instead, we should regard the category as a religious-legal one accounting for people who were especially suspect in their observance of rabbinic and Pharisaic purity and tithing laws (*m. Hagigah* 2.7). Indeed, the "people of the land" were treated identically to those who did not wash their hands before a meal, were thought suspect with liquids and utensils in relation to making food impure, and were deemed unlikely to excise care in matters of corpse impurity.[16]

This analogous context is important for understanding the

mixed audience for the Jesus movement and its approach to purity: it would have allowed the movement to emerge from and reflect agrarian interests and concerns while simultaneously facilitating association with rich sinners, many of whom would not have followed Pharisaic interpretations. In other words, part of the success behind the Jesus movement's approach to purity law was that it cut across class lines. Whether purity law or ethical teaching, the Jesus movement's core teaching was designed to reflect the needs of the peasantry while accounting for the possibility of rich sinners changing their ways and joining the movement.

Such teaching not only brought the movement into conflict with competing Jewish groups over the interpretation of the law, but also continued to attack the elites for their decadent morality and degenerate behavior. Among members and sympathizers, we see something of a shared code of behavior to maintain group discipline and help the vanguard maintain its credibility as the representative of peasant interests. The Jesus movement's disciplined behavior provided an example to the watching world and highlighted possibilities of a life of self-respect for peasants in Galilee whose world had been turned on its head by the Herodian building projects.

Chapter 8

A Preferential Option for Death

In the previous two chapters we have seen how the Jesus movement's emphasis on virtuous self-discipline and strict adherence to the Mosaic law was likely related to its self-presentation as tough, muscular, hard, and manly, in the face of ridicule over fragmenting agrarian households and the unsettledness of itinerant life. It is also reasonable to suppose the Jesus movement, through its revolutionary millenarian proclamation of divine judgment leading to a dictatorship of the peasantry, began to antagonize class enemies among influential and powerful elites, as John the Baptist had done with Herod Antipas.

In sensing heightened vulnerability, the Jesus movement may have experienced a level of paranoia, especially after John's demise, and placed even greater investment in its hopes and dreams that God would bring about the end times soon. Indeed, social positions characterized by relative powerlessness and the threat of exploitation tend to produce thoughts of paranoia. Far from an illness that takes root *ex nihilo*, paranoia is exacerbated by the belief that important outcomes may be predetermined by powerful forces beyond an individual or group's control.

The Jesus movement thus started to grasp at ideas about how their marginal or deviant social positions were, in fact, an assured path to the victory of the Golden Age and may hasten God's dramatic intervention to reverse the material hierarchies in Galilean and Judean society. As we will see below, the movement appears to have developed a theology that would justify placing themselves into situations of imminent danger with a preferential option for death. Not only would it mean they could continue to display bravado and "servant" manliness in the public domain, but it might even spur on or provide a clear indication of the installation of the anticipated kingdom, in accordance with the divine plan.

Recall one of Jesus' closest associates, Simon, held the nickname "the Zealot," perhaps because he had a prior (and even ongoing) reputation for an aggressive defense of the cause. Despite a pragmatic preference for non-violence, we know in tense and crowded situations things can escalate quickly, and a scrap here or there may have been an arousing proposition for at least some figures associated with the movement. That Mark's Gospel unsentimentally reports a sympathizer with the movement was armed (Mark 14.47) suggests we should not dismiss such notions too quickly.

Indeed, as we will see in the next chapter, entering a crowded Jerusalem at Passover was a risky business, and it is not out of the question to suppose that some in the Jesus movement saw it as an important opportunity for provocation. They would defiantly march their message of end-time comeuppance for those responsible for the economic changes occurring in Galilee and Judea out from under the armpit of the Roman Empire and right into a cherished organ of the repressive imperial apparatus: the Holy Temple in Jerusalem. Paula Fredriksen has even developed the intriguing speculation that sometime around *this* Passover was when Jesus thought the kingdom would come.[1] The glorious end times were upon them, and the fortunes of the agrarian world would be finally turned upside down!

But all this raises another salient question: did the central committee of the Jesus party go to Jerusalem knowing full well at least one of them *would* die? To answer this question, we need to explore traditions of martyrdom as they had gestated in Jewish thought in the preceding centuries, and how they once again resurfaced in the Gospel authors' portrayal of Jesus' own predictions of death as a glorious triumph.

It is important to clarify here that the word "martyr"

originally comes from an ancient Greek legal term for "witness," i.e., someone who gives testimony or evidence in a court of law. Only later, and largely through the influence of early Christians, did it come to predominantly mean someone who suffers persecution and even death for holding firm to one's religious beliefs.[2] In any case, the concept is a cross-cultural phenomenon and, as we will see, much older than the Christian movement. Accordingly, we use the language of martyrdom in this "Christian" sense to describe how the Jesus movement came to understand its own ideas about suffering a good death which benefited others, and who, of course, would in later times come to regard Jesus as the archetypal martyr to be imitated.

The Martyrs Are Immortal!

There was an established, culturally credible tradition of interpreting death redemptively available to the Jesus movement: the Maccabean martyrs. About 160 years before the birth of Jesus, the Seleucid king Antiochus IV attacked Jerusalem and the Temple and, if subsequent reports are to be believed, outlawed, tortured, and killed Jews who observed the Mosaic law. A successful guerrilla insurgency was led by the Maccabee family who eventually restored Temple worship.

Those who lost their lives in the persecution were remembered fondly as martyrs; stories about their courageous deeds were written up as heroic examples and commemorated annually at the festival of Hannukah. There was the famous story of a mother and her seven sons who were tortured and killed in an attempt to force them to eat pork (2 Macc. 7). They resisted in exemplary "manly" fashion (2 Macc. 7.21), and took their beatings with glee, for not only were they prepared to die for their laws, but they also had expectations of vindication through an ongoing existence of life after death, in addition to the belief that divine punishment would be meted out on the perpetrators (cf. Dan. 11.35). These martyrdoms were also thought to have a redemptive function in that the martyrs gave up their lives for the "laws of our ancestors" and yet they would also assuage the wrath of God after he punished the people for their sins which angered God (2 Macc. 7.32-38; cf. 4 Macc. 17.20-22).

Alongside the annual commemoration of the Maccabean martyrs, there were other shining examples of martyrdom from around the time of Jesus. In this respect, it is worth expanding on an episode noted in Chapter 3, namely, when Herod the Great had to deal with some of his Jewish subjects unhappy with his decorations in the Temple precinct (*War* 1.648-655; *Antiquities* 17.149-67). Two expert teachers called Judas and Matthias, whose teaching on the law was popular with their youthful audience, allowed an idea to develop once it was becoming clear that Herod was sinking further into illness: pulling down "those structures which had been erected" that were thought to be in defiance of Jewish laws concerning idolatry.

According to Josephus, Judas and Matthias encouraged their followers to cut down the golden eagle Herod had erected on a Temple gate because an image of a living creature should not be present in such a holy place. Josephus adds they were encouraged to prepare to die for their laws and attain immortality as well as an inspirational reputation:

> [They] now exhorted their disciples to cut down [the golden eagle], telling them that, even if the action proved hazardous, it was a noble deed to die for the law of one's country; for the souls of those who came to such an end attained immortality and an eternally abiding sense of felicity; it was only the ignoble, uninitiated in their philosophy, who clung in their ignorance of life and preferred death on a sick-bed to that of a hero. (*War* 1.650)

A number of young men managed to gain access to the eagle via the roof and began hacking away at it. But when caught and seized by a sizable guard, the perpetrators and their teachers were burned alive.

This was not the end of the episode, nor the potential for further martyrdom. In 4 BCE, Herod's son and successor Archelaus spoke to the crowds before the Passover festival and one of their demands was the liberation of the remaining prisoners, which he accepted. However, insurrectionists still wanted to avenge the deaths of the martyrs. After public mourning for Herod the Great had ended, they began their own, loud mourning for their lost ones who had died for the law and Temple: "there were piercing shrieks, a dirge directed by a conductor, and lamentations with beating of the breast which resounded throughout the city." They wanted to depose of Herod's favorites, including the High Priest, and so, with Archelaus fearing the worst, the result was the inevitable slaughter at a busy, tense Passover (*War* 2.1-13; *Antiquities* 17.200-205; on the social and political tensions at Passover see chapters 9-10).

We also saw in Chapter 3 that issues relating more directly to Roman rule brought about possibilities for martyrdom. According to Josephus, the Roman prefect Pontius Pilate's "blasphemous" act of bringing Roman standards with their images of the Emperor into Jerusalem led to hostility from the urban and rural crowds in defense of their laws. After Pilate refused to remove them, the Jewish crowds "fell prostrate around his house and for five whole days and nights remained motionless in that position." Pilate would not relent but, when armed soldiers had surrounded the protestors and threatened to cut them down, he was confronted by a remarkable sight: "the Jews, as by concerted action, flung themselves in a body on the ground, extended their necks, and exclaimed they were ready rather to die than to transgress the law." Pilate relented, astonished at the sight of such dedication (*War* 2.169-174; *Antiquities* 18.55-60; cf. Philo, *Embassy to Gaius* 299-305).

Whatever the exact historical accuracy of these accounts, the key point is these ideas were, unsurprisingly, widespread and even viable possibilities for ordinary Jews in the first century. Martyrdom may be a strange, alien, or even playful thing in the hands of the modern academic, but it was something plenty of people would have known as honorable, if carried out for the right reasons, namely, for God and country. When the situation called for it, a preferential option for death was both a radical and a sensible one.

With the Blood of Martyrs

It is apparent that the Gospel writers formulated their own understanding of Jesus' life in light of theological convictions about the redemptive significance of his death and resurrection. As will become clearer in the next chapter, John's chronology of Jesus' last week is unreliable as he redates events to have Jesus crucified at the same time the Passover lambs were being prepared for slaughter in the Holy Temple (John 19.31-33). This shift in the date of Jesus' death facilitated John's distinctive theology of Jesus as "the lamb of God who takes away the sin of the world" (John 1.29, 36). We will also see that Mark's Gospel has a clear agenda to explain the life of Jesus considering his controversial death.

But it is not just issues of death and resurrection where we should be suspicious, of course. While John is known for playing fast and loose with the facts, the process of formulating Jesus in terms of idealized agendas is clear in other Gospels. It was already well underway by the time Mark's Gospel was being circulated, and we have seen this time and again, from our analysis of the paradigmatic framing of the "call to discipleship" narratives (chapters 4 and 6), to the initial decision by the various Gospel authors to write up their accounts of Jesus' life in the form of Greco-Roman *bioi*, with all its accompanying and problematic emphasis on Jesus as a singular great individual (Chapter 1).

It may come as a surprise, then, to hear us suggest that the historical Jesus quite possibly expected his imminent demise.

We are convinced Jesus' predictions of his own execution, his martyrdom for the cause, was most likely *not* a later interpretation formulated by the Gospel authors, at least not entirely. On the contrary, it was a belief that went back to the early Jesus movement and some historical imagination can help us get there. As we will see in the next chapter, if the movement was prepared to play its part in an apparent riot or insurrection at the Holy Temple during Passover (Mark 11.15-17), then it must have known the death of a popular leader or figurehead was a possible or even likely outcome. The *expectation* of execution for a popular millenarian leader like Jesus would have almost certainly predated his execution. As noted above and as we saw with John the Baptist's arrest and execution for his role in leading a potentially seditious threat to Antipas (see Chapter 3), the early Jesus movement could have guessed that one of their own easily could be next. The close connections between John the Baptist's movement and the Jesus movement only made this more likely still. We do not know when the Jesus movement started to interpret potential deaths in redemptive or atoning terms. It is possible when the movement became publicly visible and execution an increasing possibility that such interpretations took off. Alternatively, this process could have begun after the death of John the Baptist, developed gradually, or became clear to them when they traveled to Jerusalem for Passover.

Whenever this theology of martyrdom developed, structures were in place for the authorities to deal with a public movement. As far as we can tell, the Jesus movement stayed in the public eye and mostly in Antipas' territory. Local rulers and magistrates like Antipas were reliant on intelligence networks both to maintain personal power but also to maintain "peace" within their respective jurisdictions. The elite needed to become acquainted with the nature of any potential threat which faced them, particularly in regions with a long history of rebellion. In writing of a generation before, Josephus explicitly suggested "there were spies everywhere, both in the city and in the roads, who watched those that met together" (*Antiquities* 15.366). It is likely, then, any surveillance network worth its salt in Palestine would have detected the smaller disturbances or threats to the social order, such as the activities and revolutionary millenarianism of the Jesus movement.

The Gospel tradition itself alludes to Jesus and his associates being under surveillance by the authorities both during its activities in the countryside as well as leading up to Jesus' crucifixion. Mark 6.14, for instance, reveals Antipas "had heard" of the activities of the Twelve for Jesus' name "had become known" to him. Mark and Luke also suggest legal authorities were "closely watching" Jesus (Mark 3.2; Luke 6.7; 14.1), and there may have been occasionally commissioned "spies" gathering intelligence on his ministry activity.

The authorities knew what Jesus was up to. And the Jesus movement knew the authorities knew. Coupled with a likely awareness of possible arrest or execution, there was, as we saw above, a ready-made framework for lionizing and interpreting martyrdom, particularly from the well-known and authoritative stories about the Maccabean martyrs. There were even stories about prophets who expected to die in Jerusalem (*Lives of the Prophets*; *Ascension of Isaiah* 1-5; cf. 2 Chron. 24.20-22; Matt. 23.32-36), versions of which Jesus himself may have known (Luke 13.31-35//Matt. 23.37-39). In drawing on such exhilarating accounts about Jewish radicals from the past who put their lives on the line for God and country, the Jesus movement began to formulate their own ideas of revolutionary martyrdom.

In Mark 10.35-45 we see an early account of the martyr theology of the Jesus movement. Here the sons of Zebedee, James and John (otherwise known as the Sons of Thunder), ask to sit at the right and left side of Jesus in his "glory" to which Jesus asks whether they are prepared to suffer for the cause ("Are you able to drink the cup that I drink, or be baptized with the baptism that I am baptized with?"). Martyrdom, it would appear, was required to sit in such an elevated position. The text implies a similar idea of enthronement as we saw with the Twelve judging the tribes of Israel (Matt. 19.28//Luke 22.29-30), but now with James and John having pride of place even within the politburo. Thus, when the Sons of Thunder said they were prepared to undergo sufferings this annoyed the rest of the Twelve. With clear martyrological connotations, Jesus then told them about the significance of acting as a slave or servant to become "first among you," concluding, "For the Son of Man came not to be served but to serve, and to give his life a ransom for many." To die as a "ransom" (*lutron*) appears to be an allusion back to "slave," as the term referred to the price required to redeem captives or purchase freedom for indentured servants.

The echoes of the Maccabean martyrs are clear (2 Macc. 7.32-38; 4 Macc. 17.20-22). Likewise, as such martyrdom is coupled with ideas of an afterlife (2 Macc. 7.10-13, 23; Dan 12.2–3), the Markan passage also echoes related themes, such as in the influential book of Daniel which itself was a response to the Maccabean crisis but partly read as a future prophecy by the time of Jesus, including its take on the glorification of the martyrs: "Some of the wise shall fall, so that they may be refined, purified, and cleansed, until the time of the end, for there is still an interval until the time appointed" (Dan. 11.35).

It is sometimes argued that Mark 10.35-45 was written *after* the supposed martyrdoms of James and John. While we cannot prove with certainty this prediction came from the historical Jesus, it cannot be a retrospective writing up after the event in the form of prophecy, at least not in the case of John, son of Zebedee. Indeed, later tradition remembers only one of the Sons of Thunder as a martyr, and even accounts of his martyrdom are much later and likely dependent on Mark 10.35-45. Acts (written in either the late first century or possibly as late as the early second) gives us a telling account of James' possible martyrdom around the early 40s CE when it mentions Herod Agrippa "had James, the brother of John, killed with the sword" (Acts 12.2). John does not appear to have been executed and is regarded as one of the pillars of the Jesus movement by Paul (Gal. 2.9). The version of Mark 10.35-45 developed in Luke (i.e., the first volume of Luke-Acts) makes no mention of specific names (Luke 22.24-27) and one reason for this modification is that John had not in fact been executed. There are also traditions from the second century that John "yielded up the ghost" at an old age in Ephesus (*Acts of John* 115), which are unlikely to have taken off as an idea if John had died a martyr in line with a prediction in Mark's Gospel.[3]

There are other reasons which strengthen the case for Mark 10.35-45 being an early tradition. First, the story appears to presume a Jewish-only audience, which, as we have seen on previous occasions, is consistent with what we know of the earliest memories of the Jesus movement. The passage not only criticizes non-Jews from an insider perspective and in stereotypical terms ("You know that among the Gentiles those whom they recognize as their rulers lord it over them, and their great ones are tyrants over them. But it is not so among you," 10.42-43), but there is also no indication that non-Jews would benefit from the death. If there was a conventional assumption that the nations or righteous and supportive non-Jews would also have a role in the new world order, then it is not a theme developed despite inclusion of non-Jews being a major issue in the movement that followed after Jesus' death.

Such a reading rests on a relatively restrictive reading of "the many" in the saying attributed to Jesus in verse 45: that Jesus has come "not to be served, but to serve, and to give his life a ransom for many." The "many" should be understood here not as referring to the many nations under Rome (as it might later have), but rather as shorthand for the in-group of Jesus' associates, and the righteous outsiders who would likewise benefit. This is a comparatively less restrictive but nonetheless similar use of "the many" found in the Dead Sea Scrolls to refer to its in-group (1QS 6.1, 7–25; CD 13.7; 14.7). It is reasonable, then, that the "many" was a reference to "Israel" or "Jews" (with some wider non-Jewish inclusion perhaps assumed) and, for the Jesus movement, it presumably would include a limited group focused primarily on Israel albeit excluding the unrepentant rich.

Finally, we should note the "son of man" saying in Mark's account. It could be, and probably was, understood by most of Mark's audience as a title for Jesus alone. But Mark 10.45 is an example where "son of man" would also work within a generic frame of reference to include people like Jesus himself, in this case incorporating the Sons of Thunder and at the end of a passage describing the importance of serving others: "For the son of man (/a man in my position) came not to be served but to serve, and to give his life a ransom for many." This would suggest the saying in verse 45 could have originated as a tradition or theology of martyrdom within the early Jesus movement more broadly, and only later came to be applied to Jesus' death specifically. In this sense, it is very close in sentiment to one portrayal of the collective effort of the Maccabean martyrs:

> These, then, who have been consecrated for the sake of God, are honoured, not only with this honour, but also by the fact that because of them our enemies did not rule over our nation, the tyrant was punished, and the homeland purified—they having become, as it were, a ransom for the sin of our nation. And through the blood of those devout ones and their death as an atoning sacrifice, divine Providence preserved Israel that previously had been mistreated. (4 Macc. 17.20-22)

Before going further, we should clarify that our suggestion the historical Jesus was willing to die for the cause is exactly that, a suggestion. It would be difficult to conclusively prove Jesus *intended* to die, and especially that he or others in the movement offered themselves as martyrs for the cause. This is because all our evidence comes from a time *after* he had died in the way he did, and traditions of his death were taking on a life of their own in the years and decades following the fateful events in Jerusalem.

As we mentioned in Chapter 5 regarding Jesus' messianic status, we need to be careful when determining what Jesus thought about himself. We have no way of getting back to Jesus' *self-understanding* beyond external and subjective impressions of how others came to think of him. Even so, as we have shown above, memories of the Jesus movement looking forward to a glorious death comes from very early in the tradition. This alone warrants the critical historian putting the option on the table. But there is a final (and hopefully by now familiar) reason why we should entertain this as a viable option: masculinity.

Dying to Be Great Men

L. Stephanie Cobb's book *Dying to Be Men: Gender and Language in Early Christian Martyr Texts* points to a now recurring theme in this book: martyrdom as a "manly" act.[4] Cobb persuasively argues that early Christian martyr texts functioned to shape Christian group identity and enhance the self-esteem of individual members. By remembering the assertive, perhaps even gladiatorial-like, masculinity involved in acts of martyrdom, marginal Christian groups were able to align themselves with a pivotal value of patriarchal Roman society.

As we saw in Chapter 6, embracing the life and death of a martyr was a useful and perhaps even convenient way of contesting gender dysphoria in the ancient world, and it is important to recall such ideas here as it provides a strong motive for why a movement expecting imminent death at the hands of the authorities might want to develop ideas about martyrdom. Given the violence of Rome and Roman-backed power was regularly cast in masculine terms of domination and conquest, and humiliated combatants were diminished as passive and emasculated victims, the "righteous death" of a martyr could be used to turn Roman hegemonic masculinity on its head. Masculinity was, as noted above, also a central concern in stories about Jewish martyrs such as the Maccabees,[5] which may have influenced the Jesus movement and been part of the appeal for the movement's embrace of a revolutionary and manly martyrdom.

In Mark 10.35-45 discussed above, Jesus refers to the "Great Men" (*hoi megaloi*) who are tyrants over the nations (42). "But it is not so among you," he promises, "whoever wishes to become great among you must be your servant, and whoever wishes to be first among you must be slave of all" (43). To first-century ears this would sound like a call for their transgendering: being "slavish" was a synonym for being "womanish" for all practical purposes. But somehow this would make them "butch" after all: a martyr's death was a sure path to achieve true greatness, the fulfillment of a "servant" masculinity.

Later Christians would, of course, find inspiration in this enthusiasm for emasculating punishment, sometimes going to comical levels. Ignatius, the famous Bishop of Antioch in the early second century, was arrested for engaging in Christian activities of some kind. As he was traveling under armed guard to face death by being thrown to the wild beasts of the Roman arena, he wrote to the Christians of Rome, pleading with them *not* to intervene in the proceedings. Rather, he implored, "leave me to be a meal for the beasts, for it is they who can provide my way to God. I am his wheat, ground fine by the lions' teeth to be made purest bread for Christ...let them not leave the smallest scrap of my flesh" (Ignatius, *Romans* 4.1-2).

The cult of Christian martyrs of the second and third centuries were perhaps less the victims of targeted persecution against

Christians,[6] and more like ambulance-chasers seeking out high-risk situations. Some later tales of Christian martyrdom were almost certainly embellished or fabricated entirely for propagandistic reasons. In any case, we would argue that the inspiration to embrace death fanatically and willingly can be ultimately traced back to the early Jesus movement. Instead of going meekly to their slaughter, the most serious and disciplined among them would put up a heroic and manly resistance to the death. And as it so happened, Passover provided the perfect opportunity to put their preferential option for death into practice.

Chapter 9

Passover in Jerusalem

The Gospels are dominated by Jesus' last week and the journey to Jerusalem for Passover, especially Luke which devotes considerable space to the trip (Luke 9.51-19.44). Mark provided the basic narrative for Jesus' last week that would be used by Matthew and Luke in particular (Mark 11-15; Matt. 21-27; Luke 19-23; cf. John 11.55-19.42). Through much of this book we have worked with the idea of *early themes* associated with the Jesus movement precisely because establishing detailed narratives or chronological outlines of Jesus' life is difficult. As much of the overall narrative outline is dependent on Mark, we do not have an independent source prior to (possibly) John with which to compare and examine the details.

But even in the case of Mark's Gospel, the narrative about Jesus' last week is, as we will see, full of obvious expansion and embellishment. Mark, followed by Matthew and Luke, and finally John, all sought to authorize their own ideas in the authoritative theology of the death and resurrection of Jesus. It is, therefore, even more difficult to establish the earliest narratives about Jesus' last week in Jerusalem and so we stress more than usual what follows is a tentative reconstruction. However, when we apply some historical imagination, we are (odd though it may seem) once more on firmer ground in reconstructing the details about what this particular Passover might have been like for a revolutionary millenarian movement.

Accordingly, this chapter examines what can and cannot be known about the most memorable events associated with Jesus' last week in Jerusalem up to his arrest. After exploring the context of Jewish Passover more broadly, we turn to the Jesus movement's controversial and somewhat "loud" entry into Jerusalem. We examine the contours of a disturbance that took place in the Temple precinct which we argue most likely led to Jesus' subsequent arrest. But we also make the important observation that although, according to the Gospels, Jesus was singled out for punishment, he was likely not acting alone. Following this, we decode the apocalyptic predictions Jesus is said to have uttered concerning what would come to pass following his death. While there are plenty of reasons to be suspicious of this material, it is possible at least one "prediction" may have been early, as we will see. Finally, we address Jesus' famous "Last Supper" and the defection of Judas Iscariot who ratted on Jesus to the authorities. According to the Gospels, this led to Jesus' arrest in the garden of Gethsemane and set in motion the events culminating in his death by crucifixion followed some days later by his purported resurrection from the dead. Details surrounding these events are themselves complex for the critical historian and so will be dealt with separately in the next chapter.

Passover

The Passover festival commemorated Israel's exodus from slavery under Pharaoh in Egypt. This was a founding myth of Israel, and its narrative is spread over four of the five books that make up the Pentateuch. "Passover" itself refers to the "passing over" of the angel of death: according to the book of Exodus, Moses warned the Israelite slaves in Egypt to mark a lamb's blood above their doors, so that the angel of death would "pass over" their houses and spare their children. As the Lord God said to Moses: "The blood shall be a sign for you on the houses where you live: when I see the blood, I will pass over you, and no plague shall destroy you when I strike the land of Egypt" (Ex. 12.13). The festival thus held strong associations of deliverance of God's people from oppression through miraculous divine intervention, and for prepped millennials like the early Jesus movement, such prospects were as electrifying as the boisterous crowds that descended on the holy city.

While ancient guesses at attendance numbers at Passover in Jerusalem during the first century are exaggerated, they still indicate a general point about size. So, when Josephus describes the Passover, we should not believe the impossible claim that three million were present (there could not have been), but rather the basic assumption that Jerusalem was packed to the brim (*War* 2.280; cf. *War* 6.420-27; *Antiquities* 17.217). Families, households, and entire villages attended festivities (cf. *Antiquities* 11.109) to the extent that Jerusalem was unable to contain all the attendees, many of whom sought shelter outside the city, hence why Jesus' party were associated with nearby Bethany during Passover (e.g., Mark 11.1-2, 11; 14.3; John 12.1).

Passover took place in spring during the month of Nisan. On 10 Nisan an unblemished, one-year old lamb or kid was taken and on the evening of 14 Nisan it was slaughtered in the Temple, to commemorate the "passing over" of the houses of the Israelites in Egypt, "when he struck down the Egyptians but spared our houses" (Ex. 12.27b). That night, it was roasted and eaten with unleavened bread and bitter herbs (Ex. 12.1-13; Num. 9.2-4; Lev. 23.5; cf. Mark 14.12). The Passover meal was followed by the festival of Unleavened Bread for 7 more days (Ex. 12.14-20; Lev. 23.6). Sometimes both festivals were referred to together as "the Passover and the festival of Unleavened Bread" (e.g., Mark 14.1) or collectively as either "Passover" (e.g., John 11.55) or "Unleavened Bread" (e.g., Mark 14.12; cf. *Antiquities* 18.19; Luke 22.1).

The Gospels are vague on precisely when Jesus' party

arrived in Jerusalem. Mark's account implies the group were already settled in Jerusalem 2 days before the Passover meal (Mark 14.1) and had been active for most of the week in and around the Temple (Mark 11-13). As Mark's Jesus put it, "Day after day I was with you in the temple teaching, and you did not arrest me" (Mark 14.49). Whether or not Jesus said these words or did the things said of him in Mark 11-13, the author could assume Jesus was in the vicinity of Jerusalem for at least a week in advance of the Passover meal.

Indeed, anyone who had contracted corpse impurity (which was likely many of those traveling from the countryside for whom death was a standard part of life) would have to undergo purification before entering key parts of the Temple (cf. Num. 9.6-13). Numbers 19 explains that the purification ritual (involving sprinkling of water and the ashes of a red heifer) took 7 days to complete. The week-long process is confirmed by the first-century Jewish philosopher Philo (*Special Laws* 1.261) and Josephus also indicates people congregated at Passover a week before (*War* 6.290). While John's redating of Jesus' last week to fit an obvious theological agenda (see Chapter 8) undermines its usefulness for reconstructing Jesus' last Passover, on this point it concurs with the view above: "Now the Passover of the Jews was near, and many went up from the country to Jerusalem before the Passover to purify themselves" (John 11.55; cf. 12.1).

Whatever may or may not be useful in the Gospels for reconstructing Jesus' last week in Jerusalem, we can be sure Jesus and his fellow revolutionary millenarians were entering a potentially explosive situation, perhaps willingly so. A packed Jerusalem at Passover was a tinderbox that could spark off at the tiniest provocation. There is awareness in Mark's account that one misstep at Passover (in this case the authorities arresting Jesus) could lead to a riot (Mark 14.2). The festival commemorated the liberation of Israel and in a context where enough Jews were expecting an imminent overthrow of the world powers, this meant Jewish-Roman relations were especially tense. Potential for violent outbursts was very real (as they were at other festivals where crowds gathered, e.g., *Antiquities* 17.213-18, 237, 254-55; cf. *Antiquities* 13.372).

The Roman authorities and Jewish elites were obviously keen for order to be maintained through strategic use of the repressive imperial apparatus. At one Passover in the mid-first century, a Roman solider deliberately whipped out his nether regions to festival goers which in turn provoked an angry riot and an inevitably brutal response from the Roman governor who feared for his life (*War* 2.224-26; *Antiquities* 20.105-12). Before the incident happened, the Romans were already aware of the potential for upheaval, hence Josephus noted when the crowd assembled, "the Roman cohort had taken up its position on the roof of the portico of the Temple; for a body of men in arms invariably mounts guard at the feasts, to prevent disorders arising from such a concourse of people" (*War* 2.224; cf. *War* 5.244-45).

To enter Jerusalem and the Holy Temple at Passover was thus especially dangerous for a social movement propagating its revolutionary millenarian message of end-time comeuppance for those responsible for the economic changes occurring in Galilee. Nobody in the first century, the Jesus movement included, was so naïve to think they could avoid getting seduced by the commotion of a crowd, take part in a riot, and possibly get injured or even die.

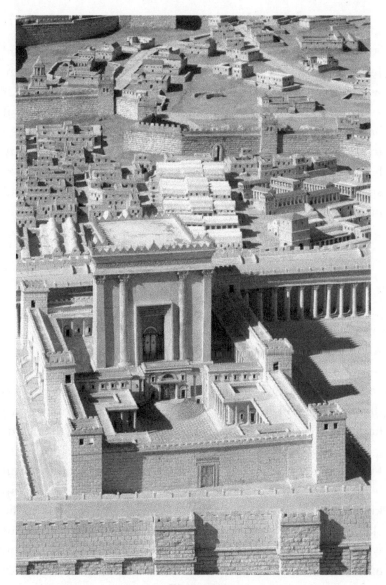

Figure 8.
Model of Jerusalem and Herod's Temple in the Late Second Temple
Period. To get a sense of the potential volatility during the
Passover festival, imagine the courtyard crowded and
the porticos patrolled by armed guards.
commons.wikimedia.org

Entering Jerusalem

According to Mark 11.1-11, as the Jesus party neared Jerusalem, two associates were sent ahead to a nearby village where they would find an unridden colt to bring back. If asked, they were to say, "the Lord needs it and will send it back here immediately," which led to them being permitted to take it. (Indeed, a "lord" could conceivably refer to any honored person.) Jesus then rode the colt as "many people" spread cloaks and leafy branches on the road before him, and many shouted:

> Hosanna!
> Blessed is the one who comes in the name of the Lord!
> Blessed is the coming kingdom of our ancestor David!
> Hosanna in the highest heaven! (Mark 11.9-10)

After looking around the Holy Temple, Jesus and the Twelve retired to Bethany for the night.

Here we start to encounter the problem of reconstructing the narrative of Jesus' last week. Could this story have happened? Maybe. Quite where fact meets fiction, however, is hard to determine. The basic outline of Jesus riding into Jerusalem with a crowd lavishing praise on a millenarian leader and exclaiming their hopes and dreams for the coming kingdom is certainly possible. Yet there are reasons to be skeptical: when elite ruling men entered cities, a ritual of welcome displayed their elevated status. Mark's description of Jesus' entry into Jerusalem both mimics and parodies such entry rituals, but in a way that neatly accords with the propagandistic function of ancient biographies to portray their subjects as Great Men.

It is conceivable, however, that the Jesus movement deliberately engaged in parodying figures like Pontius Pilate, the official Roman governor of the province of Judea. Pilate's main residence was in Caesarea Maritima, but he also would make his way to Jerusalem in advance of major festivals to maintain order. We also find in Mark's account class connotations that fit the Jesus movement's revolutionary ambitions grounded in a dictatorship of the peasantry: the fact Mark mentions those who "spread leafy branches" they themselves "had cut in the fields" suggests these were agricultural workers. Scenes of branches and hymns of thanksgiving are reminiscent of when Simon liberated Jerusalem "from the yoke of the Gentiles" (1 Macc. 13.41, 49-53) and Judas Maccabeus rededicated the Holy Temple after Antiochus Epiphanes' imperial tyranny (2 Macc. 10.7-9). Such scenes, if they happened anything like they are described in Mark, would have gestured to not only populist ambitions for the movement, but possibilities of willful martyrdom and the prestige recipients of such eventualities might enjoy.

What about the fanciful story of the acquisition of the colt? Less likely (perhaps) but still possible is that Jesus made advanced arrangements through the movement's Judean networks to have the colt made ready for him. Matthew (21.1-11) and Luke (19.29-40) certainly found Mark's story deficient as they both elaborate on it. Matthew infamously has both a donkey *and* a colt and Jesus somehow rides both simultaneously. As ridiculous as it sounds, we should not attempt to rationalize this; it is clearly Matthew's attempt to fit Jesus into the fulfillment of a prophecy without missing any detail from the scriptural prooftext of Zechariah 9.9. As Matthew explains, "This took place to fulfil what had been spoken through the prophet, saying, 'Tell the daughter of Zion, Look, your king is coming to you, humble, and mounted on a donkey, and on a colt, the foal of a donkey'" (Matt. 21.4-5).

Another detail that remains unclear in our sources is the question of who acclaims Jesus as king? Mark appears to think of those traveling with Jesus as crying out "Hosanna," rather than the crowd. This follows from verse 9 which specifies "those who went before and those who followed" were the ones doing the shouting. Matthew and John, however, unambiguously present the "crowd" as the ones proclaiming him. Luke, ever the compromiser, appears to combine both, albeit with an emphasis on those who traveled with Jesus to Jerusalem ("the whole multitude of the disciples," Luke 19.37).

In addition to isolating Jesus from the crowd, Matthew also sharpens the focus on Jesus by changing the generic hope explained in Mark about the coming kingdom of David to Jesus now being the specific holder of the Davidic title. Matthew's redactions of Mark's text are marked-up below:

> Hosanna **to the Son of David!**
> Blessed is the one who comes in the name of the Lord!
> ~~Blessed is the coming kingdom of our ancestor David!~~
> Hosanna in the highest heaven! (Matt. 21.9)

Luke similarly elevates Jesus but dampens the millenarian enthusiasm by removing references to the coming kingdom of the Jewish ancestor David and having the multitude of disciples proclaim a less nationalistic sounding, "Blessed is the king who comes in the name of the Lord! Peace in heaven, and glory in the highest heaven!" (Luke 19.38). Class connotations are also downplayed in Luke: there are no leafy branches collected from the fields and spread out on the road.

So, we are left with Mark's version which does not have an obvious reference to the prophecy of Zechariah 9.9 and does not explicitly make Jesus the king or "son of David." The emphasis on the kingdom of David is language associated with Jerusalem and the surrounding area in Mark's account (Mark 10.46-52; 12.35-37) which suggests (for Mark at least) a different support network than the usual Galilean one. Read in this light, some version of Mark 11.1-11 could have reflected Jesus' entry into Jerusalem. Unfortunately, there are not enough additional clues to think that this narrative is either an early tradition or a late fictional creation. If it did take place, quite what size of crowd was present, we cannot say, despite the educated guesses of scholars.

Nevertheless, the millenarian sentiment keeps with everything else we know about the early movement, and we can imagine how a revolutionary party would have gone down arriving at the Passover festival with its stories of liberation. A swath of hyped-up radicals, perhaps broader than the usual Jesus movement given the magnetic pull of the festival, entering the holy city, and standing by to take back Jerusalem for God. Any hints or gestures toward possibilities for martyrdom, surfacing either from the arriving party or the crowd, would have stirred up the revolutionary fervor even more. The Jesus movement had become deadly serious about its message. Again, we are left with the limitations of a disciplined historical imagination for reconstruction, but such attempts are not without merit.

Unrest in the Temple

Framed by the curious story of Jesus successfully cursing a fig-tree (Mark 11.12-14, 20-21), the next piece of action in Jerusalem involves a key event in the lead up to Jesus' arrest and execution:

> And he entered the temple and began to drive out those who were selling and those who were buying in the temple, and he overturned the tables of the moneychangers and the seats of those who sold doves; and he would not allow anyone to carry anything through the temple. He was teaching and saying, "Is it not written, 'My house shall

be called a house of prayer for all the nations?' But you have made it a den of robbers/bandits." And when the chief priests and the scribes heard it, they kept looking for a way to kill him; for they were afraid of him, because the whole crowd was spellbound by his teaching. (Mark 11.15-18)

Some interpreters argue that Jesus' actions in the Temple symbolized judgment on the Temple and its authorities, as Mark's framing of the cursed fig-tree implies. While any symbolism would not have been obvious (symbolic acts are typically explained at length in the Jewish scriptures), there may have been an implicit threat to the Temple as we will see below. If there was, we are given plenty of reasons why Mark's Jesus thought so in Mark 11.15-17, which aligns with an early theme of the Jesus movement we have seen time and again: the critique of wealth and exploitation.

According to Mark, Jesus drove out those buying and selling and turned over the tables of the moneychangers and the seats of the dove-sellers while referring to the Temple as having become a den of bandits (again, the Greek word *lēstēs* is used). Mark's Jesus thus stood alongside other prominent Jewish critics of the Temple and its leadership.[1] The Dead Sea Scrolls contain polemics against the concentration of wealth of the Temple with allegations of exploitation and corruption (e.g., 1QpHab 8.8-12; 9.4-5; 10.1; 12.10; 4QpNah 1.11; CD 6.16, 21). Elsewhere there are stories about wealthier Temple priests doing well from the tithing system as well as stories about some priests collecting their tithes through force (e.g., Josephus, *Life* 63; *Antiquities* 20.181, 206-207; t. *Menahot* 13.21; cf. *Life* 80). Rabbinic literature also records earlier complaints about the Temple. This included one by Simeon ben Gamliel who complained that the price of sacrificial doves was too expensive for the poor (m. *Keritot.* 1.7; cf. Lev. 12.6-8). When one rabbinic saying later rationalized why the Temple was destroyed by the Romans in 70 CE, it used a longstanding tradition in the allegation it was due to the greed of its functionaries (t. *Menahot* 13.22).

Alongside these parallels, the Jesus movement's uneasiness with the operations of the Temple system hardly looks special or unique. Rather, moneychangers were already perceived as on the take or exploiting people. With money changed into the Tyrian Shekel, moneychangers played an influential role in the flow of currency and the payment of the Temple Tax, an equal payment demanded of rich and poor alike. While the Jewish scriptures mention a Temple Tax (Ex. 30.11-16; 2 Chr. 24.4-16; Neh. 10.32), an annual, permanent tax appears to have been a later innovation put in place by the time of Jesus. It was not universally accepted (cf. *Mekhilta. Ex.* 19.1; Matt. 17.24-27) and one of the Dead Sea Scrolls advocated a one-off payment for life (4Q159 1.6-7). Again, it is plausible that Mark was here presenting Jesus as a critic of a Temple not living up to its ideal theocratic standards by singling out its current middle-management as benefactors of an apparently exploitative system.

This sheds light on another angle to the criticism attributed to Jesus, and which would have made many other Jews equally uncomfortable. The critique likely involved an allegation of idolatry because the Tyrian Shekel contained an image of the Tyrian god (see figure 9). Such a possibility is corroborated by Mark 14.58, where the term *cheiropoiētos* ("made with hands") which refers to an idol is used: "We heard him say, 'I will destroy this temple that is made with hands...'" As Leviticus 26.1 commanded, "You shall make for yourselves no idols [LXX: *cheiropoiēta*] and erect no carved images or pillars, and you shall not place figured stones in your land, to worship at them; for I am the LORD your God" (cf. Lev. 26.30; Judith 8.18; Wisdom 14.8; Is. 2.18; 10.11; 29.9; 31.7; 46.6).

Figure 9.

A half-shekel minted at the Phoenician city of Tyre. The human-like face is of Melkarth, the Tyrian god. On the other side is an eagle with one foot on the prow of a galley. commons.wikimedia.org

Jewish theology was distinctive in the wider Greco-Roman world for its stated preference to worship its god alone, in contrast to the many gods of the nations, which were referred to as "idols." Most people in antiquity had no issue with dividing loyalties between multiple deities as was practical. Yet as Paul explained to the Corinthian assembly, who were themselves grappling with issues of idolatry, "even though there may be so-called gods in heaven or on earth—as in fact there are many gods and many lords—yet for us there is one God, the Father, from whom are all things and for whom we exist" (1 Cor. 8.5-6a). There was broad unease about idolatry in Jerusalem and the Temple precinct during the first century, whether Herod the Great's erection of a golden eagle on the Temple gate or Pilate bringing Roman standards into Jerusalem (*War* 1.648-55; *Antiquities* 17.149-68; *Antiquities* 18.55-59; *War* 2.169-174; cf. Philo, *Embassy to Gaius* 299-305).

These criticisms of perceived economic exploitation and idolatry are possibly behind the claim that Jesus "would not allow anyone to carry anything through the temple" (Mark 11.16). Interestingly, the other Gospel authors did not know what to make of this and removed it from their own accounts. However, the action does not have to denote Jesus physically blockading against all such actions but rather may point to a legal ruling by the early Jesus movement. It was already the case that no vessel was allowed to be carried through the inner Temple (Josephus, *Apion* 2.106-107) and so Mark 11.16 could reflect a legal decision that this principle should extend throughout the Temple precincts.[2] Such a ruling would conform with the Jesus movement's emphasis on the ideal function of the Holy Temple as a house of prayer freed from idolatrous images and economic exploitation.

An emphasis on Jesus' Temple actions as primarily concerning economic exploitation is not countered (as is sometimes tried) by claims that the Temple system could not function without its monetary networks. According to such arguments, that what we have named in this book as the repressive imperial apparatus was actually there to look after the general populace, and so the passage could not possibly be about criticizing these issues. Such thinking is shared by modern attempts to discredit the actions of popular, perhaps overly utopian movements today which call for an end to the military, the police force, the prison system, and so on, without thinking of the consequences. Why would one seriously call for an end to an institution which purportedly keeps us all safe? However, this reductive line of argument imposes the genteel world of the liberal intellectual onto a context where they expect participants to behave as they do. Rather, as with any number of popular protests, in the case of the Jesus movement this was about utopian idealism and a polemical attack on a system deemed corrupt and exploitative. The millenarian organizers had probably not thought through all the detailed ramifications their actions might have for the Temple administration, the flow of goods, administration of sacrifices, or town planning.

Nor should we take seriously the old claim that Jesus was

trying to abolish the Jewish sacrificial system and its supposed exclusivity. Quotations from Jewish scriptures in Mark 11.17, sometimes cited as evidence of this position, point in the opposite direction. The first is from Isaiah 56.7: "My house shall be called a house of prayer for all the nations." If Mark wanted to signal the end of the sacrificial system, then Isaiah 56.7 was not a good choice because it also talks about the importance of "burnt offerings and sacrifices." Having Jesus express this sentiment in his critique of the economic use of the Temple merely points to the ideal function of a theocratic Temple system which included a Court of the Gentiles where *anyone* could participate, and the accompanying hope that in the end times righteous non-Jews would join in with sacrifice at worship. Indeed, in a packed Jerusalem, the various economic activities would have been squeezed into the Court of the Gentiles, giving this reference to Isaiah additional relevance.

The second scriptural reference concerns the Temple becoming a "den of robbers/bandits" from Jeremiah 7.11 which may function as a threat to the Temple as it did in Jeremiah where the Temple custodians of centuries past were denounced for theft, murder, adultery, and swearing falsely, as well as idolatry in their offerings to foreign gods (Jer. 7.9). If there was a conditional or implicit threat to the Temple system, then it would have been in line with what we already know about the Jesus movement's critique of wealth and the demand for the rich to repent before it was too late.

Some of these intra-Jewish issues suggest we may be in touch with an earlier theme which had minimal concern for debates happening in the later Christian movement after Jesus' death. We can speculate that the disturbance in the Temple was probably why Jesus was arrested (and ultimately executed) and that his arrest had to be carried out with caution given a riot could easily ensue (cf. Mark 11.18; 14.1-2). This explanation for Jesus' arrest and subsequent execution is far more plausible than the reason given in John's Gospel, which relocates the actions in the Temple to the beginning of his Gospel with typical elaborations (John 2.12-22) and has Jesus' miraculous raising of Lazarus back from the (very) dead as the reason why Jesus' opponents wanted him killed (John 11).

Once again, some historical imagination can help us here: it is not difficult to imagine the potential for trouble when a revolutionary millenarian movement entered Jerusalem with murmurings of exploitative wealth amid trading activity in the Temple which many Jews believed was precisely part of this ongoing corrupt behavior. Given we have shown conclusively above that judgment on the Temple system was not unique to the Jesus movement, and thus such ideas did not simply manifest from Jesus' individual genius *ex nihilo*, can we afford to maintain the view that Jesus was acting alone during the Temple disturbance?

A Crowded Temple

Whatever the case for Jesus' individual circumstances, it is reasonable to infer he was accompanied by party members and sympathizers during the Temple disturbance in Jerusalem. In addition to these agents, we would do well not to underrate the presence and power of bulging and potentially explosive festive crowds. The Gospels suggest it was Jesus who ultimately lit the match, and the authorities would certainly come to regard him as a, if not the, central perpetrator, especially after Judas' defection (see below). Despite the Gospels' intense focus on Jesus' individual actions, however, there are sober reasons to approach their framing of events with caution.

In line with the literary conventions of Greco-Roman *bioi*, the Gospels exhibit a pattern of *isolating* Jesus from the crowds, who were clearly present in the Temple, as indicated by Mark 11.18. This is not unique to the Temple commotion, but a common pattern throughout the Gospels: crowds engage with John the

Baptist (Luke 3.7-10; cf. Matt. 7-12); they throng around and listen to Jesus or witness his healings and deeds (Mark 2.4, 13; 3.9, 20, 32; 4.1-2, 36, 5.21, 24, 27, 30-31; 6.34, 45; 7.14, 17, 33; 8.1-2; 9.14-17, 25; 10.1, 46; Luke 7.24//Matt. 11.7; Luke 6.19; 13.10-17); they are depicted as "following" after Jesus (Mark 8.34; Matt. 4.25; 8.1; 12.15; 19.2; 20.29) to mirror the disciples following after him; they react with astonishment and awe at Jesus' teaching and deeds (Mark 2.4-12; 12.21; Matt. 7.28; 9.8, 33; 12.23; 15.31; 22.33; Luke 11.14-15 [cf. Matt. 12.23-24; Mark 3.20-23]; Luke 13.17); they occasionally take orders from Jesus (Mark 6.45; 8.6; Matt. 15.39; cf. Mark 5.30; 7.14); and when involved in disputes with the scribal elite, Jesus steps in and sometimes has "compassion" for them when hungry (Mark 6.34; 8.2; 9.14-18). We see this same exaggeration in the Temple incident where the chief priests and scribes were afraid of Jesus "because the whole crowd was spellbound by his teaching" (Mark 11.18). In pushing *collective* subjects to the margins or background, the Gospels accentuate Jesus' *individual* importance.

Neil Elliott has provocatively suggested, following the careful work of S. G. F. Brandon, that the Gospels offer hints that the Temple incident may have been initially remembered as a *collective* action. The Gospel authors, however, subsequently suppressed this for their own apologetic and ideological ends. As evidence, Elliott points to incidental remnants of an attempted insurrection in Mark's account of Jesus' trial:

> Mark identifies the man whom Pilate offers to the crowd instead of Jesus as Barabbas, who was in prison "with the rebels who had committed murder during the insurrection" (15:7)...The reference is peculiar, since Mark has made no previous mention of a lethal "insurrection."...Brandon interprets this reference as a clear indication that there had in fact been an insurrection in the city shortly before Jesus's arrest and trial—one that none of the Gospels bothers to

narrate. Further, he infers that Pilate crucified Jesus because he considered him at least partially responsible for it.[3]

The hypothesis of an attempted insurrection having taken place during Jesus' last week is corroborated by the further observation that Jesus was later crucified between two bandits or insurrectionists (*lēstai*), at least according to our earliest account in Mark 15.27. The same characterization is present in Matthew 27.38, but Luke 23.33 changed these men into "wrongdoers" or "criminals" (*kakourgoi*), convenient foils that morally contrast with Jesus' purported innocence. In any case, where did these other crucified men come from? Were they terrorists from an attempted insurrection in Jerusalem? The Gospels remain silent on how these men came to find themselves fellow travelers in Jesus' execution. The obvious point, and the gap in the text we can exploit with historical imagination, is that despite the Gospels' intense focus on Jesus the individual, he was *not* crucified alone, but in the disreputable company of bandits.

We thus stress that whatever the specific historical details of Jesus' actions in the Temple, including the precise nature of who and what was involved, the possibility that the Jesus party were caught up in the tumultuous effects of the crowd is not inconceivable. In fact, quite the opposite. Crowd theorists often remark that crowds have power and influence over events precisely because of their uncontrollable urge for growth and thoroughly chaotic energy. Jodi Dean, for instance, observes that "crowds are more than large numbers of people concentrated in a location. They are effects of collectivity, the influence— whether conscious, affective, or unconscious—of others." Furthermore, the crowd, manifesting a desire of the people, "forces the intrusion of the people into politics. Whether the people is the subject of a crowd even is up for grabs. The crowd opens up a site of struggle over its subject."[4] We will return to the power and unpredictability of the Jerusalem crowd in the next chapter when we consider Jesus' trial before Pilate, for it is here where they apparently, and scandalously, turn on Jesus and call for him to be crucified.

The End?

Following the Temple incident, Jesus is presented in various discussions in and around the Temple complex (Mark 11.27-12.44). These included questions of the movement's authority, an ominous parable aimed at the authorities who wanted Jesus killed (cf. *Thomas* 65), an ambiguous answer on whether to pay taxes to Caesar, an elaboration about marriage (or not) in the age to come, an agreed principle with a legal teacher that loving God and the neighbor was more important than (though does not replace) sacrifices, further connections (or not) between the Messiah and King David, a criticism of allegedly flamboyant and exploitative religious behavior and who will eventually be punished, and a story of Jesus praising a poor widow who gave a paltry Temple offering (with the usual critique of the rich). Additional parables about repentance and the end times, extensive legal teaching, and polemics against opponents were added by Matthew while both Matthew and Luke continued their use of Mark (Matt. 21.23-23.39; Luke 20.1-21.4).

Certainly, the gist of all these events is in line with early themes associated with the Jesus movement. But not only do we give the usual caveat that we cannot know the extent to which any of them goes back to the historical Jesus and which is later embellishment, we would add it remains possible that Mark's Gospel, like Matthew's and Luke's, includes reworked earlier material from different settings and times in the history of the early church, as well as inventions of their own unique material. In other words, some of these events may or may not have happened and they may or may not have happened during Jesus' final week or at some other time. Indeed, there is good evidence material reflecting themes developed *after* Jesus' death was added to the story of Jesus' last week. A sustained example is the end-time discourse in Mark 13.

This extended discourse involves a series of informative questions and answers between Jesus and his core associates, Peter, James, John, and Andrew. It begins with one associate pointing to the "large stones and large buildings," to which Jesus replies, "Do you see these great buildings? Not one stone will be left here upon another; all will be thrown down." Moving to the Mount of Olives opposite the Temple, the four associates ask Jesus "privately" about "the sign that all these things are about to be accomplished." Sensing another good teaching moment, Jesus proceeds to give an extended response.

First, "Beware that no one leads you astray." According to Jesus, many will come and declare "I am he" and lead many off track. Second, before the end itself, there will be wars, rumors of wars, earthquakes, and famines. But Jesus' advice is, "do not be alarmed; this must take place, but the end is still to come." Third, on a personal note, Jesus predicts his associates will be handed over to councils, beaten in synagogues, and stand before governors, all because of him and the need for the "good news" or gospel to be preached among the nations. Fourth, Jesus predicts a "desolating sacrilege set up where it not ought to be" (i.e., something idolatrous placed in the Temple; cf. Dan. 9.27; 11.31; 12.11) and so those in Judea must flee to the mountains because this particular event will precipitate a period of unprecedented terror and suffering. False Messiahs and false prophets will also come, and so the elect should stay vigilant. Fifth, after all these tribulations, the sun and the moon will be darkened and the stars will fall from heaven, before they see "the Son of Man coming in clouds with great power and glory" who will send out angels to collect the elect from the ends of the earth. Finally, we are provided with a timeframe for when these events will take place: specifically, before "this generation" passes away. With that said, however, no one apart from the Father (i.e., God) knows the exact date, not even "the Son" (i.e., Jesus) or the angels. But these events are coming...soon.

Vigorously millenarian though the Jesus movement was, we can still differentiate between types of expectation and their evolution in the Gospel tradition, and Mark 13 is an excellent example of how millenarian themes were developed *after* Jesus' death. There are stock features of end-time thinking that could have plausibly emerged before or after Jesus' death, such as reference to earthquakes, famines, and the fate of the stars, moon, and sun, but overall, there are plenty of indications of post-Jesus innovation. Mark 13 is a lengthy discourse, however, and includes no reference to the "kingdom of God" which itself is suspicious given the central role this concept was afforded in the revolutionary millenarism of the movement (see Chapter 5). The passage is also packed with allusions to events and theological beliefs that took shape after Jesus' death. For example, the beatings in synagogues and standing before governors and kings (Mark 13.9) is described elsewhere as happening to the movement later in the first century (e.g., 2 Cor. 11.32-33; Acts 12.1-3; 18.12-17; 23.23; 25.6, 23; Rev. 1.9). Furthermore, taking the "good news" to the nations (Mark 13.10) is a development *after* the time of the historical Jesus as his movement was primarily concerned with Jewish restoration. All this points to the common practice of writing up prophecies after events, or at least as they were happening or looked likely to happen.

The dramatic prediction about the "desolating sacrilege" in the Temple (Mark 13.14) is not found elsewhere in the Synoptic tradition (other than the parallel in Matt. 24.15) which we might expect had such a spectacular claim come from the lips of Jesus. Indeed, this prophecy is more likely to have originated around 39/40 CE when the Roman Emperor Caligula threated to put a statue of himself in the Temple, hence Mark's grammatically unusual Greek when he mismatched the neuter "abomination" (*bdelygma*) with a masculine "set up" or "standing" (*hestēkota*).[5]

The language mirrors 1 Maccabees 1.54 which describes when the Seleucid ruler Antiochus desecrated the Holy Temple by sacrificing to foreign gods. The injunction for those in Judea to "flee to the mountains" is what the zealous supporters of Israel's ancestral traditions did in 1 Maccabees 2.28, and hence the coded warning, "let the reader understand" (Mark 13.14).

The Markan Jesus' titular reference to himself as "the Son" (Mark 13.32) is likewise used only in explicit self-reference in Mark 13 (Mark 12.6 and 14.62 are not explicit) and its use as self-reference is at the beginning of a rapidly increasing tradition taken up afterward and with zest in John's Gospel. "The Son" in Mark 13.32 belongs, then, to a developing tradition and not from the time of the Jesus movement, otherwise we would have more early evidence for such a title on Jesus' lips. As we have seen, the Jesus movement possibly believed the core associates would hold elevated stations in the cosmic and end-time hierarchy, but we can see how later interpreters also molded their own end-time fantasies in the face of new challenges.

The prediction of "the Son of Man coming in clouds with great power and glory" (Mark 13.26) looks like a reference to the Second Coming (or *Parousia*) of Jesus and with a titular use of "Son of Man" removed from the historical Jesus. The idea of the Second Coming gives expression to the early Christian belief that Jesus would appear again in the future to sit as judge on the coming day of judgment. The Second Coming was invented *after* Jesus' death, however, and was a development of Jesus' predictions about end times, given that the kingdom the Jesus movement had proclaimed did not materialize immediately after Jesus' death or at his resurrection (e.g., Acts 1.11; 3.19-21; 1 Cor. 15.22-28; 16.22; 1 Thess. 4.15-17; Rev. 19.11-21; 22). Indeed, we can see how Matthew develops Mark in this respect and by ensuring the "Son on Man" is a title for Jesus alone, as Matthew did elsewhere (Matt. 12.8//Mark 2.27-28):

> Truly I tell you, there are some standing here who will not taste death until they see that the kingdom of God has come with power. (Mark 9.1)
>
> Truly I tell you, there are some standing here who will not taste death before they see the Son of Man coming in his kingdom. (Matt. 16.28)

Such end-time uses of the Son of Man as a unique title belong to a tradition that took off after Jesus' death.

As we have seen, Mark's Gospel begins its use of "son of man" in an ambiguous manner (Mark 2.10, 28), in the sense that the term could still have been seen as a translation of the idiomatic Aramaic term for "man" or a "man in my position." Subsequent uses, however, were so thoroughly worked over with post-Jesus theology and knowledge after the events where the phrase unambiguously functions as a title for Jesus alone (e.g., Mark 8.31, 38; 9.31; 10.33-34). In the final chapters of Mark, the title refers to Jesus alone with reference to the prediction in the book of Daniel to the Son of Man "coming with the clouds of heaven" (Dan. 7.13). Coupled with the absence of "kingdom of God" in Mark 13, we can suggest that Mark 13.26 most likely reflects a post-Jesus development of the term.

Similarly, in the trial of Jesus we have the culmination of Markan theology and the main Markan titles for Jesus (Messiah, Son of the Blessed/God, Son of Man's divine authority, and the Son of Man coming with the clouds of heaven) given as reasons for Jesus' execution (Mark 14.61-65). As we will see in the next chapter, the trial was almost certainly written up to reflect issues after Jesus' death rather than ones during any actual trial. Mark shifts away from the most plausible known reason for Jesus' arrest (i.e., playing a pivotal role in a Temple disturbance) and onto grounding Jesus' authority in what was at the heart of the author's theology: Jesus' death.

Predictions of the Temple's Destruction

Despite its improbable historicity, is there anything we can salvage from Mark 13? We would suggest the "prediction" of the destruction of the Temple that opens Mark 13 cannot be ruled out as going back to the early Jesus movement, and possibly to the lips of the historical Jesus himself. Recall that in 70 CE, after 4 years of Jewish revolt, Roman legions descended on Jerusalem, encircled the city, and ultimately razed it to the ground, including its Holy Temple. This was a world-changing event for first-century Jews, and although it took place several decades after the activities of the early Jesus movement, it would have a profound impact on the subsequent development of Judaism and what would ultimately become a separate religion: Christianity.

There are clues in the end-time discourse in Mark 13 that a prediction about the Temple's destruction may have been uttered by the early Jesus movement. Although providing the narrative frame for the extended discourse, verses 1-2 appear out of kilter with what follows which does not then refer to the actual destruction of the Temple (though it is arguably implied in passing, Mark 13.14). The tradition of Jesus predicting the destruction of Jerusalem and the Temple is also spread through multiple sources which, conceivably, the Gospel writers inherited (e.g., Luke 19.41-44; 21.20, 24-; John 2.19). However, we do need to be cautious as these passages could be additions made by the Gospel authors themselves, writing up their narratives in light of the destruction of the Temple and Jerusalem (see below). For instance, we can see this possibility in the development of the Q tradition, the Parable of the Great Feast (Matt. 22.1-14// Luke 14.15-24), where Matthew 22.7 ("The king was enraged. He sent his troops, destroyed those murderers, and burned their city") is absent from Luke. Matthew could have had access to an earlier version; equally, Matthew could have added this comment to the parable to reflect the destruction of Jerusalem.

Yet predictions about the destruction of the Temple and Jerusalem could still have been a working assumption of the Jesus movement. The Temple had already fallen once before, to the Babylonians in 587 BCE, and this is a major theme in Jewish scriptures. Closer to the time of Jesus, according to 4QpHab 9.5-7, the city would fall again to an army of the "Kittim" (world empire). Such ideas would have been especially invigorating if members of the Jesus movement felt the ideal function of the Temple, as a house of God rather than a den of robbers, had been corrupted. Dreams of the Temple's destruction and/or rebuilding, as part of appropriately meted out divine judgment, were live options likely to find a home among radical and revolutionary millenarian types in and around Galilee and Judea.

And so, it is certainly possible that vague sentiments about "great buildings...thrown down" were tied in with the movement's millenarian expectation of divine judgment on the rich and corrupt. The overarching problem remains, the destruction of Jerusalem and/or the Temple were more predictable, as it were, at the time scholars typically date Mark, that is, during the 4 years of Jewish revolt that resulted in Jerusalem's destruction in 70 CE, especially for those perceptive enough to read "the signs" of the devastation that could be brought by Roman might. Even Josephus, when things were not going the expected way, switched sides late in the war and served as a translator for the emperor's son when he led the siege on Jerusalem.

A common view is that Mark 13 originated in response to the Caligula crisis (cf. Mark 13.14), with scholars suggesting it was later reapplied to the Jewish uprising against Rome or, alternatively, that this is evidence in favor of an earlier dating of Mark's Gospel around 40 CE.[6] But the issue remains: this still means it could function as a prediction that Mark or an earlier writer made at that time, even if they did not ultimately eventuate because of that episode. Indeed, we can see why such

a prediction would continue to be popular as there is evidence
that Jews were expecting a repeat action by a Roman emperor in
the decades following the Caligula crisis (Tacitus, *Annals* 12.54.1).

Be that as it may, even if Mark was written before 70 CE, the
other Gospels were most certainly written *after* the destruction
of Jerusalem and so any independent traditions about the fall
of the Temple and/or the city would have been developed in
retrospect and with knowledge of the event in mind. We see
evidence of this in their accounts. For example, right before
Jesus cleanses the Temple, Luke has Jesus weep over it and
predict "the days will come upon you, when your enemies will
set up ramparts around you and surround you and hem you
in on every side" (Luke 19.41-44). This rather detailed outline
approximates the actual tactic of the Roman forces during the
siege, when they ringed the city with a stone wall manned
by guards, and so cut off valuable supplies to the city and
starved the population.[7] Even if Luke had an earlier tradition, it
remains difficult to disentangle from Luke's explanation of the
destruction of Jerusalem. This is clearer still when Luke changes
Mark's prediction of a "desolating sacrilege set up where it
not ought to be" (Mark 13.14) to: "When you see Jerusalem
surrounded by armies, then know that its desolation has come
near" (Luke 21.20; cf. Luke 21.24).

Whatever the case, it is possible, but still an educated guess,
that there was a kernel of truth in what those "false witnesses"
implied at Jesus' trial, namely, that *he predicted a new Temple
would replace the old* (Mark 14.57-59). Although certainly
possible, there is not, however, enough corroborating evidence
to make a conclusive stand on whether Jesus himself specifically
predicted the fall of the Temple.

Jesus' Last Passover Meal

In Mark 14, the narrative moves on to describe Jesus' activities
around the Passover meal, followed by the defection of Judas

from the Jesus party. As we saw in Chapter 4, Mark depicts the meal taking place in a "large room upstairs" (Mark 14.15) which, in a crowded Jerusalem, is a vital detail given the range of associates and sympathizers, including women (cf. Mark 15.40-41), who were likely present in addition to the Twelve (Mark 14.12-26). Hence, Jesus narrows down the suspected defector to "one of the twelve, one who is dipping bread into the bowl with me" (14.20).

As scholars like to point out, other details in Mark's account complement what we know of Passover meals. The reference to "the first day of Unleavened Bread" in Mark 14.12 refers to one of the generic labels for the festival of "Passover and Unleavened Bread" we saw above and so the date must be 14 Nisan. Mark also indicates this was the time when the Passover lamb or kid was being slaughtered, that is, during the afternoon. Presumably, as one of party's leaders, Jesus was directly involved in the slaughter of the animal before a priest in the Temple. As Mark implies, Jesus' accompanying delegates were eager to make plans for the meal preparation. Mention of "a man carrying a jar of water will meet you" (Mark 14.13) is another coded reference of the sort we saw in the preparation for the colt to ride into Jerusalem (Mark 11.1-6) and several commentators have suggested the idea of a man carrying water would have stood out as this was a task usually undertaken by a woman.

After the preparations had been made, the meal was consumed and this would have involved the lamb or goat, unleavened bread, bitter herbs, haroseth sauce, and wine (cf. Mark 14.20, 22-25), with the party leader giving the appropriate words and interpretation of the key elements of the meal a reminder of the liberation from slavery under Pharaoh. At the conclusion of the meal, they sung Psalms 113-118, known as the "Hallel Psalms." Or, as Mark put it, "When they had sung the hymn, they went out to the Mount of Olives" (Mark 14.26).

While we can dispute whether an arrangement was in

place enabled by a man carrying water on his head, or indeed any number of specific details for their historical accuracy, the fact that the general outline in Mark 14.12-26 is consistent with a traditional Passover meal gives us clues to historical reconstruction in a different way. Even if Mark had made up this event from scratch, we could at least say the general outline reflects the sort of Passover Jesus would have experienced in his life.

Be that as it may, Mark 14 remains a contentious text with details that go far beyond a standard Passover meal. First is the interpretation of key elements of the meal Jesus is reported to have provided:

> While they were eating, he took a loaf of bread, and after blessing it he broke it, gave it to them, and said, "Take; this is my body." Then he took a cup, and after giving thanks he gave it to them, and all of them drank from it. He said to them, "This is my blood of the covenant, which is poured out for many. Truly I tell you, I will never again drink of the fruit of the vine until that day when I drink it new in the kingdom of God." (Mark 14.22-25)

This picks up and develops the martyrological imagery we saw previously in Chapter 8. Understood in a Passover setting, Jesus' interpretation of the meal's elements would renew hopes of liberation as the Israelites were once liberated from slavery under Pharaoh. Reference to the kingdom of God suggests the next liberation was understood as the (imminent) end of the present rulers of the world or this age, i.e., the Roman Empire and their lackeys. Reference to blood pouring out for "the many" not only echoed Passover language (cf. Ex. 24.8) but also Mark 10.45, which likely places the emphases on willful martyrdom for the salvation of Israel (minus the unrepentant). The fate of the martyr in the end-time scheme of revolutionary transformation in Mark 14.25 was relatively standard in Jewish martyr theology, as we saw from the influential book of Daniel ("Some of the wise shall fall, so that they may be refined, purified, and cleansed, until the time of the end, for there is still an interval until the time appointed"; Dan. 11.35). These concerns about Jewish salvation and liberation are in line with what we have seen of both the revolutionary millenarianism and martyr theology of the early Jesus movement. They also appear removed from later concerns about the salvation of non-Jews. As part of a general theme, then, these sentiments point to their emergence in early tradition.

There is also evidence that a similar version of Jesus' words about the meal was known independently and predated the Gospels, hence it turns up in Paul's first letter to the Corinthians written in the mid-50s CE. 1 Cor. 11.23-26 clearly refers to the same event, but Passover is no longer the setting and instead Paul uses the story to address the chaotic lack of discipline in the Corinthian branch when they were coming together to eat the "Lord's supper" (1 Cor. 11.20). We follow those scholars who argue Paul was working with an inherited tradition he (or someone before him) updated to reflect post-Jesus concerns. Where Mark's version has Jesus reference traditional Passover language by referring to the drink as the "blood of the covenant" (Mark 14.24; cf. Ex. 24.8), Paul instead claims that Jesus said: "This cup is the *new* covenant in my blood" which suggests the movement now emphasized non-Jewish inclusion and presented itself as moving beyond the internal Jewish concerns of the Markan passage. Whereas Mark's Jesus talks in terms of Jesus meeting the associates again in the coming kingdom, Paul's version refers to the Second Coming of Jesus ("you proclaim the Lord's death until he comes"; 1 Cor. 11.26). And whereas Mark's Jesus presents this as his final Passover meal, Paul's account has this as an ongoing memorial meal in the post-Jesus movement. Paul seems to have had a direct or indirect influence on Luke's version, or at least on a section added to Luke's version (Luke 22.19-20), which also includes reference to this "new covenant" (also added to Mark in some later manuscripts) as well as the declaration to "Do this in remembrance of me." Even if we cannot reconstruct the precise details of what happened at Jesus' last meal, the most obvious conclusion to draw from all this is that the story itself was early, circulated independently, and although possibly written later, Mark's version nonetheless reflects an *earlier* tradition than Paul's, whose version reflects an interpretation influenced by concerns removed from the time of the early Jesus movement. -

Defection of a Comrade

The other contentious part of Mark's account of Jesus' last Passover is the defection of Judas. Mark explains that Judas was one of the Twelve and defected to the Temple authorities for which he received payment (Mark 14.10-11).

The theme of "betrayal" runs throughout Mark's portrayal of the meal and its aftermath, with Peter and other associates presumably indulging in a little too much festive food and drink (Mark 14.37-38, 40-41). As Jesus was noticeably anxious about his fate, Judas and his new associates arrived as a mob to arrest him (Matt. 26.47//Mark 14.43//Luke 22.47; cf. John 18.3, where Judas brings not a crowd but "a detachment of soldiers together with police from the chief priests and the Pharisees"). Judas famously and scandalously kissed Jesus to identify him to the authorities. The kiss itself was a gesture of affection and inclusion. It would have suggested familiarity, closeness, and homosocial intimacy. And yet, in the case of Judas it resulted in an act of betrayal, and the arrest (and ultimately death) of his close associate. After a scuffle where a slave of the high priest was said to have lost his ear, Jesus is arrested, and remarked to the arresting party "Have you come out with swords and clubs to arrest me as though I were a bandit?" (Mark 14.48).

It is difficult to know what to do with this. Some perceive a clue in the other part of Judas' name: "Iscariot," which in Hebrew means "man of Kerioth," i.e., a town understood to be in the south of Judea. This would have meant Judas was an outsider to the otherwise Galilean Twelve which could in turn be one factor behind his defection. Sometimes linked to this argument is the possibility that Judas was horrified by the lack of respect shown by Jesus in the Temple. Another, perhaps more sensational, option is that Judas' act was performed in obedience to special instructions given him by Jesus. This would have provided the opportunity for Jesus to faithfully see through his willful martyrdom (see, e.g., heated discussion surrounding the second-century CE "Gnostic" *Gospel of Judas*). Both explanations are possible, but they remain speculative, and in the case of the latter are based on a specific reading of a late and unreliable source. Alternatively, it is occasionally argued that Judas was a coded but fictional reference to "Jews" (or a similar label) to shift blame for Jesus' death onto Jews as a whole. While we cannot rule out creative storytelling here, Mark does not generalize Jewish blame and his story of Jesus' death and makes it clear that Jewish and Roman *authorities* were responsible for Jesus' death, *not* the Jewish people.

If the story of defection and betrayal was invented then it was probably early on, as Paul in the mid-first century appears to reference it (minus Judas' name) in the tradition he received (1 Cor. 11.23). We can be content with the general picture again and our best guess is that Jesus was arrested for his involvement in the Temple disturbance, whatever that entailed. Volatile crowds and the potential for further riots meant the authorities arrested this perceived rabble-rouser as carefully as possible. As we will see in our penultimate chapter, the revolutionary millenarianism of the Jesus movement, with its seditious implications for the end of the Roman Empire, only heightened the justification the authorities needed to have Jesus arrested and executed. As Mark's Jesus indicates, he was arrested as a "bandit" or violent insurrectionist. And there are clues in the over-embellished story of his trial and execution that *this* was the real reason he would end up martyred on a Roman cross.

Chapter 10

A Ransom for the Many

A popular scholarly view of Jesus' death is that it was relatively unexpected and caught the movement by surprise. Those who regarded or came to regard Jesus as the Messiah would have expected him to fulfill his divinely appointed duty of liberating the Jewish people from their Roman overlords. The shock and grief at his sudden death, combined with many post-mortem appearances, influenced the movement to subsequently develop a theology of martyrdom to account for how Jesus ended up dead on a Roman cross. But what if the opposite were true?

We have argued it is entirely possible the Jesus movement was deadly serious when they marched on Jerusalem. They had been developing fantasies about a glorious martyrs' death, and the most disciplined among them were prepared to die for the cause, to give their life as a ransom for many (Mark 10.45). We saw in Chapter 8 this tradition was likely an early one associated with the movement. In Christian theology, to die as a "ransom" (*lutron*) would come to have associations with Jesus' death as an atonement for sin. But as Morna Hooker observes, "the word **ransom** bears no relation, in spite of many statements to the contrary, to the Hebrew word *'āšām* used in Isa. 53.10, which means 'an offering for sin.'"[1] Rather, in the first century the term was a clear allusion to a number of transactions including the money given to free a slave (cf. Lev. 25.47-55). That the movement conceived of their sacrifice for the national interest in economic terms is another important link, whether intentional or not, to the perceived wrongs of the social and economic changes in Galilee that had first sparked the revolutionary millenarianism of the Jesus movement. Payment with one's life was thus a viable and indeed manly option for propelling their end-time expectation of a divine reversal of fortunes forward (cf. 4 Macc. 17.20-22).

The death and resurrection of Jesus would become the most important factor of his life in the global religion that emerged after him. But how much of the well-known story of Jesus' trial, death, and burial goes back to the earliest Palestinian tradition? We have already seen that reconstructing Jesus' last week during the Passover festival requires a disciplined historical imagination. The problem is our earliest sources the Gospels have plenty of holes, questionable motives, obvious embellishments, and rhetorical flourishes. The same is true of the events surrounding his death, and so once again we must apply cautious and sober criticism to our primary sources. In doing so, however, we come away with a far more positive assessment than the skeptics among us might initially suppose.

In this penultimate chapter, we determine what can and cannot be known about the earliest ideas surrounding Jesus' death and subsequent reports of his resurrection. We begin by discerning the historical veracity (or not) of Jesus' trials in front of the ruling elite, noting the power of crowds which should not be underestimated in shaping the course of history. Jesus was famously put to death on a Roman cross, and so we explore the various accounts of his martyrdom, drawing attention to its ideological ramifications for the early Jesus movement. We uncover class concerns in the narratives of Jesus' burial in a rich man's tomb. Finally, we address the cultural conditions and martyr theology that may have played a role in shaping the movement's subsequent experiences of a post-mortem Jesus. Despite the dearth of reliable and consistent evidence, one idea comes through strongly in our sources: from very early on Jesus' death and resurrection was thought to have had cosmic ramifications. The end times were now truly at hand!

Trial and Punishment

After his arrest in the garden of Gethsemane, Mark's Gospel, our earliest narrative account, suggests that Jesus underwent two trials: first, in front of the Jewish authorities, and second, in front of the Roman prefect.

In the first trial scene, Mark 14.53-65 reports that Jesus appeared before the High Priest (which Matthew, expanding on Mark's account, rightly identifies as Caiaphas) and a gathering of "all the chief priests, the elders, and the scribes." Peter, we are told, was following nearby (Mark 14.66) and had not been arrested himself. Remarkably, the council could find no one to provide testimony to put Jesus to death and so provided false witnesses instead. This involved garbled and contradictory allegations, including a claim that Jesus was heard saying "I will destroy this temple that is made with hands, and in 3 days I will build another, not made with hands." The High Priest then intervened but Jesus remained silent and so the High Priest asked directly, "Are you the Messiah, the Son of the Blessed One?", to which Jesus replied, "I am; and 'you will see the Son of Man seated at the right hand of the Power,' and 'coming with the clouds of heaven.'" This was deemed enough for the High Priest to charge Jesus with "blasphemy," and so the council agreed Jesus must die.

There are good reasons to doubt the historicity of the first trial in Mark 14.53-65, despite the hint of the Temple disturbance which, as we saw in the previous chapter, is the most likely reason why Jesus was arrested by the authorities. According to later rabbinic law, trials were not meant to take place during a festival or at night (m. *Sanhedrin* 4.1), which is contrary to Mark's presentation, and Luke notably omits the night trial and has a gathering take place in the morning (Luke 22.66-71) prior to an extended trial before Pontius Pilate and Herod Antipas (Luke 23.1-22). If such rules were in place during the time of Jesus, even as an ideal, then Mark's skewed version was not an innocent mistake. As we saw in Chapter 7, Mark knew Jewish law in detail (e.g., Mark 7.1-5) and so instead the trial scene is rhetorically designed to show how due process was blatantly breached by the authorities. As Helen K. Bond puts it: "with its rowdy false witnesses, accusations and formal verdict, Mark's trial scene resembles a kangaroo court...the whole affair is presented by the evangelist as a travesty of justice."[2]

The brief report in Mark 15.1 is scarce in detail but a far more probable representation of what happened: "As soon as it was morning, the chief priests held a consultation with the elders and scribes and the whole council. They bound Jesus, led him away, and handed him over to Pilate." Here again we need to use our imagination. The High Priest (unnamed in Mark's account) was Caiaphas whose term of office (18-36 CE) overlapped with Pontius Pilate's term as Roman prefect or governor (26-37 CE). Their relatively lengthy tenures suggest a good working relationship, and Pilate would have had to be involved for Jesus to be executed, not that it would take much for Pilate to execute someone (see e.g., Philo, *Embassy to Gaius* 302).

The second trial scene before the Roman prefect in Mark 15.2-5 is surprisingly brief and informal. It is often noted that Pilate had a reputation for cruelty, but the Gospel accounts do not accurately reflect this. The short account of Jesus before Pilate in Mark's Gospel suggests Pilate was perhaps indifferent to the fate of Jesus, and merely surprised Jesus did not bother to defend himself when asked if he was the "King of the Jews" (15.1-2), an especially loaded title when faced with the council of the chief priests and the Roman prefect. Perhaps Pilate sensed Jesus was willing to die for his cause, and so, without too much concern, sent the fool along to his cross.

Mark may or may not provide accurate information of what happened on that day, but his portrayal of Pilate is not out of the ordinary. It is not difficult to imagine Pilate was easily persuaded that Jesus, a revolutionary millenarian from Galilee, was an insurrectionary threat, who had whipped up the Passover crowds with his Temple actions, who wanted rid of the Romans, and, further, who appeared wild, deranged, and mad.[3] As with John the Baptist and later Theudas, the ruling class rarely cared enough about the specifics of threatening-looking movements. Rather, they worked with the principle of acting first to suppress them and (maybe) asking questions later. Thus, Jesus was treated like any other violent insurrectionist once sentenced to death by crucifixion. A "whole cohort" (about 500 soldiers) was apparently summoned (Mark 15.16) and may well have forced someone like Simon of Cyrene to carry part of the cross, as presumably retold by his sons Alexander and Rufus (Mark 15.21). Jesus was then crucified as an insurrectionist between two insurrectionists (using the now familiar Greekword lēstēs) (Mark 15.27).

In terms of possibilities, the idea that Jesus was unceremoniously executed for being a deranged insurrectionist is the most likely scenario. A straightforward path from arrest to death would reflect the brutal realities of the smooth functioning of Roman power in its imperial outposts. There are plenty of other details in the trial of Jesus that look like later embellishments or creations. For instance, Luke's insertion of a third trial before Herod, through which we learn the charming details of how "Herod and Pilate became friends" (verse 12), is pure fabrication (Luke 23.6-16). We can be assured whatever went down during the trial(s) of Jesus, that the *authority* to crucify him began and ended with Pilate. Indeed, after Jesus' death, even Joseph of Arimathea, who Mark identifies as a "prominent member of the council" (i.e., an influential person at the first trial), required "courage" to approach Pilate to ask for Jesus' corpse: authority which Pilate held to grant or deny.

The Crowd's Preferential Option for Jesus' Death

Another prominent example of embellishment, this time immediately following Jesus' second trial in Mark, is the famous story of Pilate allowing one lucky prisoner to be released at festival time. Barabbas was let go on account of the chief priests stirring up a crowd against Jesus. Given the importance of crowds in writing the history from below, however, it is worth spending some time on this story, even if we are unsure of the extent to which it goes back to the earliest tradition. Mark narrates the event as follows:

> Now at the festival he used to release a prisoner for them, anyone for whom they asked. Now a man called Barabbas was in prison with the rebels who had committed murder during the insurrection. So the crowd came and began to ask Pilate to do for them according to his custom. Then he asked them, "Do you want me to release for you the King of the Jews?"...the chief priests stirred up the crowd to have him release Barabbas for them instead. Pilate spoke to them again, "Then what do you wish me to do with the man you call the King of the Jews?" They shouted back, "Crucify him!" (Mark 15.6-13)

We saw in the previous chapter the incidental reference to a murderous insurrection suggests a violent upheaval may have taken place during Jesus' last week, an event the Jesus movement was possibly caught up in, but of which our Gospel authors do not bother to provide details.

Quite what transpired between Pilate and the crowd that Passover, there are plenty of reasons to be suspicious of Mark's account of Jesus' sentencing in front of the crowd. For starters, the so-called "custom" of releasing a prisoner during Passover is not otherwise known. Given everything else we know about Roman rule in the provinces, it is difficult to imagine Pilate offering the choice between a (possibly indistinguishable?) insurrectionist and deranged royal pretender.

If not a pure literary fabrication, the idea could be based on the account of the imprisonment of the associates of Matthias and Judas who attacked the golden eagle Herod the Great had erected at the Temple (see Chapter 8).[4] Recall too, in 4 BCE, Herod's son Archelaus spoke to the crowds before Passover and one of their demands, which he accepted, was the liberation of these prisoners. But in any case, with episodes like these circulating in popular memory, the release of the murderer and insurrectionist Barabbas might have reflected Mark's absurdist portrayal of elite rulers in a world turned upside down.

The name "Barabbas" is itself doubly suspicious because it literally means "son of a father" in Aramaic (some versions of Matt. 27.16-17 even call him "Jesus Barabbas"). Given Jesus is unambiguously presented as *the* son of God the father by Mark (e.g., Mark 1.11; 9.7; 12.6; 13.32; cf. 14.61-62), the inclusion of the release of Barabbas continues Mark's theme of perversion of justice. The life of a murderer and "son of the father" is spared, but the innocent son of the father is put to death. This theme of misunderstanding the "son" continues through the crucifixion (see also Matt. 27.40-44) and also appears in the confession of the Roman centurion when he watched Jesus die: "Truly this man was God's Son!" (Mark 15.39). Unlike other presentations of Jesus as "the son" in Mark (1.11; 9.7), Mark 15.39 lacks the definite article and is in the imperfect past tense and so the centurion's claim can be read as another misunderstanding (or perhaps mocking) of Jesus' identity.[5]

But again, we should not be too quick to throw out the baby with the bathwater. Whatever the likely embellishments around the sentencing of Jesus, the Synoptic tradition and Josephus both repeatedly attest to the potential for uproar around Passover, and such forces are on full display in the portrayal of the prisoner exchange scene in the Temple complex. Crowds engage in, or have the potential to engage in, riotous acts, and have the capacity to occasionally bring the elite to their knees.[6] Whatever the reality behind the story of Pilate's interrogation of the crowd, it was not out of compassion but basic *realpolitik* that he agreed to the release of Barabbas ("Pilate, wishing to satisfy the crowd...", Mark 15.15). A small concession could go a long way, especially if it facilitated the smooth and uninterrupted functioning of the social and political orders at what was otherwise a turbulent few days in Jerusalem.

The crowd's sudden and unexplained turn on Jesus overnight has similarly raised doubts about their portrayal in the Gospel accounts. But such arguments, when put forth by scholars, are typically reductionist in their understanding of how crowds work. Such arguments naïvely assume crowds are always consistent rather than chaotic, predictable rather than disruptive, focused rather than diffuse. Other factors could explain the crowd's sudden turn against Jesus. We should not rule out the possibility, although speculative, that some supporters of the movement, finding themselves caught up in the tumultuous effects of the crowd, willingly joined the chorus calling for his execution, insofar as it would lead to his righteous martyrdom.

Elias Canetti's anthropological study *Crowds and Power* categorizes crowds according to their prevailing emotion: first, the *baiting crowd* forms with reference to a quickly attainable goal. "This crowd is out for killing and it knows whom it wants to kill."[7] This is a riotous crowd focused and determined on this one outcome; second, the flight crowd is created when people flee together because of an external threat. Flight crowds have a force of direction, away from danger; third, a prohibition crowd, much like an industrial strike, is created by many people together refusing to continue to do what is normally expected of them; fourth, a reversal crowd is where, in a stratified society, the exploited classes lash out against those in power, such as in a revolutionary situation. Reversal crowds direct power toward achieving liberation from the burdens of submission to domination; finally, feast crowds, centered on the shared goal of a feast, are limited spaces, full of abundance, and where many prohibitions and distinctions are waived.

Through the lens of Canetti, the emotional crowd type present at Jesus' trial scene is *not* a feast crowd but a baiting crowd. It is thus useful to distinguish between the *feast* crowd already present in Jerusalem (and alluded to in the previous chapter) and the *baiting* crowd that participates in Jesus' sentencing before Pilate. In moving away from history as the individual exploits of Great Men, Canetti suggests that in a public execution, "The real executioner is the crowd gathered round the scaffold. It approves the spectacle and, with passionate excitement, gathers from far and near to watch it from beginning to end." In fact, Canetti offers Jesus' sentencing as a primary example of this phenomenon. He writes:

> The cry of "Crucify Him!" comes from the crowd; it is the crowd which is truly active here. On another occasion it might have done everything itself and stoned Jesus. The tribunal pronouncing judgment—normally in front of a limited number of people only—stands for the multitude which later attends the execution...It is actually for the sake of the crowd that justice is done and it is the crowd we have in mind when we speak of the importance of justice being public...Once a baiting crowd has attained its victim it disintegrates rapidly. Rulers in danger are well aware of this fact and throw a victim to the crowd in order to impede its growth.[8]

Our point is that we do not have to dismiss the *possibility* of the active involvement of a crowd based on the grounds of seemingly contradictory or irrational behavior. And we raise the *possibility* that some of them too may have embraced the willful martyrdom promoted by the Jesus movement. Jesus was, accordingly, offered over as a ransom for the many. Nevertheless, it remains difficult to establish what may (or may not) have happened between Pilate and the crowd. And so, we come to no firm conclusions. At this point in Mark's Gospel, Jesus' death has been presented as such a perverse miscarriage of justice that we may be dealing with more ironic Markan commentary with minimal relevance for reconstructing the historical Jesus' last hours.

Other aspects of Jesus' fate mentioned in Mark 15.1-39 may reflect early themes, though much cannot be proven and could be fictional for all we know. Severe beatings and corporal punishment would not have been unusual. It is conceivable that soldiers dressed Jesus up as a mock king in "soft" or "effeminate" clothing, that a mocking inscription "The King of the Jews" hung above his body on the cross (see below), and that bystanders at his crucifixion mocked him for prophesying about the Temple (if a garbled version of the claim) and his millenarianism (Mark 15.16-20). All these details are consistent with the total humiliation underscored by Jesus' death. That Jesus suffered a shameful death on a Roman cross is one of the most historically certain facts about Jesus' life we have, and so it is to this particular event we now turn.

Total Humiliation: The Shame of Crucifixion

The Romans used crucifixion to punish "bandits" in the provinces for acts of incitement to rebellion. Of the options available, the chosen means of Jesus' extermination was a drawn-out and excruciating way to die, although it did have the advantage of a comparatively quicker death than the prolonged brutality of economic exploitation.

Evidence for Jesus' death by crucifixion is strong. Such a fate is attested independently in Mark (followed by Matthew and Luke) and Paul (e.g., Mark 15.13-15, 20-27; 16.6; 1 Cor. 1.13, 23; 2.2, 8; 2 Cor. 13.4; Gal. 3.1; 5.24. 6.14; Phil. 2.8) which shows that Jesus' death by crucifixion was an accepted and uncontested assumption in the earliest material we have. Jesus' crucifixion is further corroborated by the observation that it would have been embarrassing for the early Christians, yet it remained within the tradition as something that had to be explained and defended. Surprising as it may sound, for Paul, although Jesus' death (and resurrection) was central to his theology, the method of his death was not. Indeed, Paul has little to say specifically about Jesus' "crucifixion" or the "cross" in his letters. When he did draw attention to Jesus' crucifixion, Paul revealed it could be perceived as a problem: "For the message about the cross is foolishness to those who are perishing...we proclaim Christ crucified, a stumbling-block to Jews and foolishness to Gentiles" (1 Cor. 1.18, 23). Accordingly, the embarrassing death would occasionally prove rhetorically useful, such as when Paul wrote to the "foolish Galatians" (Gal. 3.1) or attempted to bring down the hubris of the Corinthians (1 Cor. 1.17). It looks unlikely, then, that the Jesus movement would have invented Jesus' crucifixion; rather, it was a problem they had to deal with and explain.

According to the Gospel accounts, Jesus was crucified at a place called Golgotha, a name based on the Aramaic word for "skull," as Mark implies (Mark 15.22). There are speculations about why this place was labeled with reference to "skull" and the simplest explanation is probably the best guess: in a place where people were crucified, the land would have been littered with skulls. The strongest case for the location of the site of crucifixion is not the hill of later Christian imagination but outside Gennath Gate and near two main roads.[9] In either case, however, the location of Jesus' crucifixion would have served the Roman goal of engineering the punishment as a public warning.

Indeed, crucifixion was a public, highly choreographed, and sadistic spectacle, intended to serve as an example to others they needed to respect and obey Roman rule. While crucifixion was used by societies before the Romans, including the Persians and Macedonians, under Roman rule crucifixion became widespread and notorious, in some cases involving mass deaths. Josephus described crucifixion as "the most wretched of deaths" (*War* 7.203). It was reserved primarily for traitors of the empire, and generally meted out on the lower classes, slaves, and foreigners (cf. Tacitus, *Hist.* 2.172.1-2). Cicero, for instance, expressed disgust at the thought of possibly crucifying a Roman citizen (*In Verrum* 2.5.63, 66). Crucifixion of Jews became a matter of policy as Roman armies increasingly interfered in the administration of Judea.

As noted above, crucifixion was also widely understood as a shameful death, and for Jews in particular the victim was thought to be under a curse (Deut. 21.22-23; cf. 4Q169 3-4, I.6-9; 11Q19 64.6-13). The intent of dishonoring Jesus was indicated by the inscription of the charge against him placed above his head: "The King of the Jews" (Mark 15.26). Following the important work of Wongi Park, we should not miss the ethnoracial dimensions to the Roman charge "The King of the Jews."[10] The charge would draw attention not only to Jesus' deranged political pretensions, but also functioned as a racial slur: the Jesus movement's mistake was to assume their Jewish identity, grounded in radical allegiance to their Jewish God, obedience to their Jewish law, and aligned to the material interests of the native population, was a viable challenge to Roman power. Such thinking would have appeared absurd from the position of Roman dominance and so needed to be put rightly in its place. Jesus' public execution was intended to humiliate and, in Park's language, "minoritize" Jesus, as well as to propagate ideas about Roman superiority over ethnic Judean inferiority.

Such a reading of Jesus' death also grafts comfortably onto the gender dynamics inherent within Roman understandings of crucifixion. We saw in Chapter 6 how crucifixion was understood as a grotesque display of Roman hyper-masculine dominance over their defeated, passive, and feminized combatants. Ancient audiences would have been familiar with the ritualized stripping of masculinity in crucifixion: the Greek term commonly used for crucifixion in the New Testament, *stauroō*, has connotations of being nailed or impaled; victims were hung naked, exposed, and vulnerable; they experienced a lack of control over their breathing; and their ritual humiliation was further compounded by the contempt of onlookers.

Alongside this, we saw in Chapter 8 how the early Jesus movement, possibly in advance of their journey to Jerusalem, developed theologies about how to confront death head on, to "take it like a man," and to keep their masculinity intact through their principled submission to death. There appears to have been a diversity of ways to deal with the emasculation of Jesus' shameful death among our sources. Colleen M. Conway has noted the varying ways Jesus' death is constructed in the New Testament, including as a passive emasculated victim (Mark 14-16) alongside more "manly" presentations (also found in Paul) of a heroic strong man (Mark 1-8) and noble martyr (Mark 8-10).[11] That these various options existed is important for understanding the historical Jesus, irrespective of the historicity of specific passages. It appears competing narratives about Jesus' death were already known, discussed, or assumed among Jesus' close associates, but also by his enemies. As we have seen, emasculating constructions of Jesus' death could have been both acknowledged and countered by the Jesus movement with hyper-masculinized constructions. These conflicting and ironic explanations likely already surrounded Jesus as he hung dying on the cross.

Other details of the portrayal of Jesus' crucifixion in Mark's Gospel have been much discussed. Having experienced the brutal realities of martyrdom with no signs of divine intervention, it is possible, but difficult to prove, that a dying Jesus called out in anguish to God (in Aramaic), "Eloi, Eloi, lema sabachthani?" ("My God, my God, why have you forsaken me?"; Mark 15.34). The general point that there were women watching from a distance (Mark 15.40-41) is possible (see below), perhaps likely, because the male associates had fled. That the male associates could continue to be active in Jerusalem shortly afterwards should not be a surprise. They would not have been well-known faces (cf. Mark 14.66-72) but that may be beside the point as the Temple authorities would have known that teachings of the Jesus movement were not those of the violent insurrectionist in the here and now, even if Jesus was seen to have gone too far at Passover. The associates of Jesus may have been allowed further distance from any alleged crime committed by Jesus if, as Justin Meggitt argues, their leader was understood to have been uniquely mad.[12]

What happened immediately following Jesus' death? According to Mark, the "curtain of the temple" was torn in two from top to bottom (Mark 15.38). Mark is probably referring to the inner curtain that separated off the Holy of Holies, through which only the High Priest was allowed to enter, and that only once per year. Given there was obviously no possibility for an eyewitness to this supernatural occurrence, Mark appears to be marking the moment of Jesus' death as highly symbolic and the Greek verb *schizensthai* ("torn apart") appears only once elsewhere in Mark to denote the tearing apart of the heavens at the precise moment of Jesus' baptism (Mark 1.10). Some commentators argue that the rending of the Temple curtain was a vivid gesture toward the removal of barriers between heaven and earth. However, this theme is not developed in Mark's Gospel and the more likely scenario, as Roger Aus has shown in detail, is that Mark was presenting the most extreme form of mourning in fully ripping the garment, in this case God mourning for his beloved son by rending his garment (the Temple curtain) "from top to bottom."[13]

A direct association between Jesus' martyrdom and the dramatic breaking-in of God's kingdom appears to be the motivation behind Matthew's embellishments here. Following the torn curtain, Matthew adds an earthquake followed directly by a remarkable if not confusing miracle: "The tombs also were opened, and many bodies of the saints who had fallen asleep were raised. After his resurrection they came out of the tombs and entered the holy city and appeared to many" (Matt. 27.52-53). There is no corroborating evidence to support this story of numerous resurrections. It is clearly Matthean fiction; Mark and others would not have omitted such a wonderous event had it happened. Even so, apologetic claims are occasionally made by scholars, such as that by Bishop Tom Wright: "Some stories are so odd that they may just have happened. This may be one of them, but in historical terms there is no way of finding out."[14] Against Wright, we claim the exact opposite is true: some stories are just so odd precisely because they *did not* happen. Another reason why Matthew 27.53 did not happen is that only the *wealthy* dead saints of Jerusalem were raised back to life. This is clearly in conflict with the class politics of the early Jesus movement which demanded the rich give up their wealth. Indeed, only the elite could afford rock-cut tombs, and Jesus' burial in such a tomb itself cuts against the funerary practices of the non-elite, as we will see below. What this later addition by Matthew does show, however, is that early Christians were capable of formulating resurrection stories that aligned to pre-existing cultural beliefs about a general resurrection at the end times. But more on this later.

Reversing Burial: Tombs for the Poor, Pits for the Rich?

The Gospels tell us that, following his death, Jesus was taken down from his cross and placed into a rock-cut tomb (which later would be found empty). Accepting such an idea as an early account of Jesus' burial is more complicated than often thought, and once more, as hinted above, intersects with the issue of class. Burial conditions in first-century Judea and Galilee varied according to a household's means. Where the elite in Jerusalem could expect to be buried in elaborate and ornate rock-hewn family tombs, most Jews, especially the peasantry, were buried at some distance from cities or towns in simple and inconspicuous shaft graves. Had Jesus died in Nazareth, he would have been afforded a simple burial in a pit grave or trench grave. But Jesus died in extraordinary circumstances: not only was he away from his hometown, he was put to death as a bandit. What, then, became of Jesus' body?

One provocative suggestion is that Jesus' body was treated like any other body of a Roman crucifixion victim, perhaps left outside for the wild animals, or otherwise thrown unceremoniously into a pit with the corpses of other criminals.[15] This would mean that the Gospel accounts of Jesus' burial are entirely fictitious and designed to cover up what was seen as an especially shameful death. Although possible, and certainly consistent with the total humiliation of crucifixion, there are good reasons we should be skeptical of claims that such victims would *never* be released for burial. Although unusual, it was not impossible (e.g., Justinian, *Digest* 48.24.1 3; Josephus, *War* 4.317).

A second option is that Jesus was buried in a pit grave or trench grave, and thus not in a tomb. This would be the assumption for any lower-class Jew who was buried at the time (assuming their body was released). The tradition of the "potter's field as a place to bury foreigners" in Matthew 27.7-8 speaks to this sort of burial. Curiously, none of Paul's letters specifically mention Jesus was buried in a tomb. Without the Gospel accounts, then, one might reasonably deduce that Jesus, who Paul describes as "poor" (2 Cor. 8.9), was simply buried in the ground.

A third option is that there is some degree of truth to the Gospel accounts, or at least Mark's account which reads as follows:

> When evening had come, and since it was the day of Preparation, that is, the day before the sabbath, Joseph of Arimathea, a respected member of the council, who was

also himself waiting expectantly for the kingdom of God, went boldly to Pilate and asked for the body of Jesus. Then Pilate wondered if he were already dead; and summoning the centurion, he asked him whether he had been dead for some time. When he learned from the centurion that he was dead, he granted the body to Joseph. Then Joseph bought a linen cloth, and taking down the body, wrapped it in the linen cloth, and laid it in a tomb that had been hewn out of the rock. He then rolled a stone against the door of the tomb. (Mark 15.42-46)

Mark explains Jesus was buried by a Sanhedrin member, Joseph of Arimathea, with the beginning of the Sabbath approaching which suggests it happened in haste to comply with Jewish law. Deuteronomy 21.22-23 requires burial within 24 hours of death (cf. 4Q169 3-4, 1.6-9; 11Q19 64.6-13; Acts 5.5-6, 10). Moreover, the law prohibited burial on the Sabbath. Given Jesus died on the eve of the Sabbath, there was a narrow window for burial. It could not wait until after the Sabbath, as that would mean exceeding the 24-hour time limit. Accordingly, Jesus was buried before sundown on Friday. Joseph asked Pilate for permission to take Jesus' body and have him buried in a tomb hewn out of rock and a stone rolled against the door of the tomb to seal it. We are probably meant to assume these tombs were usually communal, so there would have been allotted space for other bodies, as Mark later implies (Mark 16.5).[16]

If the tradition of Joseph of Arimathea is early, however, then it provides another clue that the first trial of Jesus before the High Priest and the Sanhedrin was not. If Joseph was both a "respected member of the council," but also "himself looking for the kingdom of God," why did he not speak up during Jesus' trial? Matthew and Luke both saw the problem and tried to smooth it over in different ways: for Matthew, Joseph was no longer a member of the council that condemned Jesus but "a rich man" (Matt. 27.57); for Luke, he was "a good and righteous man, who had not consented to their purpose and deed" (Luke 23.50b-51). Such gaps have generated a variety of interesting receptions through the centuries,[17] but it is the confusing discrepancies contained in the Gospels that concern us here. If Jesus really was buried in Joseph's tomb, it would suggest that the Jesus movement's "mission to the rich" was having a moderate token of success. The movement had been loudly promoting its ideas for several days now in Jerusalem, and one of its chief proponents had been (willingly?) put to death for the cause, absolutely convinced divine judgment was imminent. We saw in Chapter 5 how the revolutionary millenarianism of the movement implored that at the coming judgment the rich would be damned, and the poor would be afforded a life of plenty. The powerful Joseph's offer of a tomb for Jesus' burial was precisely the kind of handing over of property to the movement that was required to assuage God's wrath and get on the right side of history before it was too late.

According to Jodi Magness, "There is no need to assume that the Gospel accounts of Joseph of Arimathea offering Jesus a place in his family tomb are legendary or apologetic. The Gospel accounts of Jesus' burial appear to be largely consistent with the archaeological evidence." Indeed, as she observes further, "The source(s) of these accounts were familiar with the manner in which wealthy Jews living in Jerusalem during the time of Jesus disposed of their dead."[18] But aside from the legal obligations, was Joseph also motivated by the Jesus movement's "mission to the rich?" Put another way, what was Joseph's exact relationship to the early Jesus movement?

Interestingly, Mark and Luke's accounts do not *explicitly* designate Joseph of Arimathea as a "disciple" of Jesus. The idea that Joseph was remembered as a disciple or at least a strong supporter of the Jesus movement in the earliest tradition is generally inferred by some combination of the following: (1) the mention in Mark and Luke that he was "waiting expectantly for the kingdom of God" (Mark 15.43; Luke 23.51); (2) the added detail in Luke that Joseph, a member of the council, had not himself consented to the council's plan regarding Jesus; (3) that Joseph intervened to request Jesus' body for burial, a fitting action for a supporter; and (4) that both Matthew 27.57 and John 19.38 explicitly name Joseph as a disciple.

If we read Mark (and Luke) on its own terms, however, it is difficult to discern how close Joseph was to the Jesus movement. Readings that posit Joseph was a disciple or strongly acquainted with the movement are, in fact, already the product of a harmonizing tendency that obscures the underlying ambiguity in Mark's earlier account. That Mark's assessment is especially ambiguous is evidenced by the fact Matthew and Luke read him in opposite ways: Matthew explicitly designates Joseph as a "disciple" of Jesus, whereas Luke stresses Joseph's piety as a law-abiding Jew and gives no indication of his relationship to the Jesus movement. Consequently, Luke provides an entirely different rationale for why Joseph intervened to secure Jesus' body. Specifically, Joseph, a "good and righteous man" (Luke 23.50) from a "Jewish town," was a law-observant Jew who dutifully saw another Jewish man was properly buried (Deut. 21:23). Such a characterization of Joseph accords nicely with the trope of the "righteous" and "upstanding" man in the Hebrew Bible (e.g., Gen. 6.9; Job 1.1). What is especially noteworthy is the use of similar language elsewhere in Luke to describe Jewish characters who are "righteous before God, living blamelessly according to all the commandments and regulations of the Lord" (Luke 1.6; cf. 2.25), and so on. While such a characterization of Joseph is not incompatible with him being a sympathizer of the Jesus movement, it nonetheless provides sufficient explanation for his actions on its own terms. In other words, on these issues alone, Joseph is not necessarily a follower or strong supporter of Jesus.

But what of the aside in Mark and Luke that Joseph was anticipating the kingdom of God? Surely, given the importance of the kingdom for Jesus' teaching, this would mean they both depict Joseph as a disciple or at least a strong supporter of the Jesus movement's revolutionary millenarianism? As we saw in Chapter 5, the concept of divine kingship was not original or unique to the Jesus movement but was rather part of a longer millenarian tendency in Jewish thought. Feasibly, Joseph could have been anticipating the kingdom understood in a broad sense and not necessarily the specific regime change from the heavens envisaged by the Jesus movement.

Our tentative suggestion, based on the earliest account in Mark's Gospel, is that Joseph was probably *not* a known associate or supporter of the movement. His precise motivation for intervening to secure Jesus' body for burial was not known. Hence the ambiguity in Mark's version, and the inconsistent embellishments we find in the other Gospels which took over this story. Was it because he was a dutiful Jew who wanted to avoid this man's shameful burial? Was it because he was a sympathizer with the movement? Not knowing precisely why Joseph did what he did would not quell speculation. Quite the opposite: the tradition of a wealthy and/or powerful man handing over a tomb provided useful propaganda for the Jesus movement's "mission to the rich."

Post-mortem Visions of a Millenarian Martyr

The next part of the story is the most difficult, and interesting, for the critical historian. Three days after Jesus was buried, there were reports he was seen alive by many of his associates.[19] We have seen that Jesus ending up bleeding out on a Roman cross, as shocking and gruesome as it was, was not completely unexpected. And nor, as we shall see, were subsequent reports that he had been raised back to life. We suggested in Chapter 8 that resurrection was one possible outcome for steadfast martyrs in the cultural matrix of early Judaism, and such ideas had likely provided encouragement as the movement advanced on Jerusalem. Among the millenarian fervor surrounding Passover, a life handed over as a ransom for many could, God willing, lead to great things.

After Jesus' crucifixion, according to Mark's narrative, we are left with prominent female members and sympathizers of the Jesus movement looking on (the male associates having already fled the scene much earlier). Specifically, we are told that Mary Magdalene and Mary the mother of Joses saw where Jesus' corpse had been placed (15.40-41, 47). We are then provided with a brief account about what happened next (Mark 16.1-8): once the Sabbath was over, the two Marys and Salome went to treat Jesus' body, a role usually assigned to women. They saw the massive stone blocking the entrance had been rolled away and there on the inner right-hand side of the tomb was a young man, dressed in a white robe (possibly an angel) who calmed them, explained that Jesus had risen, pointed to Jesus' vacant burial slot as proof, and told them to tell the other associates and Peter that Jesus would see them in Galilee. The women fled the tomb in terror and "they said nothing to anyone, for they were afraid."

Surprisingly, according to early and authoritative manuscripts, this is where Mark's Gospel ends. There is an empty tomb, but no accounts of the resurrected Jesus. Claims there is a lost ending to Mark are speculative, and suggestions the author was arrested, got sick, or died before completing the Gospel cannot be substantiated. Another possibility, that the last page of a codex containing the resurrection accounts fell off, may again explain the abrupt ending, but it cannot be proven. Whatever the case, it is difficult to see how something as important to the emerging Christian movement as the stories of the resurrected Jesus would have been lost. Certainly, later scribes, desiring a more complete resolution to Mark, added endings, but these were not included in the earliest versions of the Gospel. Modern English translations often include a small handful of these varied endings, but they are usually bracketed off as secondary given their absence from early and authoritative manuscripts. We can only conclude that Mark's Gospel from early on ended abruptly with the women telling no one because they were afraid.

The Gospels of Matthew and Luke, drawing on Mark as a source, were clearly unsatisfied and provide extended but remarkably different narrative accounts of the empty tomb and appearances of a resurrected Jesus. Matthew 28 adds another earthquake to accompany the appearance of an (unambiguous) angel who rolled away the stone and the women went to tell the other associates, though not before an appearance by Jesus who is then worshiped. In addition to explaining away a counternarrative that had been likely circulating about Jesus' resurrection (i.e., the claim his body had been stolen by Jesus' associates), Matthew's Gospel concludes by grounding emerging Christian theology and inclusion of non-Jews in the story of the resurrection of Jesus:

> Now the eleven disciples went to Galilee, to the mountain to which Jesus had directed them. When they saw him, they worshipped him; but some doubted. And Jesus came and said to them, "All authority in heaven and on earth has been given to me. Go therefore and make disciples of all nations, baptizing them in the name of the Father and of the Son and of the Holy Spirit, and teaching them to obey everything that I have commanded you. And remember, I am with you always, to the end of the age." (Matt. 28.16-20)

Luke 24 includes more details still. Now we have not one, but two men in dazzling clothes (presumably angels). These figures not only explain that Jesus had risen but change the story. Jesus would no longer meet his other associates in Galilee in the near future, rather this was something that had happened already in the past: "Remember how he told you, while he was still in Galilee, that the Son of Man must be handed over to sinners, and be crucified, and on the third day rise again" (Luke 24.6-7). Luke does this because he directly changes and contradicts Mark by locating an extended account of resurrection appearances in and around Jerusalem. Jerusalem appears central to Luke's theological geography over the course of Luke-Acts as a whole: by locating Christian origins after Jesus' death in Jerusalem and then moving out to the heart of the Empire in Rome, the author constructs a spatial narrative of Christianity radiating out around the Greco-Roman world. Luke also includes an additional story about Peter running to the tomb and looking in.

Whether independent from the Synoptics or not (there is no firm consensus among scholars), John takes the resurrection appearances of Jesus in a different direction again. In John 20.1-21, Mary Magdalene immediately tells Peter *and* a "beloved disciple," with the latter outpacing Peter to the tomb to see the results, though he graciously allows Peter to go in first. Jesus then appears to Mary Magdalene and then to the others. John also includes the famous story of the "doubting Thomas" who had to inspect the wounds of Jesus to believe. When he gets his confirmation by inserting his protruding finger into Jesus' wound, Thomas answered, "My Lord and my God!" and Jesus responded, "Have you believed because you have seen me? Blessed are those who have not seen and yet have come to believe" (John 20.26-28). Probably written in the last decade of the first century, John's Gospel here justifies the inclusion of new believers joining the movement decades after the death of Jesus who themselves had not "seen" the risen Jesus. It is apparent John's account of the resurrection is molded to meet the emerging theological needs of his readers. Indeed, immediately following the story of Thomas is a summary statement of John's purpose for writing: "these [signs] are written so that you may come to believe that Jesus is the Messiah, the Son of God, and that through believing you may have life in his name" (John 20:31).

After what looks like the end of John's Gospel, John 21 has a series of encore appearances: Jesus appears in Galilee with a story of a miraculous catch of fish, he orders Peter to look after the flock and hints at his likely martyrdom, and Jesus provides an explanation about why the Second Coming had not yet taken place. If the story about Peter's authority and the claim about the delay in the Second Coming of Jesus were much earlier, they would have possibly found their way into the other Gospels. Moreover, they are stories which reflect developments long after the death of Jesus. The hint about Peter's martyrdom (John 21.18-19) reflects a tradition emerging at the turn of the second century that Peter was executed (in Rome, according to other traditions) rather than the historical likelihood that he died of natural causes in the mid-first century.[20] As with 2 Peter 3, a text from roughly the same period as John, the indefinite postponement of the Second Coming in John 21.23 is an instance of rewriting earlier millenarian predictions after they had not come to pass: "the rumor spread in the community that this disciple would not die. Yet Jesus did not say to him that he would not die, but, 'If it is my will that he remain until I come, what is that to you?'"

The evidence for what likely took place after Jesus' burial, then, is a complete mess. The Gospel accounts of Jesus' resurrection are so thoroughly written up in light of later concerns faced by the church decades after Jesus' death they are of little use in reconstructing what may or may not have happened. The Gospel writers grounded their anxieties and theological concerns in a central belief in emerging Christianity: the resurrection of Jesus. It would be premature, however, to conclude that Jesus' associates did not experience what they thought were post-mortem appearances. Rather, the Gospel accounts gesture toward one thing we do know: despite all the contradictions and elaborations, the first associates sincerely believed God had risen Jesus from the dead, and many believed they had also seen him.

The best evidence for this is from Paul, and it is arguably as good a piece of evidence we have for the earliest days of the movement:

> For I handed on to you as of first importance what I in turn had received: that Christ died for our sins in accordance with the scriptures, and that he was buried, and that he was raised on the third day in accordance with the scriptures, and that he appeared to Cephas [Peter], then to the twelve. Then he appeared to more than five hundred brothers at one time, most of whom are still alive, though some have died. Then he appeared to James, then to all the apostles. Last of all, as to someone untimely born, he appeared also to me. (1 Cor. 15.3-8)

Paul has provided his own first-hand eyewitness account and referred to many more eyewitness accounts of people who were still alive and could verify such claims. The tradition of Jesus' death and resurrection had itself been "received" by Paul who as of first importance "handed (it) on" to the Corinthian assembly which he had founded several years prior to writing this letter in the mid-50s CE. A powerful case can be thus made that the tradition of post-mortem appearances of Jesus was very early and genuinely believed.

Some argue that the language of being "risen" in Paul's account typically assumes a body being raised up ("that he was buried, that he was raised") in the sense it would leave a tomb (or a place in a tomb) empty. This is certainly possible, but it is not an argument that shows the necessity for an empty tomb (or an equivalent space in a tomb). Mark 16.1-8 and 1 Corinthians 15.3-8 are the oldest independent traditions we have, and they do not provide much support for the argument that an empty space in a tomb was a known idea circulating in the immediate aftermath of Jesus' burial. Mark suspiciously says the women told no one about the missing body (which could, conceivably, be Mark's explanation of why no one knew where this tomb was), and Paul only provides evidence for people experiencing "appearances" of Jesus, not an empty tomb. As we saw above, without the Gospel accounts one might conclude a lower-class individual like Jesus was simply buried in the ground. As this is all the evidence we have for the discovery of an empty (slot in a) tomb, it is not particularly useful for historical reconstruction in this respect.

A common argument is that as women were the first witnesses at the tomb then this is a sign of its historical accuracy because women were supposedly deemed unreliable witnesses in early Judaism and the Greco-Roman world, and so it is unlikely it would be invented. This argument is not as strong as it may first appear. To begin with, according to Mark, women were not in fact the *first* witnesses to the empty tomb at all, rather it was a young man. (Though perhaps understanding Mark correctly, only Matthew explicitly says this man was an angel.) It could be argued women were still regarded as the first witnesses and Mark placed the young man in the tomb to alleviate the difficulty of women being deemed problematic witnesses. But were they regarded as problematic? It depends. It is true, as some apologists like to point out, that the elite male Josephus implores the testimony of women (as well as slaves) not be admitted (*Antiquities* 4.219). The Mosaic law, however, does not specify the gender requirements of witnesses in legal hearings (Deut. 17.6; 19.15), and while it probably did assume they would be men (given the patriarchal constraints of the time), Josephus' direction implies that by the first century, at least, there were some anxieties that women and slaves might be used as legitimate witnesses in legal hearings, hence his needing to specifically react against it.

Even so, witnesses to an empty slot in a tomb was not the same kind of legal category, though predictably the gender of witnesses could be contested and controversial (cf. Origen, *Contra Celsus* 2.55). In any case, we know a relative degree of prominence for women was not a problem for Mark. Indeed, when the men scattered prior to the crucifixion, Mark was left only with the remaining female associates (Mark 15.40-41). Other Jewish texts include heroic women, such as Judith or Esther, who played prominent roles despite being implicated by patriarchy. Given this, could not the early followers of Jesus after his death have done the same and written stories about heroic women in a given context? Yes. Could other followers have taken a more misogynistic line? Yes (as is perhaps implied in Luke and John's accounts). Could both tendencies have existed in this movement? Yes. The argument about problematic women only works if we hold to an old fashioned, monolithic view of beliefs about gender in early Judaism and the ancient world.

For historical reconstruction of the events after Jesus' death, we should focus on the earliest appearances in the earliest sources. The claim found in Paul, and quoted above, that Jesus appeared to Peter, the Twelve, members of the wider movement, over five hundred associates, Jesus' brother, and Paul is the earliest "eyewitness" material available (1 Cor. 15.3-8). We can make educated guesses about what people claimed they saw. For instance, we have later narrative accounts of Paul's vision in Acts. Here is the most famous account:

Now as he was going along and approaching Damascus, suddenly a light from heaven flashed around him. He fell to the ground and heard a voice saying to him, "Saul, Saul, why do you persecute me?" He asked, "Who are you, Lord?" The reply came, "I am Jesus, whom you are persecuting. But get up and enter the city, and you will be told what you are to do." The men who were travelling with him stood speechless because they heard the voice but saw no one. (Acts 9.3-7; cf. Acts 9.13-19; 22.16-21; Gal. 1.11–16)

Irrespective of whether Luke got this report from Paul, or it came from the imagination of the author or reported tradition, it still gives insight into how visions might have been experienced or understood. Indeed, a bright light and an authoritative voice are common features of visions cross culturally. Given what we end up with in the Gospel resurrection accounts, it is likely that some would have had visions where they sincerely experienced the risen Jesus resembling his familiar physical body, though (as the Gospel accounts imply) one that was notably different from the usual in that this body was understood to vanish and reappear (cf. Mark 9.2-8). Understandings of "ghost"/"spirit" and "human" overlapped or could be easily confused in the ancient world (cf. Mark 6.49). Indeed, Luke's Gospel stresses that the resurrected Jesus was *not* a ghost (Luke 24.36-43), no doubt because reports of the resurrected Jesus sounded somewhat ghostly.

The contents of such visions across cultures also differ according to local contexts and are, not surprisingly, guided by local cultural assumptions. In the case of the visions of a post-mortem Jesus, pre-existing traditions of resurrection, and especially traditions about the resurrection of Jewish martyrs, were an important influence not only on possible expectations of vindication, but also on the *interpretation* of any visionary experiences. The following account from one of the important texts associated with the Maccabean martyrs (see Chapter 8) offers a template for such beliefs:

And when he was at his last breath, he said, "You accursed wretch, you dismissed us from this present life, but the king of the universe will raise us up to an everlasting renewal of life, because we have died for his laws"... "I got these (hands) from Heaven and because of his laws I disdain them, and from him I hope to get them back again." (2 Macc. 7.9, 11)

Texts like this one provided the kind of local cultural assumptions that would shape the content of a vision and why those who saw the post-mortem Jesus could claim he still had a physical body in some way. These assumptions were also influenced by more general Jewish ideas about bodily resurrection from the dead. Stories like the resurrection of the dead saints in Matthew 27.52-53 mentioned above reveal the pre-existing cultural ideas that influenced how visionary experiences of dead associates might be interpreted. Raised bodies could leave tombs, enter the holy city, and appear to many.

Despite its lack of historicity, the resurrection of the dead saints in Matthew points to an important cultural understanding for Jesus' resurrection: it was not thought of as an isolated event. In first-century Judaism, those groups which believed in resurrection, such as the Pharisees, thought of it not as a separate event for each individual at death but as a corporate event in which God would raise all of the elect at the end times. The earliest associates of Jesus believed he had been raised and thus concluded the end of the age had already begun. The resurrection of allegiant saints would follow Jesus' resurrection and was, in fact, guaranteed by God's resurrection of Jesus. Accordingly, Paul understood Jesus' resurrection not as a one-off event in history but as the "first fruits" (1 Cor. 15.23) of a general resurrection which was tethered to the revolutionary millenarianism of the early movement. As Paul wrote immediately after mention of Jesus' resurrection, following the Second Coming of Christ, "comes the end, when he [Christ] hands over the kingdom to God the Father, after he has destroyed every ruler and every authority and power. For he must reign until he has put all his enemies under his feet" (1. Cor. 15.24-25).

Whatever the cause behind these visions of a post-mortem Jesus (and on the specific cause, as critical historians, we cannot be sure), the associates interpreted their experiences within a pre-existing cultural framework that was primed with millennial enthusiasm and expectation. They believed God had vindicated the martyrdom of Jesus by raising him back to life and thus had inaugurated the transformation to the next age as well as the general resurrection of the dead. This was a dramatic and fantastical consequence of a ransom paid for the many. The end times had arrived, and the world would be finally turned on its head. It was, as one scholar puts it, the day the revolution began. Or was it?

Chapter 11

What Happened Next?

The Failed Revolution of the Jesus Movement

A peculiar fetish in late capitalist society is found in the notion of a "change agent." Such individuals are recognized for instigating or managing change within an organization. Changes implemented, however, are generally superficial, perhaps leading to slight increases in productivity or revenue. Radical innovations that would dramatically disrupt business practices, such as reversing the hierarchies between managers and employees, are obviously not tolerated or rewarded by the careerists in power. Under late-stage capitalism, so-called change agents are reactionary instruments that facilitate the perpetuation, rather than the overturning, of the status quo.

A similar overemphasis on isolated and entrepreneurial initiatives of atomized individuals endures in the writing of bourgeois history. E. P. Sanders ended his influential life of Jesus by claiming the "perhaps most important" thing to emerge from the historical reconstruction of Jesus is that "we know how much he inspired his followers, who sometimes themselves did not understand him, but who were so loyal to him that they changed history."[1] Our life of Jesus has demonstrated the exact opposite. The most important thing to emerge from our historical reconstruction is how Jesus' life was, as all hitherto history is, engulfed in the history of class conflict.

In direct contrast to Sanders above, Jesus and his associates were changed *by* and *through* history from below. The Jesus movement emerged not merely due to magnetic or heroic individuals changing history *per se*, but rather was generated by the changing economic landscape of first-century Palestine. The Jewish peasantry were bound by, and responding to, real-existing material premises and definite conditions interwoven with their historical life-circumstances. This gave rise to pivotal conceptions, ideas, and activities of the Jesus movement. The popular attraction of the movement owed as much to these changing material conditions as it did to pre-existing social and religious networks or structures, and indeed to the religious organizers it helped to inspire and form.

We do not doubt the relative importance of charismatic individuals as suitable conduits for group interests. But the effective elimination of materialist explanations, and an overreliance on the individual genius of so-called Great Men, is typical of the cottage industry of historical Jesus research, and it needs to end. Likewise, attractive or edgy claims that Jesus' death was "the day the revolution began," or that Jesus' associates found in his ministry, and especially in his resurrection, a new commissioning that subsequently "changed history," should be avoided for their similarly reductionistic approach to history.

Of course, on one level Jesus' associates and those who spoke of their visions of Jesus after his death did indeed keep the movement alive. But "changing history" can mean different things to different people. And ultimately, nothing much changed, at least not along the lines the early movement had envisaged. The end-times did not come about. Nor did a reversal of the material hierarchies in Galilee and Judea. Put simply: the millenarian manifesto of the Jesus movement culminated in a failed revolution.

Walter Benjamin famously expressed the thesis that behind every case of fascism there is a failed revolution. When reapplied to pre-capitalist societies, something of this observation rings true concerning the broader history of Christianity, stuck as it were between "a complex tension of reaction and revolution."[2] Rather than overturning the hierarchies of the imperial world, Christianity would later become the ideological handmaiden of the Roman Empire. It would drive anti-Jewish hatred and provide a foundation for reactionary violence. In the longer run, it would also feature as an ideological basis for European colonialism and various expressions of patriarchy which have still not been fully deconstructed. But alongside this, Christianity provided credible and compelling justification for numerous peasant revolts and resistance movements. And let us not forget the powerful impact Christianity has made on the development of radical movements in the modern age, responding to the ravages of capitalism: from abolitionism to Christian socialism and liberation theology, to name but a few prominent examples.

If we are to look at the bigger materialist picture outlined in the opening chapter, then, the Jesus movement's initial revolutionary impulses were subsumed into the longer historical materialist process itself, as different class antagonisms and technological developments drove the transformation from ancient societies into feudal ones and feudal ones into capitalism. Christianity provided ideological justification for these changes and provided ideological opposition to these changes, as well as shades of difference in-between. What we want to do in this concluding chapter, then, is to underscore how Christianity became such a dominant reactionary and revolutionary ideology. We do this by looking back to the inherent tension between these opposing and contradictory forces within the ideological texture of the early Jesus movement itself.

Spread of Christianity

One of the crucial decisions emerging from the Jesus movement and the material conditions in Galilee and Judea was the "mission to the rich." Coupled with the concern for poverty, an emphasis on saving the wealthy laid the ideological framework for a movement inclusive of people of different social standings and competing class interests. Ultimately, the movement's base would shift from a mostly rural constituency of peasants and fisherman to urban environments with a much greater diversity of people and material issues. Along the way, the movement's original concerns were modified or adapted to make sense of the Jesus movement's peculiar brand of "revolutionary millenarianism" in these new habitats: it would become millenarianism with urban characteristics.

This shift from rural to urban took place very quickly after Jesus' death. If the book of Acts is to be believed, Jerusalem immediately became a base of operations from which the movement sent out apostles to other urban centers, first in Palestine and Syria, but then all over the Roman Empire. It is worth observing that our primary sources for Christian origins, even when describing rural situations such as in the Gospels, do so through the lens of urban habitats. Even some of our earliest sources, Paul's letters (written mostly in the 50s) were predominantly addressed to millenarian assemblies in urban centers (and in the case of Romans and 1-2 Corinthians, major urban centers).

What resulted was a significant shift through the Jesus movement's emphasis on saving rich "sinners." We saw in Chapter 5 how this term referred to oppressive rich lawbreakers, but, crucially, non-Jews were categorized by the same term; in other words, they were behaving in the exact same manner as non-Jews were "sinners" by default (cf. Gal. 2.15: "We ourselves are Jews by birth and not Gentile sinners"). In such contexts, "sinners" was thus a term to stereotypically describe non-Jews and the non-Jewish nations as oppressive, rich, greedy idolators who acted beyond the law and as if there were no Jewish God.[3] In urban environments, especially cosmopolitan ones, one's "neighbor" was no longer necessarily another Jew, but more likely a non-Jew, and thus a lawbreaker and a sinner. But the edict to "love your neighbor as yourself" (Mark 12.31a) was still strongly felt.

This provided a compelling impetus for active inclusion of

non-Jews into the movement that emerged after Jesus' death. Such views of bringing gentiles onboard mapped onto pre-existing Jewish understandings of the end times where righteous non-Jews were sometimes incorporated into the salvific scheme. Again, we do not have to resort to individual magnetism, spectacular miracles, charismatic missionaries, or soaring rhetoric to account for how the movement soon included a noticeable number of non-Jews in its ranks. A positive result of sociological studies of conversion and the spread of ideas is that social networks, such as the workplace, friendships, and wider geographical contacts, in tandem with other material forces and factors, lay much of the groundwork.[4] Already in place around the Greco-Roman world were synagogues which welcomed interested non-Jews (sometimes referred to as "Godfearers") who had varying levels of attachment to and interest in Jewish law.

Non-Jews simultaneously had different affiliations beyond synagogues, whether trade associations or their own households. These other networks brought with them countervailing influences. Paul gives some indication of different levels of attachment among the movement in Corinth where he had to deal with Jesus' teaching on divorce in the case of believing and unbelieving partners (1 Cor. 7.10-16). By analogy, those who were interested in emergent Christianity through Jewish synagogue networks would have behaved in a different manner in different networks where issues such as avoidance of pork, resting on the Sabbath, or talk of adult male circumcision would have been strange. We can imagine a situation where interested non-Jews would, as a matter of routine, respect Jewish law in synagogues, while in another context eat pork, praise another god, or work on the Sabbath. By the 40s CE, these networks had thrown up the question of observance of the law in relation to non-Jews as it started to become a significant issue which Paul and his associates had to deal with.

It is notable too that we have stories of women interested in

Judaism (Josephus, *War* 2.560-61; cf. *Antiquities* 18.81-84; 20.34-48), because for adult men circumcision was a risk to life itself, though some were still interested even if it meant circumcision (e.g., *Antiquities* 20.34-48). While women with means to support the Jesus party played an important part in the early spread of the movement (cf. e.g., Rom. 16.1-2; 1 Cor 1.11; Col. 4.15; Acts 12.12-17; Acts 16.14-15),[5] the possibility for interested non-Jewish men not having to undergo a painful and potentially deadly circumcision was a useful option known in some branches of early Judaism (though not undisputed), and one taken up by factions in the emerging Christian movement. Of course, this issue was hardly without controversy within the movement as Paul's letters to the Galatians and Romans would show.

For all the complexities surrounding Paul's theology and the clashes over what to do with relations and eating arrangements among Jews and non-Jews, the idea that non-Jews were accepted as full and equal members of the movement would soon become non-controversial as it began to work out (in different ways) whether it was to be understood as a primarily Jewish or non-Jewish organization. Language of an alternative, non-biological family inherited from early Judaism and the earliest Jesus movement became useful for the emerging movement in expressing and constructing relationships. The stories about specifically Jewish purity laws in the Jesus tradition had no immediate concern for non-Jews (who were outside the category of Jewish impurity laws), but they partly survived because a heavy emphasis on morality matched stereotypes about non-Jewish behavior and provided the grounding for Christian ethics, identity, and group boundary-making in the ancient world.

God of Empire

Meanwhile, building on Jesus as an elevated figure within the movement and the visions of Jesus in the period following his death, speculations about his person and his connection to divine forces took off. This included the belief that he was an emperor-like figure who would return soon to command the world, itself an outworking of the predictions of the kingdom/ empire/dictatorship of God. As Paul put it, "God also highly exalted him and gave him the name that is above every name, so that at the name of Jesus every knee should bend, in heaven and on earth and under the earth, and every tongue should confess that Jesus Christ is Lord" (Phil. 2.9-11).

One of the major shifts in the development of the Jesus movement is that by the end of the first century it had transformed from a purely or primarily Jewish movement into becoming a majority non-Jewish or gentile one, and in some cases, an anti-Jewish one. And we can push the notion of the Jesus movement's failed revolution further for a moment by detecting some of the chilling "fascist-like" tendencies that gestated toward the end of this early period. We need go no further than John's Gospel, written toward the end of the first century, to observe how in some strands of emerging Christian thought a proto-fascist ideology developed that replaced the initial revolutionary impulses that had failed to take root.

We mentioned in the opening chapter the Gospel of John's curious obsession with denigrating a character group known as "the Jews."[6] Not unlike the reactionary political ideology of twentieth-century Nazism, the Gospel of John similarly insisted Jesus' followers must have a pure bloodline (i.e., be born of the correct Father, John 3.1-15). By prioritizing the "spiritual purity" of Jesus' followers, John's text relied on a peculiar kind of racial logic: Jewish ethnicity was replaced with a new form of divine ethnicity in which the elect must be "born again" of the same Father. Near the beginning of the Gospel this logic is clearly spelled out: "to all who received him, to those who believed in his name, he gave the right to become children of God—children born not of natural descent, nor of human decision or a husband's will, but born of God" (John 1.12-13).

Amid the complex questions of identity and whether, how, or the extent to which this new movement was to be understood as "Jewish" (or "anti-Jewish"), was the idea that Jesus was to be *equated* with God, a point which was most evidently developed in John where elevated theological claims are tellingly framed in disputes with "the Jews" (e.g., John 5.17-18; 10.29-33). The Gospel of John's dramatic denigration and suspicion of opposing groups likely reflected sociological and possibly "sectarian" realities behind the text. High among the controversies was an intra-Jewish disagreement about whether Jesus "and the Father are one" (John 10.30), though now showing signs of the movement moving beyond Jewish self-identity.

As a reactionary text, the Gospel of John thus constructed uncompromising boundaries between true believers and outsiders. But whereas the revolutionary millenarianism of the early movement was focused on the reversal of the material hierarchies of Galilee and Judea at the end times, John's Gospel focused on the "spiritual" truth of the "good news" in the here and now. Those who would not consent to John's assessment of Jesus were to be left out in the dark, deprived of light and direction (John 12.35-36). They remained in the "world" below and would die in their sins (John 8.23-24). By contrast, members of the community were destined to move up spiritually. In the purest of totalitarian language, John's Jesus declared, "I am the way, and the truth, and the life. No one comes to the Father except through me" (John 14.6).

But the other side of the coin to an overly exclusive worldview is an overly inclusive one. That Jesus was to be equated *with* the God of the universe meant that, in time, Christianity was seen to provide a theological system which was compatible with, and appropriate for, a Roman Empire covering a range of colonized peoples and unified by trade routes and communication networks. It is often thought the pre-Christian Roman Empire was "polytheistic" (many gods) in contrast to Christianity and

Judaism which emphasized (not without controversy in the case of Christianity) "monotheism" (one God). These descriptions are not always helpful. For example, Jewish and Christian ideas about an overarching God sounded a lot like ideas about Zeus or Greek philosophical speculations while ideas about angels and elevated human figures sounded a lot like the lesser gods in other Greco-Roman ways of understanding the supernatural world.[7]

Nevertheless, Christianity had a notion of an overarching and unifying divine rulership which did not necessarily prioritize one nation or ethnic grouping as Judaism did, so long as one was "in Christ." Christianity was, over the second and third centuries, spreading through networks of friends of friends of friends until it was large enough and credible enough to become the dominant religion of the Roman Empire. It is telling that when Julian the Emperor (or "Apostate") tried to reinstate the old supernatural system during his time as Emperor (361-363 CE), he saw local gods as manifestations of the creator, Moses' god of one people as too parochial and restricting for an empire, and Christian conceptions of the divine as not even matching Moses' lower standard of an imperial god because Christians were understood to worship two or three gods.[8] Julian may have wanted to show that Christianity was ideologically unsuitable for the scope and reach of the Roman Empire but to the historian it reveals the opposite: it did precisely this and would soon resume as the successful religion of empire.

Even though Christianity became the handmaiden of empire, it could still provide the language of resistance where needed. In Medieval Europe, Christianity came to justify the feudal system and monarchical social hierarchies, but just as equally justified those peasant millenarians and insurgents who attempted to usurp the existing order, as the Jesus movement had done before. The Protestant split from Catholicism, as well as the colonial drive to go out and "make disciples of all nations" (Matt. 28.19), may have aided the transformation from feudalism to capitalism and the ongoing consolidation of the emerging middle class, but the old concerns of millenarians and insurrectionists were taken up in new ways, including their absorption into the agendas of socialist and communist parties, and new Protestant (and Catholic) oppositional thinking emerged too. The hardened masculinity of the early Jesus movement, inherited from its wider patriarchal context, never really left during these transitions from one mode of production to the next. Only since the latter half of the twentieth century did a sustained feminist investigation into Christianity's entanglement with the patriarchy begin. Yet the ways gender and power were negotiated by this socially deviant movement has provided sustenance and impetus for those on the margins in a variety of contexts and situations. Of course, any number of interests and ideological positions in between have been justified by multiple variations of Christianity because, in "the West" at least, it has formed the dominant ideology for well over a millennium.

Indeed, it is remarkable to behold that what began as the parochial ideologies of the disaffected peasantry in Galilee and Judea would in turn come to ground a dominant global ideology, one that continues to be embedded in subtle ways within the now capitalist mode of production of our own age.[9] The historical Jesus is part of the deep ideological fabric that has simultaneously framed the world but has also generated forces to change it. For this reason, understanding the life of Jesus as a life in class conflict is inescapable to appreciating the class struggles of today. To paraphrase Marx's eleventh thesis on Feuerbach, however, the point is not simply to understand the world in various ways, rather the point is to change it. Perhaps agents of radical change are what we need after all.

Endnotes

Chapter 1

1. See further, e.g., John Dominic Crossan, *The Historical Jesus: The Life of a Mediterranean Jewish Peasant* (San Francisco: Harper, 1991); Douglas E. Oakman, *Jesus and the Peasants* (Eugene: Cascade, 2008); Roland Boer and Christina Petterson, *Time of Troubles: A New Economic Framework for Early Christianity* (Minneapolis: Fortress, 2017).

2. And the classic treatment is by Eric J. Hobsbawm in *Primitive Rebels: Studies in Archaic Forms of Social Movement in the 19th and 20th Centuries* (Manchester: Manchester University Press, 1959) and *Bandits* (London: Weidenfeld and Nicolson, 1969). The classic treatments of the historical Jesus and his context in the tradition of Hobsbawm are Richard A. Horsley with John S. Hanson, *Bandits, Prophets, and Messiahs: Popular Movements in the Time of Jesus* (Minneapolis: Winston, 1985) and Richard A. Horsley, *Jesus and the Spiral of Violence: Popular Jewish Resistance in Roman Palestine* (San Francisco: Harper & Row, 1987).

3. See now Helen K. Bond, *The First Biography of Jesus: Genre and Meaning in Mark's Gospel* (Grand Rapids: Eerdmans, 2020).

4. Halvor Moxnes, *Jesus and the Rise of Nationalism: A New Quest for the Nineteenth-Century Historical Jesus* (London: I.B. Tauris, 2012), 26.

5. See, e.g., Larry Siedentop, *Inventing the Individual: The Origins of Western-Liberalism* (London: Penguin, 2015).

6. For the latest theories see Eve-Marie Becker, Helen K. Bond, and Catrin H. Williams (eds.), *John's Transformation of Mark* (London: T&T Clark, 2021).

7. For the critique, see Chris Keith and Anthony Le Donne (eds.), *Jesus, Criteria, and the Demise of Authenticity* (London:

T&T Clark, 2012).

8. Karl Marx and Friedrich Engels, *The German Ideology: Parts I & III* (New York: International Publishers Inc, 1939), 39.

Chapter 2

1. See the argument in Alan Saxby, *James, Brother of Jesus, and the Jerusalem Church: A Radical Exploration of Christian Origins* (Eugene: Wipf & Stock, 2015).

2. See, e.g., Jane Schaberg, *The Illegitimacy of Jesus: A Feminist Theological Interpretation of the Infancy Narratives* (San Francisco: Harper & Row, 1987).

3. Maurice Casey, *Jesus of Nazareth: An Independent Historian's Account of His Life and Teaching* (London: Bloomsbury/T&T Clark, 2010), 158-62.

4. Chris Keith, *Jesus against the Scribal Elite: The Origins of The Conflict* (Ada: Baker Academic, 2014).

5. E. P. Sanders, *The Historical Figure of Jesus* (London: Penguin, 1993), 21.

6. Morten Hørning Jensen, *Herod Antipas in Galilee* (Tübingen: Mohr Siebeck, 2006); Morten Hørning Jensen, "Herod Antipas in Galilee: Friend or Foe of the Historical Jesus?", *Journal for the Study of the Historical Jesus* 5 (2007): 7-32; Helen K. Bond, *The Historical Jesus: A Guide for the Perplexed* (London: Bloomsbury/T&T Clark, 2012), 75-77.

7. G.E.M. de Ste. Croix, *The Class Struggle in the Ancient Greek World: From the Archaic Age to the Arab Conquests* (London: Duckworth, 1981); Roland Boer, "Marxism and the Spatial Analysis of Early Christianity: The Contribution of G.E.M. de Ste. Croix," *Religion* 41 (2011): 1-20; Deane Galbraith, "Interpellation, Not Interpolation: Reconsidering Textual Disunity in Numbers 13–14 as Variant Articulations of a Single Ideology," *Bible and Critical Theory* 10 (2014): 29-48; Roland Boer and Christina Petterson, *Time of Troubles: A New Economic Framework for Early Christianity* (Minneapolis:

Fortress Press, 2017).

8. Jodi Magness, "How Romanized Was Galilee in the Time of Jesus?" in Markus Tiwald and Jürgen K. Zangenberg (eds.), *Early Christian Encounters with Town and Countryside: Essays on the Urban and Rural Worlds of Early Christianity* (Göttingen: Vandenhoeck & Ruprecht, 2021), 113-128.

9. Sean Freyne, *Jesus, a Jewish Galilean: A New Reading of the Story* (London: T&T Clark, 2004), 46-47.

10. Eric Hobsbawm, *Uncommon People: Resistance, Rebellion and Jazz* (London: Abacus 1998), 224.

11. de Ste. Croix, *The Class Struggle in the Ancient Greek World*, 427.

12. Sarah E. Rollens, *Framing Social Criticism in the Jesus Movement: The Ideological Project of the Sayings Gospel Q* (Tübingen: Mohr Siebeck, 2014).

13. The classic treatment of this issue (which we develop here) is Gerhard E. Lenski, *Power and Privilege: A Theory of Social Stratification* (New York: McGraw-Hill, 1966), 263-65.

14. James Crossley, *Spectres of John Ball: The Peasants' Revolt in English Political History, 1381-2020* (Sheffield: Equinox, 2022).

Chapter 3

1. Two exceptions, the former arguing for lower-class and the latter arguing for upper-class, are John Dominic Crossan, *Jesus: A Revolutionary Biography* (San Francisco: Harper, 1994), 36–38; Johan Strijdom, "The Social Class of the Baptist: Dissident Retainer or Peasant Millennialist?" *Teologiese Studies/Theological Studies* 60, no. 1/2 (2004). See also Robert J. Myles, "John the Baptist in Memory, Judaism and Historical Materialism," *Journal for the Study of the Historical Jesus* 19 (2021): 62-73.

2. See Joan E. Taylor, *The Immerser: John the Baptist within Second Temple Judaism* (Grand Rapids: Eerdmans, 1997),

109-110.

3. Maurice Casey went one step further and argued that an Aramaic reconstruction bolsters this argument. See Maurice Casey, *An Aramaic Approach to Q: Sources for the Gospels of Matthew and Luke* (Cambridge: Cambridge University Press, 2002), 105-15.

4. Roger D. Aus, *Water into Wine and the Beheading of John the Baptist: Early Jewish-Christian Interpretation of Esther 1 in John 2:1-11 and Mark 6:17-29* (Atlanta: Scholars Press, 1988); James Crossley, *Jesus and the Chaos of History: Redirecting the Quest for the Historical Jesus* (Oxford: Oxford University Press, 2015), 147-160.

5. See further Nathan L. Shedd, *A Dangerous Parting: The Beheading of John the Baptist in Early Christianity* (Waco: Baylor University Press, 2021).

Chapter 4

1. Or *kyriarchal.* See e.g., Elisabeth Schüssler Fiorenza, *Jesus and the Politics of Interpretation* (New York: Continuum, 2001).

2. See the fuller discussion on "Magdala and the Fishing Industry" in Richard Bauckham, *Magdala of Galilee: A Jewish City in the Hellenistic and Roman Period* (Waco: Baylor University Press, 2018), 185-268. See also K. C. Hanson, "The Galilean Fishing Economy and the Jesus Tradition," *Biblical Theology Bulletin* 27 (1997): 99-111.

3. Jonathan L. Reed, "Archaeological Contributions to the Study of Jesus and the Gospels," in Amy-Jill Levine, Dale C. Allison, and John Dominic Crossan (eds.) *The Historical Jesus in Context* (Princeton: Princeton University Press, 2006), 51.

4. Maurice Casey, *Jesus of Nazareth: An Independent Historian's Account of His Life and Teaching* (London: Bloomsbury/T&T Clark, 2010), pp. 431-32.

5. For the latter, see e.g., John P. Meier, *A Marginal Jew: Rethinking the Historical Jesus*, vol 3. (New York: Doubleday, 2001), 19-39.

6. Joan E. Taylor, "Jesus as News: Crises of Health and Overpopulation in Galilee," *Journal for the Study of the New Testament* 44 (2021): 8–30.

7. See, e.g., Josephus, *War* 2.136; *Jewish Antiquities* 8.45-49; m. *Berakhot* 5.1, 5; y. *Berakhot* 5,6/2(9d); b. *Berakhot* 34b; cf. Philo, *On the Contemplative Life* 2; Josephus, *Antiquities* 14.22-24; m. *Taanit* 3.8. The classic contextualization of Jesus among contemporary and near-contemporary healers, exorcists, and miracles workers is Geza Vermes, *Jesus the Jew* (London: SCM, 1973), 58-82.

8. For an important work on the role of gender in healings in the Jesus movement, see: Elaine M. Wainwright, *Women Healing/Healing Women: The Genderization of Healing in Early Christianity* (London: Equinox, 2006).

9. Joan E. Taylor, "Missing Magdala and the Name of Mary 'Magdalene,'" *Palestine Exploration Quarterly* 146/3 (2014), 205-223.

10. For more detailed discussion of anthropological understandings of phenomena such as healings, sickness, exorcisms, as well as related comparisons with "shamanic" figures, see e.g., John Dominic Crossan, *The Historical Jesus: The Life of a Mediterranean Jewish Peasant* (San Francisco: Harper, 1991), 303-353; Stevan L. Davies, *Jesus the Healer: Possession, Trance, and the Origins of Christianity* (London: SCM Press, 1995); Pieter F. Craffert, *The Life of a Galilean Shaman: Jesus of Nazareth in Anthropological-Historical Perspective* (Cambridge: James Clarke & Co., 2008); Maurice Casey, *Jesus of Nazareth: An Independent Historian's Account of His Life and Teaching* (London: Bloomsbury/T&T Clark, 2010), 237-279.

Chapter 5

1. The classic treatment of apocalyptic literature is John J. Collins, *The Apocalyptic Imagination: An Introduction to Jewish Apocalyptic Literature* (3rd ed, Grand Rapids: Eerdmans, 2016). For a general application of "apocalypticism" as a cross-cultural phenomenon, see CenSAMM, "Apocalypticism," in James Crossley and Alastair Lockhart (eds.), *Critical Dictionary of Apocalyptic and Millenarian Movements* (2021), www.cdamm.org/articles/apocalypticism.

2. See now Anthony Keddie, *Revelations of Ideology: Apocalyptic Class Politics in Early Roman Palestine* (Leiden: Brill, 2018).

3. Randall W. Reed, *A Clash of Ideologies: Marxism, Liberation Theology, and Apocalypticism in New Testament Studies* (Eugene: Pickwick, 2010), 45-46, 55.

4. Reed, *A Clash of Ideologies*, 52-54, 56.

5. Reed, *A Clash of Ideologies*, 95-98.

6. Dale C. Allison, *Constructing Jesus: Memory, Imagination and History* (London: SPCK, 2010), 180-81.

7. Warren Carter, *Matthew and Empire: Initial Explorations* (Harrisburg: Trinity Press International, 2001).

8. For Gospel texts, see, e.g., Mark 1.15; 9.1; 13.30, 33-37; Matt. 10.23; Matt. 25.1-13; Matt. 6.10//Luke 11.2; Matt. 23.34-35//Luke 11.49-51; Matt. 24.42-44//Luke 12.39-40; Matt. 24.45-51//Luke 12.42-46; Luke 12.35-38; 21.34-36; cf. Mark 15.43; Luke 2.25; *Thom.* 21, 111.

9. See further James Crossley, *Jesus and the Chaos of History: Redirecting the Life of the Historical Jesus* (Oxford: Oxford University Press, 2015), 67-71.

10. See, e.g., Deut. 28.1-14; Job 1.10; 42.10; Is. 3.10; Prov. 10.22; Tob. 12.9; Sir. 3.1, 6; 25.7-11; 35.13; 44.10-15; 51.27-30; Bar. 4.1.

11. See, e.g., CD 4.15-19; 1QS 11.1-2; *Ps. Sol.* 5.16; cf. *1 Enoch* 98.2; 102.9-11.

12. Luise Schottroff, "Das Magnificat und die älteste Tradition über Jesus von Nazareth," *Evangelische Theologie* 38 (1978): 298-313.

13. Richard J. Bauckham, "Rich Man and Lazarus: The Parable and the Parallels," *New Testament Studies* 37 (1991), 225-46.

14. Crossley, *Jesus and the Chaos of History*, 96-111.

15. *Testament of Abraham* [A] 10.13-15; *t. Qiddushin* 1.16; cf. Tobit 13.6; Wisd. 19.13; *Testament of Benjamin* 4.2; Pr. Man. 5-8; *Targum Is.* 28.24-25.

16. E. P. Sanders, *The Historical Figure of Jesus* (London: Penguin, 1993), 236.

17. The classic argument was made by Wilhelm Wrede, *The Messianic Secret* (Cambridge: James Clarke, 1971 [German original: 1901]).

18. See, e.g., *Ps. Sol.* 17; 4Q246 II 1-9; 1QM VI 4-6; 4Q252 V, 1-4; 4Q521 2 II 1-13; 11Q13 2.13; 2 Syr. Bar. 72.2-73.2.

19. Mark Fisher, *Capitalist Realism: Is There No Alternative?* (Winchester: Zer0 Books, 2009).

Chapter 6

1. R. T. France, *The Gospel according to Matthew: An Introduction and Commentary* (Leicester: InterVarsity, 1985), 160.

2. See further Robert J. Myles, *The Homeless Jesus in the Gospel of Matthew* (Sheffield: Sheffield Phoenix Press, 2014).

3. John P. Meier, *A Marginal Jew: Rethinking the Historical Jesus*, vol. 1 (New York: Doubleday, 1991), 8.

4. See further Robert J. Myles, "Fishing for Entrepreneurs in the Sea of Galilee? Unmasking Neoliberal Interpretation in Biblical Interpretation," in Robert J. Myles (ed.) *Class Struggle in the New Testament* (Lanham: Fortress Academic/ Lexington Books, 2019), 115-138.

5. Halvor Moxnes, *Putting Jesus in His Place: A Radical Vision of Household and Kingdom* (Louisville: WJK, 2003), 5; cf. Halvor Moxnes, *Memories of Jesus: A Journey through Time*

(Eugene: Cascade, 2021), 210-213.

6. Moxnes, *Jesus in His Place,* 97-98.

7. Christopher Hill, *The World Turned Upside Down: Radical Ideas During the English Revolution* (London: Penguin, 1972), 31.

8. Moxnes, *Jesus in His Place,* 46-107.

9. Dale C. Allison, *Constructing Jesus: Memory, Imagination and History* (London: SPCK, 2010), 135.

10. Maia Kotrosis, *Rethinking Early Christian Identity: Affect, Violence, and Belonging* (Minneapolis: Fortress Press, 2015), 51-53.

11. Colleen M. Conway, *Behold the Man: Jesus and Greco-Roman Masculinity* (Oxford: Oxford University Press, 2008).

12. For texts on women and assumptions of gendered roles, see, e.g., 1 Cor. 7.25-35; 11.2-16; 14.33-36; Eph. 5.21-33; 1 Tim. 5.3-16; 2 Tim. 3.6; Rev. 2.20-23; Irenaeus, *Against Heresies* 1.25.6.

13. Tom Wright, *The New Testament for Everyone* (London: SPCK, 2019), 366.

14. See, e.g., Sir. 4.10; Wisd. 2.17-18; *Ps. Sol.* 17.26-29; Philo, *Special Laws* 1.138; *Jubilees* 1.24-25; m. *Abot* 3.14; b. *Berakhot* 17b.

15. P. M. Casey, *Jewish Prophet to Gentile God: The Origins of New Testament Christology* (Cambridge: James Clarke, 1991), 44-46.

16. Carolyn Osiek and Margaret Y. MacDonald with Janet H. Tulloch, *A Woman's Place: House Churches in Earliest Christianity* (Minneapolis: Fortress, 2006), 144-63, 194-243.

Chapter 7

1. N. T. Wright, *Jesus and the Victory of God* (Minneapolis: Fortress, 1996), 291.

2. Wright, *Jesus and the Victory of God,* 594.

3. Cf. Lam. 3.30; 1QS 10.17-18; m. *Baba Qamma* 8.1; b. *Baba*

Qamma 83b-84a; *Targum Ps-J.* and *Targum Neof.* Ex. 21.24; *Mekhilta Ex.* 21.24 [III:67].

4. See further Robert J. Myles, "The Fetish for a Subversive Jesus," *Journal for the Study of the Historical Jesus* 14 (2016): 52-70.

5. For an overview, see John J. Collins, *Introduction to the Hebrew Bible*, 3rd ed (Minneapolis: Fortress Press, 2018), 53-69.

6. For a comprehensive exploration, see Dale C. Allison, *The New Moses: A Matthean Typology* (Minneapolis: Augsburg Fortress, 1994).

7. Whether "the Pharisees" (and/or "the Scribes") were Jesus' chief opponents in his own day is complicated, and we are not able to pursue all the issues in detail here. It is possible the Gospel authors were retrojecting their perceived antagonists from later times. When the Gospels were being composed, the Pharisees had emerged as a significant force against whom Christ-followers felt they needed to defend themselves and carve out their own identity.

8. Maurice Casey, *Aramaic Sources of Mark's Gospel* (Cambridge: Cambridge University Press, 1998), 158.

9. Luke's version also reveals adjustments in an abridged version of the teaching: "Anyone who divorces his wife and marries another commits adultery, and whoever marries a woman divorced from her husband commits adultery" (Luke 16.18). Luke omits the longer passage on divorce in Mark and so arguably downplays the restriction on divorce emphasized in Mark 10.2-9. Luke narrows in on *remarriage* as the sole problem. This may well have been influenced by Paul's interpretation (cf. 1 Cor. 7.10-11).

10. See Matthew Thiessen, *Jesus and the Forces of Death: The Gospels' Portrayal of Ritual Impurity within First Century Judaism* (Grand Rapids: Baker Academic, 2020).

11. There are many texts which refer to "sinners" in such

Endnotes

language. See, e.g., Pss. 49[50].16-23; 93[94].13; 119; Ezek.
33.8, 19; 1 Macc. 1.34; 2.45-48; Sir. 11.9; 15.7-9 35[32].17; *Ps. Sol.* 1.1; 2.1; 4.8; 14.6; 15.5, 8; 17.5; 1 Enoch 102.5-10; 103.11-15; 104.2-7, 10; 4Q511 frags 63-64, col. 3.1-5; m. *Kiddushin* 4.14; b. *Sanhedrin* 109a-b; *Genesis Rabbah* 49.6).

12. The Greek term *harpaz*, translated by the NRSV in 1 Cor. 6.10 as "robber," is better rendered "swindler" or "rogue" and most definitely should be differentiated from "bandits" which has its own term: *lēstēs*. Matt. 7.15 uses *harpaz* to speak of the "ravenous" wolves who come in sheep's clothing, and Luke 18.11 lists them alongside thieves, adulterers, and a tax collector, underscoring associations with unjust economic extraction.

13. Cf. m. *Niddah* 4.2; m. *Sheb.* 8.10; b. *Kidd.* 75b.

14. Cf. *War* 2.129-31, 150; 1QS 5.1-2, 8-9, 13, 14; m. *Berakhot* 8.2; m. *Hagigah* 2.5; m. *Yadayim* 3.1; t. *Berakhot* 5.26.

15. The classic treatment is Aharon Oppenheimer, *The 'Am Ha-aretz: A Study in the Social History of the Jewish People in the Hellenistic-Roman Period* (Leiden: Brill, 1977), 18-22.

16. See further, e.g., m. *Tohorot* 7.1-2; 8.2; m. *Makhshirin* 5.7; m. *Demai* 2.3; t. *Tohorot* 8.1; t. *Abodah Zarah* 3.10; 4.11; y. *Demai* 2, 22d; b. *Berakhot.* 43b, 47b; b. *Gittin* 61a; b. *Nedarim* 90b; *ARN* [A] 41.

Chapter 8

1. Paula Fredriksen, *When Christians Were Jews: The First Generation* (New Haven: Yale University Press, 2018), 67-70.

2. For a broader overview of Christian martyrdom, we recommend Paul Middleton (ed.), *The Wiley Blackwell Companion to Christian Martyrdom* (Hoboken: John Wiley & Sons, 2020).

3. See further, e.g., Günther Zuntz, 'Wann wurde das Evangelium Marci geschrieben?', in Herbert Cancik

273

(ed.) *Markus-Philologie: Historische, literargeschichtiche und stilistische Untersuchungen zum zweiten Evangelium* (Tübingen: Mohr Siebeck, 1984), 47-71 (50-51); Maurice Casey, *Aramaic Sources of Mark's Gospel* (Cambridge: Cambridge University Press, 1998), 206.

4. L. Stephanie Cobb, *Dying to be Men: Gender and Language in Early Christian Martyr Texts* (New York: Columbia University Press, 2008).

5. See, e.g., Stephen D. Moore and Janice Capel Anderson, 'Taking It Like a Man: Masculinity in 4 Maccabees,' *Journal of Biblical Literature* 117 (1998): 249–273.

6. See further Candida Moss, *The Myth of Persecution: How Early Christians Invented a Story of Martyrdom* (New York: HarperOne, 2013).

Chapter 9

1. Craig A. Evans, *Jesus and His Contemporaries: Comparative Studies* (Leiden: Brill, 1995), 319-380.

2. Maurice Casey, *Jesus of Nazareth: An Independent Historian's Account of His Life and Teaching* (London: Bloomsbury/T&T Clark, 2010), 412.

3. Neil Elliott, "Jesus, the Temple, and the Crowd: A Way Less Traveled," in Robert J. Myles (ed.) *Class Struggle in the New Testament* (Lanham: Fortress Academic/Lexington Books, 2019), 36-37. See also S. G. F. Brandon, *The Trial of Jesus of Nazareth* (New York: Dorset, 1968).

4. Jodi Dean, *Crowds and Party* (London: Verso, 2016), 8.

5. Mark 13.14 is "corrected" in Matt. 24.15 to make both words neuter.

6. For discussion, see e.g., Günther Zuntz, "Wann wurde das Evangelium Marci geschrieben?" in Herbert Cancik (ed.) *Markus-Philologie: Historische, literargeschichtiche und stilistische Untersuchungen zum zweiten Evangelium* (Tübingen: Mohr Siebeck, 1984), 47-71; Gerd Theissen, *The*

Gospels in Context: Social and Political History in the Synoptic Tradition (Edinburgh: T&T Clark, 1992); Nicholas H. Taylor, "Palestinian Christianity and the Caligula Crisis. Part I. Social and Historical Reconstruction," *Journal for the Study of the New Testament* 61 (1996): 101-123; Nicholas H. Taylor, "Palestinian Christianity and the Caligula Crisis. Part II. The Markan Eschatological Discourse," *Journal for the Study of the New Testament* 62 (1996): 13-41; James G. Crossley, *The Date of Mark's Gospel: Insight from the Law in Earliest Christianity* (London: T&T Clark, 2004).

7. Martin Goodman, *Rome and Jerusalem: The Clash of Ancient Civilizations* (New York: Alfred A. Knopf, 2007), 18.

Chapter 10

1. Morna D. Hooker, *The Gospel According to Saint Mark* (London: A&C Black, 1991), 248.

2. Helen K. Bond, *The Historical Jesus: A Guide for the Perplexed* (London: T&T Clark, 2012), 156. Peter, conveniently placed in the vicinity, also added a hint of eyewitness authority to Mark's rewriting of the trial.

3. Justin J. Meggitt, "The Madness of King Jesus: Why Was Jesus Put to Death, but His Followers Not?" *Journal for the Study of the New Testament* 29 (2007): 379-413.

4. Roger David Aus, *"Caught in the Act," Walking on the Sea, and the Release of Barabbas Revisited* (Atlanta: Scholars Press, 1998), 135-170.

5. Earl S. Johnson, "Is Mark 15.39 the Key to Mark's Christology?" *Journal for the Study of the New Testament* 31 (1987): 3-22; Earl S. Johnson, "Mark 15.39 and the So-Called Confession of the Roman Centurion," *Biblica* 81 (2000): 406-413.

6. For a fascinating and oft-neglected analysis of the crowd associated with Jesus' sentencing within the context of political and riotous crowds commonplace in Jerusalem in

the first century, see the chapter "Popular Mass Protests" in Richard A. Horsley, *Jesus and the Spiral of Violence* (Minneapolis: Fortress Press, 1993), 90-120. See also Robert J. Myles, "Crowds and Power in the Early Palestinian Tradition," *Journal for the Study of the Historical Jesus* 18 (2020): 124-140.

7. Elias Canetti, *Crowds and Power,* trans. Carol Stewart (New York: Continuum, 1973), 49.

8. Canetti, *Crowds and Power*, 52.

9. Joan E. Taylor, "Golgotha: A Reconsideration of the Evidence for Sites of Jesus' Crucifixion and Burial," *New Testament Studies* 44 (1998): 180-203.

10. Wongi Park, *The Politics of Race and Ethnicity in Matthew's Passion Narrative* (Cham: Palgrave Macmillan, 2019).

11. Colleen M. Conway, *Behold the Man: Jesus and Greco-Roman Masculinity* (Oxford: Oxford University Press, 2008), 89, 100 (cf. 73).

12. Meggitt, "The Madness of King Jesus."

13. Roger D. Aus, *Samuel, Saul, and Jesus: Three Early Palestinian Jewish Christian Haggadoth* (Atlanta: Scholars' Press, 1994).

14. N. T. Wright, *The Resurrection of the Son of God* (London: SPCK, 2003), 636.

15. See, e.g., John Dominic Crossan, *Who Killed Jesus? Exposing the Roots of Anti-Semitism in the Gospel Story of the Death of Jesus* (San Francisco: HarperSanFrancisco, 1995), 160-188.

16. Mark Goodacre, "How Empty Was the Tomb?" *Journal for the Study of the New Testament* 44 (2021): 134-148.

17. See, for instance, the important work of William John Lyons, *Joseph of Arimathea: A Study in Reception History* (Oxford: Oxford University Press, 2014).

18. Jodi Magness, *Stone and Dung, Oil and Spit: Jewish Daily Life in the Time of Jesus* (Grand Rapids: Eerdmans, 2011), 171.

19. For an up-to-date and balanced approach to the subject of Jesus' resurrection, see Dale C. Allison, *The Resurrection of*

Jesus: Apologetics, Polemics, History (London: Bloomsbury, 2021).

20. Michael D. Goulder, "Did Peter Ever Go to Rome?" *Scottish Journal of Theology* 57 (2004): 377-396.

Chapter 11

1. E. P. Sanders, *The Historical Figure of Jesus* (London: Penguin, 1993), 281.
2. Roland Boer, *Criticism of Earth: On Marx, Engels and Theology* (Leiden: Brill, 2012), 225.
3. See, e.g., Pss. 9.15-17; 9.36 [10.15]; 83[84].10; Tob. 13.6; Wisd. 19.13; 1 Macc. 1.10; 2.45-48; *1 Enoch* 99.6-7; 104.7-9; *Pss. Sol.* 1.1; 2.1; *m. Nedarim* 3.11; *t. Sanhedrin.* 13.2.
4. See, e.g., Rodney Stark, *The Rise of Christianity: A Sociologist Reconsiders History* (Princeton: Princeton University Press, 1996); Wayne A. Meeks, *The First Urban Christians: The Social World of the Apostle Paul* (2nd ed, New Haven: Yale University Press, 2003); Jack T. Sanders, *Charisma, Converts, Competitors: Societal and Sociological Factors in the Success of Early Christianity* (London, SCM, 2000); Philip A. Harland, *Associations, Synagogues, and Congregations: Claiming a Place in Ancient Mediterranean Society* (Minneapolis: Fortress, 2003); James Crossley, *Why Christianity Happened: A Sociohistorical Account of Christian Origins (26-50 CE)* (Louisville: WJK, 2006); John S. Kloppenborg, *Christ's Associations: Connecting and Belonging in the Ancient City* (New Haven: Yale University Press, 2019).
5. See Carolyn Osiek and Margaret Y. MacDonald with Janet H. Tulloch, *A Woman's Place: House Churches in Earliest Christianity* (Minneapolis: Fortress, 2006).
6. See further Maurice Casey, *Is John's Gospel True?* (New York: Routledge, 1996); Adele Reinhartz, *Cast Out of the Covenant: Jews and Anti-Judaism in the Gospel of John* (Lanham: Fortress Academic/Lexington Books, 2018).

7. E.g., *Letter of Aristeas* 16; Origen, *Contra Celsus* 5.41; Justin Martyr, *First Apology* 20; Macarius Magnes, *Monogenes* 4.21.
8. Julian, *Against the Galileans* 65b-c; 100c; 143ab; 290b-291a.
9. See, e.g., Roland Boer and Christina Petterson, *Idols of Nations: Biblical Myth at the Origins of Capitalism* (Fortress Press: Minneapolis, 2014).

Glossary of Important Terms, People, and Places

Agrarian Realism The predominant conception in pre-feudal societies that the agrarian mode of production, including its corresponding set of social relations, was the only viable political and economic system.

Antipas Son of Herod the Great and who was tetrarch of Galilee and Perea after the death of his father in 4 BCE until 39 CE. Responsible for major building projects in Galilee, such as at Tiberias and Sepphoris.

Archelaus Son of Herod the Great and who became ethnarch of Judea, Samaria, and Idumea, when his father died in 4 BCE. His rule was short, and his territory came under direct Roman rule in 6 CE.

Caiaphas High Priest in Jerusalem during the organizing of the early Jesus movement and at the time of Jesus' execution.

Capernaum Village on the northwest shore of the Sea of Galilee. An important location for the early Jesus movement. From where the fisherman associates were recruited.

Dead Sea Scrolls A large number of Jewish scrolls and fragments discovered between 1947 and 1956 in caves near Qumran.

Eschatology Beliefs or teachings about the end times. Early Jewish and Christian writings often contrast the present age with a coming, future age in which the world would be radically transformed.

Essenes A party in Judaism at the time of the Jesus movement. Most likely the inhabitants of Qumran and producers of (some of) the Dead Sea Scrolls.

Galilee Geographical region of northern Palestine. Under the rule of Herod Antipas during the organizing of the early Jesus movement.

Herod the Great Appointed King of the Jews by the Roman

Senate in 37 BCE and reigned until his death in 4 BCE. Initiated many building projects around Galilee and Judea including major renovations to the Temple in Jerusalem (not completed until many decades after his death) and a number of famous fortifications such as at Masada and Herodium.

Ideological Imperial Apparatus The "soft power" that generated and regulated the ideas and perspectives of the ruling elite, as evidenced by ancient literary sources as well as archaeological remains of the elite.

Jerusalem Major urban center in Judea and location of the Holy Temple.

Josephus Jewish historian from the first century who produced some of the most important works in our understanding of early Judaism (*Jewish War*, *Jewish Antiquities*, *Against Apion*, and the autobiographical *Life*). During the Jewish revolt he led revolutionary forces in Galilee, until captured by Roman forces, after which he worked on behalf of the Romans as an interpreter.

Judea Geographical region of southern Palestine. After Archelaus was ousted in 6 CE, Judea was under the authority of a Roman procurator. Its urban population was concentrated in Jerusalem.

Mosaic Law God's instruction to Israel, revealed through Moses. Commonly referred to as "Torah" or simply the "law."

Nazareth Insignificant agricultural village in Galilee from which Jesus originated.

Passover Jewish festival commemorating God's liberation of the Jews from slavery in Egypt, such as described in the book of Exodus.

Paul An important religious organizer in the spread of the early Jesus movement after Jesus' death. Responsible for writing many letters which provide evidence of early Christian beliefs and controversies.

Pentateuch First five books of the Hebrew Bible or Christian Old Testament (Genesis, Exodus, Leviticus, Numbers, Deuteronomy). Contains the Mosaic law or Torah.

Pharisees A group of particularly observant and influential Jews in the first century.

Pontius Pilate Roman Prefect of Judea and man ultimately responsible for ordering the crucifixion of Jesus.

Repressive Imperial Apparatus The "hard power" that promoted elite interests on the masses. This included the military, tax collection, the Sanhedrin and royal courts, and other violence-backed mechanisms and methods associated with enforcing laws.

Sadducees A group of influential Jews in the first century. Unlike the Pharisees and (possibly) Essenes, none of their own literature has survived.

Sanhedrin Council of Jewish leaders in Jerusalem, including priests and aristocrats.

Sepphoris Jewish city in Galilee, about 6 kilometers from Nazareth. Antipas rebuilt the city prior to making Tiberias his capital.

Septuagint Greek translation of the Hebrew Bible that began in the third century BCE. Abbreviated LXX.

Synoptic Gospels The Gospels of Matthew, Mark, and Luke (but not John) which have clear literary similarities and so can be seen ("optic") together ("syn").

Tiberias Jewish city built by Antipas as his capital and completed in 19 CE. Named in honor of the Roman Emperor at the time.

Torah God's instructions to Israel. Commonly translated as "law" and/or referred to as the Mosaic law.

CULTURE, SOCIETY & POLITICS

Contemporary culture has eliminated the concept and public figure of the intellectual. A cretinous anti-intellectualism presides, cheer-led by hacks in the pay of multinational corporations who reassure their bored readers that there is no need to rouse themselves from their stupor. Zer0 Books knows that another kind of discourse - intellectual without being academic, popular without being populist - is not only possible: it is already flourishing. Zer0 is convinced that in the unthinking, blandly consensual culture in which we live, critical and engaged theoretical reflection is more important than ever before.

If you have enjoyed this book, why not tell other readers by posting a review on your preferred book site.

You may also wish to
subscribe to our Zer0 Books YouTube Channel.

Bestsellers from Zer0 Books include:

Give Them An Argument
Logic for the Left
Ben Burgis
Many serious leftists have learned to distrust talk of logic. This is
a serious mistake.
Paperback: 978-1-78904-210-8 ebook: 978-1-78904-211-5

Poor but Sexy
Culture Clashes in Europe East and West
Agata Pyzik
How the East stayed East and the West stayed West.
Paperback: 978-1-78099-394-2 ebook: 978-1-78099-395-9

An Anthropology of Nothing in Particular
Martin Demant Frederiksen
A journey into the social lives of meaninglessness.
Paperback: 978-1-78535-699-5 ebook: 978-1-78535-700-8

In the Dust of This Planet
Horror of Philosophy vol. 1
Eugene Thacker
In the first of a series of three books on the Horror of Philosophy,
In the Dust of This Planet offers the genre of horror as a way of
thinking about the unthinkable.
Paperback: 978-1-84694-676-9 ebook: 978-1-78099-010-1

The End of Oulipo?
An Attempt to Exhaust a Movement
Lauren Elkin, Veronica Esposito
Paperback: 978-1-78099-655-4 ebook: 978-1-78099-656-1

Capitalist Realism
Is There No Alternative?
Mark Fisher
An analysis of the ways in which capitalism has presented itself
as the only realistic political-economic system.
Paperback: 978-1-84694-317-1 ebook: 978-1-78099-734-6

Rebel Rebel
Chris O'Leary
David Bowie: every single song. Everything you want to know,
everything you didn't know.
Paperback: 978-1-78099-244-0 ebook: 978-1-78099-713-1

Kill All Normies
Angela Nagle
Online culture wars from 4chan and Tumblr to Trump.
Paperback: 978-1-78535-543-1 ebook: 978-1-78535-544-8

Cartographies of the Absolute
Alberto Toscano, Jeff Kinkle
An aesthetics of the economy for the twenty-first century.
Paperback: 978-1-78099-275-4 ebook: 978-1-78279-973-3

Malign Velocities
Accelerationism and Capitalism
Benjamin Noys
Long listed for the Bread and Roses Prize 2015, *Malign Velocities*
argues against the need for speed, tracking acceleration
as the symptom of the ongoing crises of capitalism.
Paperback: 978-1-78279-300-7 ebook: 978-1-78279-299-4

Meat Market
Female Flesh under Capitalism
Laurie Penny
A feminist dissection of women's bodies as the fleshy fulcrum of
capitalist cannibalism, whereby women are both consumers and
consumed.
Paperback: 978-1-84694-521-2 ebook: 978-1-84694-782-7

Babbling Corpse
Vaporwave and the Commodification of Ghosts
Grafton Tanner
Paperback: 978-1-78279-759-3 ebook: 978-1-78279-760-9

New Work New Culture
Work we want and a culture that strengthens us
Frithjof Bergmann
A serious alternative for mankind and the planet.
Paperback: 978-1-78904-064-7 ebook: 978-1-78904-065-4

Romeo and Juliet in Palestine
Teaching Under Occupation
Tom Sperlinger
Life in the West Bank, the nature of pedagogy and the role of a
university under occupation.
Paperback: 978-1-78279-637-4 ebook: 978-1-78279-636-7

Color, Facture, Art and Design
Iona Singh
This materialist definition of fine-art develops guidelines for
architecture, design, cultural-studies and ultimately social
change.
Paperback: 978-1-78099-629-5 ebook: 978-1-78099-630-1

Sweetening the Pill
or How We Got Hooked on Hormonal Birth Control
Holly Grigg-Spall
Has contraception liberated or oppressed women?
Sweetening the Pill breaks the silence on the dark side of hormonal
contraception.
Paperback: 978-1-78099-607-3 ebook: 978-1-78099-608-0

Why Are We The Good Guys?
Reclaiming Your Mind from the Delusions of Propaganda
David Cromwell
A provocative challenge to the standard ideology that Western
power is a benevolent force in the world.
Paperback: 978-1-78099-365-2 ebook: 978-1-78099-366-9

The Writing on the Wall
On the Decomposition of Capitalism and its Critics
Anselm Jappe, Alastair Hemmens
A new approach to the meaning of social emancipation.
Paperback: 978-1-78535-581-3 ebook: 978-1-78535-582-0

Enjoying It
Candy Crush and Capitalism
Alfie Bown
A study of enjoyment and of the enjoyment of studying. Bown
asks what enjoyment says about us and what we say about
enjoyment, and why.
Paperback: 978-1-78535-155-6 ebook: 978-1-78535-156-3

Ghosts of My Life
Writings on Depression, Hauntology and Lost Futures
Mark Fisher
Paperback: 978-1-78099-226-6 ebook: 978-1-78279-624-4

Neglected or Misunderstood
The Radical Feminism of Shulamith Firestone
Victoria Margree
An interrogation of issues surrounding gender, biology,
sexuality, work and technology, and the ways in which our
imaginations continue to be in thrall to ideologies of maternity
and the nuclear family.
Paperback: 978-1-78535-539-4 ebook: 978-1-78535-540-0

How to Dismantle the NHS in 10 Easy Steps (Second Edition)
Youssef El-Gingihy
The story of how your NHS was sold off and why you will have
to buy private health insurance soon. A new expanded second
edition with chapters on junior doctors' strikes and government
blueprints for US-style healthcare.
Paperback: 978-1-78904-178-1 ebook: 978-1-78904-179-8

Digesting Recipes
The Art of Culinary Notation
Susannah Worth
A recipe is an instruction, the imperative tone of the expert, but
this constraint can offer its own kind of potential. A recipe need
not be a domestic trap but might instead offer escape – something
to fantasise about or aspire to.
Paperback: 978-1-78279-860-6 ebook: 978-1-78279-859-0

Most titles are published in paperback and as an ebook.
Paperbacks are available in traditional bookshops. Both print and
ebook formats are available online.
Follow us at:
https://www.facebook.com/ZeroBooks
https://twitter.com/Zer0Books
https://www.instagram.com/zero.books